Drive-Thru USA:
A tale of two road trips

Drive-Thru USA: A tale of two road trips

Copyright © Rich Bradwell, 2014

All rights reserved. Please respect the copyright of this work. No part of this book may be reproduced, stored, or transmitted by any means without written permission of the author, except in the case of brief excerpts used in articles and reviews.

This book is based on true events but some details have been changed. Any similarity to real persons, living or dead, is purely coincidental and not intended by the author.

For more information visit www.drivethruusa.com or www.richbradwell.com

To follow Rich on Twitter: @RichBradwell

Contents

1. Introduction: Fit for a king 6
2. Florida: Zombieland 8
3. Georgia: Sweetness and light 26
4. South Carolina: "They started it" 38
5. North Carolina: The wolfpack 49
6. Virginia: Sing-a-long 61
7. Washington DC – Car trouble 71
8. Maryland: Ahoy pirates! 83
9. Delaware: The Taxman 96
10. Pennsylvania: Independence 105
11. New Jersey: Mischief 125
12. New York: The melting pot 141
13. Connecticut: Half and half 156
14. Rhode Island: The small-time 164
15. Massachusetts: The ballgame 172
16. Maine: The forest 186
17. New Hampshire: The leaves 195
18. Vermont: Liveability 208
19. Illinois: The middle 217
20. Alabama: Division 226
21. Tennessee: The beat 235

22.	Louisiana: Influences	248
23.	Nebraska: The law	263
24.	Colorado: The mountains	274
25.	Wyoming: Cowboys	284
26.	South Dakota: Native Americans	295
27.	Washington: Popular culture	310
28.	Oregon: Pioneers	321
29.	Arizona: Geology	333
30.	Nevada: A gamble	342
31.	California: The American Dream	356

It was the best of times, it was the worst of times, it was the age of wisdom, it was the age of foolishness ... we had everything before us, we had nothing before us, we were all going direct to Heaven, we were all going direct the other way.

Charles Dickens, A Tale of Two Cities

1. Introduction: Fit for a king

I bit down and there it was, pure heaven. Heaven in a roll. I'd come a long way to get this roll, more than 2,000 miles to the middle of New England, halfway up the coast of Maine. It was a full pound of fresh lobster covered in the most delicious melted butter, stuffed into a bun that was struggling valiantly to keep hold of its meaty treasure. I felt like a king, with my fistful of lobster just waiting to be devoured, like Henry VIII presiding over some wildly indulgent feast. Then I looked around and saw the shack that was serving the rolls and across at the haphazardly placed picnic tables. I took in the nearby road where cars meandered through the small town and across the bridge on their journeys up the New England coast. Ok, so perhaps I was eating in surroundings more fit for a tramp than a king, but that roll was fit for a king. America you had delivered.

I was halfway through a journey to cross America, trying to get off the beaten path as much as possible and eating as much great food along the way as I could. It would be a challenge to do it all, not least because I wasn't sure if my travel insurance covered a fast food induced heart attack.

I wanted to undertake an epic road trip and clearly the place to go was the US. With its fearsome mountains, awesome desert roads and golden coasts, the US is the home of the road trip. But I wanted more than just a journey, I'd done that 10 years earlier and it had been shambolic, chaotic even. My friend Jack and I had driven the length and breadth of the country, sleeping in the car, hanging with the crazies and eating $1 burgers from McDonalds. On that trip, straight out of university, we'd made the mistake of thinking that having a ticket into Miami and a return ticket from San Francisco constituted "a pretty good plan" and that being almost broke would be "real travelling".

Then it struck me, I could do things differently this time. I could right a few wrongs, for one, I could eat a hell of a lot better. American food is iconic after all. I could eat my way across the States and prove there really was more to it than burgers and fries. I'd see the country and have a reason to go a little deeper, searching for the local delicacies and hidden gems. It would be a long journey, over 10,000 miles, up the whole of the East Coast, across America on the famous route 66 and down the whole of the West Coast, but the open road beckoned and I was hungry.

2. Florida: Zombieland

Florida – retirement home of America and dream holiday destination of every seven year old British child. A land of contrasts indeed. My wife, Robyn, and I flew into the coastal city of Tampa to start our trip right at the bottom of the US's East Coast. We were keen to start the trip with a few days by the beach and had picked Siesta Key, supposedly the number one beach in America. We were excited at the prospect of a white crystal sand beach and turquoise blue seas with year round warm waters. It would sure beat the beaches of our home, England, where the choice is Blackpool, which is like a trip back in time but without any of the excitement of time travel, or Brighton, a beachside resort without a beach. Pebbles don't count as a beach, they really don't.

We walked from the airport terminal to the rental car facility. One thing I like about renting cars in America is that they don't seem to care that much about the car, by which I mean, they've got loads to rent out, they assume you'll bring it back in good condition and off you go. For the most part they don't even accompany you to go and get the car, often they'll say, "Pick any from row C" and away you go. In other countries an employee normally accompanies you while you run round the car trying desperately to see the tiny scratches that they will inevitably find when you return it. When you do bring it back to them, they bring out their sternest looking employee to check the car over as if it were a fine jewel or rare specimen from faraway lands.

"Tis a scratch here!" they proclaim.

"It was there before," you say immediately, trying to sound as confident as you can.

"Hmmm..." the stern employee says cryptically.

And woe betide you if there's a dent. At that point it's time to sell the house to pay for the damages. The good thing in America is they just don't seem to care about rental cars. They just thank you for bringing it back and then move on down the line. I'm not really sure why in other countries they think renting a car requires all that faffing. I can't remember the last time I heard of a car being out of action on the grounds of scratches.

We arrived at the rental facility to pick up our compact car. I'd confidently chosen the compact model, since it was one step up from the economy model. *'Second cheapest never fails,'* I thought happily to myself as we approached the car. I was thinking about a sporty hatchback, but the gods, or more accurately, the car rental company, were thinking about a tiny, 1 litre, lemon-yellow Suzuki. It was shaped like a shoe. The boot (trunk) was more akin to a second glove box. We cursed the rental company and for about 5 minutes we played a desperate and unpleasant game of Tetris with the boot and our luggage. It refused to go in.

I looked at Robyn, it was obvious what needed to be done: we needed to go back in to the rental desk and ask if this tiny, matchbox car really was the right one, and if not get another one.

"Do you want to nip back inside and see if we can switch?" I said it casually, trying to pretend it was an easy little task. I knew it would be an unpleasant, administrative headache, dealing with robotic staff and a computer system resistant to any changes. She didn't fall for it.

"No you're alright, you go if you want," she said, equally as casually. Clearly *I didn't want to* and neither did she.

"It's fine, I'll stay here and keep trying with the luggage, so you can just quickly check and see if there are other cars available. I reckon I might be able to get them to fit." I leaned on one of them, it was stuck firmly. She looked at me, the game was over, the subterfuge was up. Neither of us wanted to go and speak to the rental people.

"Fine!" she said, "Let's do rock, paper, scissors." The simple game had long been our method to divvy up unpleasant tasks. She still held a vague dislike for the game, which stemmed from the six-months where she'd slipped into an absent-minded *always go for scissors* strategy. It had been a remarkably unsuccessful period for her. She'd almost insisted that we give up the game. Eventually I had to reveal to her my secret of winning (the rock). Since then she'd always remembered to vary her hand and had come back to winning ways. This time she won and I had to make the trek back to the desk.

The rental desk insisted the car was the right type. They didn't even have any cars of the next class up. We were stuck with the one we had. I returned to Robyn and told her the bad news. I looked at the car once more and christened it "The Lemon". We drove the car out of the airport and towards the city.

The city of Tampa, like a lot of Florida, is heavily influenced by Spanish and Caribbean influences. A lot of Cuban immigrants have made Florida their home and they've brought their food with them. We headed into Ybor City which is probably the most Cuban district in Tampa. Back in the late 19th century and early 20th century travel between Florida and Cuba was common – there's only 90 miles of sea that separate them at their narrowest point. So influences were pretty readily mixed between the two. Now though with the restrictions placed by the US on communist Cuba it's actually one of the hardest places for Americans to get to, despite being so close.

We were looking for one of the most famous Cuban foods, the Cuban sandwich. It is a food which has become very popular in the US. It's basically a big sandwich with ham, cheese, salami, pickle and mustard, so it's pretty spicy. Ironically, during my visit to Cuba I don't recall anyone making, offering or eating a Cuban sandwich. The Cuban diet to me seemed to consist of black beans, rice, chicken and mojitos.

The Ybor City district was pretty pleasant to walk around in and was clearly Tampa's designated "walking district." Some American cities (e.g. New York, Chicago) thrive with life and are filled with people on the streets, resembling metropolises pretty much everywhere else in the world. However, there are a lot of mid-size and larger American cities, especially those in the South (Atlanta, Phoenix, LA etc) which seem to be pretty much dominated by the car, to the extent that you don't see people walking around that much. It could be because of the heat or because these cities largely evolved after the invention of the car, either way they tend to be more sprawling and have far fewer pedestrians.

Even these cities though tend to have a walking district where people like to actually get out of the car and use their legs a bit. We did just that in Ybor City and wandered around the pleasant but vaguely Disneyified storefronts and streets. It looked like the area also doubled as the late night going out spot, so every other place was a bar with tequila specials being advertised. Some were open despite it being a Thursday lunchtime. Unsurprisingly take up on the tequila shots seemed low.

We went to Carmine's to get our Cuban sandwiches. They were the perfect mix of pork and melted cheese, with a tangy, spicy overtone of the zingy mustard. It occurred to me though that it was (at its most elemental) a ham and cheese sandwich, not dissimilar to what is served back in England, nor even too dissimilar to the French version, the croque monsieur. What even is a ham pizza, with its cheese, ham and bready base, if not some kind of ham and cheese sandwich? Startled by my own incredible insight into the interconnectivity of all things I agreed with Robyn that it was time to head back to The Lemon.

The Lemon carried us away to our motel and off for a couple of days at the beach. The next morning it was raining, but being beside the number one beach in the US we weren't going to let that stop us. We drove to the beach and as we were approaching the rained eased off. We were practically the first ones there. The beach was absolutely wonderful: wide, expansive, white sand and as the sun came out the sea turned turquoise. Perfect we thought, setting up our parasol and towels.

We had a great day, hanging out, going in to the sea and back out again, wandering to get ice creams. However, being in the subtropical environment of Florida the sun was pretty fierce and we inevitably got some ankles and knees burnt that had not been covered by the parasol or sun cream.

"Well we've both got some sunburn," I said to Robyn.

"I can see that," she replied.

"Isn't it funny how attracted we are to the sun? Yet if we get too much of it - it burns us. We're like moths going towards the flame," I said, startled again by my own incredible insight.

"Be quiet" she replied, inspecting her burnt leg.

* * *

I was reminded of my trip with Jack 10 years previously. That had also unfolded in Florida, in similarly confident beginnings. We arrived in Miami where we had organized a hostel while we tried to procure a car, with the aim of driving all the way to San Francisco on the other side of the country. The hostel was an eye-opener with its walls of peeling paint, a pool you wouldn't dare to venture into, and a breakfast limited to two slices of toast and an orange-flavoured sugary drink.

Our roommates were already preparing for later life as alcoholics. On the first night one of them stumbled in to the room in the early hours of the morning, collapsed into his bunk bed and immediately fell asleep. An hour or so later we were awoken by a massive crash. He was so drunk he'd fallen out of his bed, on to the floor and carried on sleeping. The remarkable thing was he'd fallen out of the top bunk.

"Is he ok?" I asked the rest of the darkened room.

"He must be; he's still sleeping. He seems fine," replied his friend.

"So do we just leave him there?" I asked, a little concerned.

"He seems happy."

"Ok ... so goodnight then?" It wasn't usual to say goodnight as a question, but there wasn't any reply forthcoming so I rolled over and went back to sleep.

Our search to find a car wasn't going any better. We assumed that we could simply rent a car from

Miami either to New York or all the way to San Francisco. We called a few car rental companies, but they didn't want to rent a car to a pair of twenty-two year olds and there would be a massive fee for a one-way rental. We were despondent and feared we might have to get the bus. We didn't want to do a road trip on a bus, that would be like going swimming and finding out the pool was a paddling pool. Yes you'd get wet, but it wasn't really what you had in mind. While we were weighing up our options we were flicking through a guide and we came across a small advert for one-way car rentals, specifically for young penniless travellers.

We phoned the number and a German man called Don told us he had just the vehicle for us, a 12 year old Dodge Ram Minivan.

"I don't know about a minivan, we were really thinking we wanted a car," I told him.

Don was insistent, "I think this is the car for you, it's in Miami and I need it in New York. You can have it for a month and it's only $800."

"What's the fuel economy like?" I asked naively.

"It doesn't matter," said Don, who was getting exasperated now. "You're in America now and gas is cheap!"

"Well, what else have you got?" I asked.

"I've got a minivan. Are you taking it or not?"

Needless to say we took the van.

We needed to get the Greyhound bus from Miami to the neighbouring town of Fort Lauderdale to pick up the van. We decided to take a local bus from where we were staying in Miami Beach to the Greyhound station, which was located downtown. The bus driver said that he didn't stop there but we could walk to it from one of the stops. Twenty minutes later, he made a stop, and told us it was about 8 blocks away, gesturing in a vague direction.

On stepping out of the bus with all of our worldly belongings we realised we'd made a mistake. The area looked at best like the setting of the drug crime drama *The Wire* and at worst like the setting of zombie apocalypse drama, *The Walking Dead*. Either way it was a little out of the comfort zone of us two young Englishmen.

"Let's just keep our heads down and start walking," I said to Jack.

"This isn't ideal is it?" he replied. "I'm rather regretting bringing my Macbook computer." He surveyed the wasteland of empty parking lots, surrounded by chain link fences, the derelict houses and abandoned storefronts.

"I reckon the less chat out loud about your Macbook right now the better," I said as we cast a look into the middle distance where we could see a dark human-like shape huddled over in the doorway of one of the abandoned shops.

We walked a few blocks of the concrete badlands with only the occasional car sailing ominously by. Nobody else was walking. Since all we had was a vague direction and an approximate number of blocks, we didn't really know where we were. We saw a lone construction worker sitting in the shell of a building eating his lunch and approached him.

"Excuse us. Do you happen to know where the Greyhound station is?" we asked. He chewed his sandwich slowly. He spoke ponderously.

"There was one about one block that way," he said, pointing.

"Was? Has it closed down?" we asked nervously.

"Yep," he said. He paused and we waited to see if there was more information. Slowly he seemed to summon up the effort to speak again. "I think they moved it to a temporary one about 8 blocks that way," he gestured.

"8 blocks!" we repeated. How dispiriting. We'd already walked 8 blocks in this zombiefied hellscape. Plus this guy didn't really seem sure of anything. He was speaking so slowly that I wondered if he had already been bitten by the zombies. We thanked him and shuffled away.

"Right well we'll just have to press on that way," I told Jack.

"Look, if we can't find our way, we can always sell the Macbook and return to Miami Beach," Jack said unhelpfully.

We walked on and by now it was increasingly clear we were lost.

"It's pretty obvious we've got all our stuff on us, isn't it?" said Jack, seemingly taking a perverse pleasure in the hopelessness of the situation.

"I would say that given we're laden with our backpacks and carrying bags in each arm, that yes it's pretty bloody obvious that we've got all our stuff on us," I said, annoyed that he was managing to see any humour in our predicament.

"And I've got my Macbook."

"Shut up about the bloody Macbook," I replied.

We kept walking along, the heat increased as the sun rose higher in the sky. The area of abandoned homes, empty car parks and half-finished buildings went on and on. Weighed down by our backpacks and clutching our possessions, I started to feel like we were two mules in one of those old Westerns, being transported through some treacherous valley, just waiting for the bandits to rise up on the ridgeline and gun us down mercilessly.

Eventually we came across another man, clearly homeless, dressed in rags and sitting on the pavement. As we approached, we considered asking him for directions.

"He doesn't look like he'd know much about buses," Jack declared.

We made the mistake of looking at him twice and as we approached he barked at us, "Hey you."

"Heads down and carry on walking Jack," I said under my breath.

"Hey you guys, where you going?" he shouted as we moved a few paces past him. "Where you going?" he repeated. "Come back here!" His voice rose in volume and desperation with each unanswered call. "Come back here!"

"I'm thinking we don't go back there," Jack said under his breath as we quickened our pace, eyes locked forward.

Eventually we saw a group of people milling around a tatty shack of a building. It felt like the first time we'd seen life in a long time, even though we'd only been walking around the zombie wasteland for an hour. Massively relieved, we boarded the bus, went to Fort Lauderdale and found the second hand car dealership where the Dodge Ram Minivan was waiting for us. It was dark green, boxy with darkened windows on the side and a vaguely aggressive looking front. Since they didn't really sell minivans of this style in the UK at the time, we decided that it looked like a mix of the A-team van and a motorhome.

Jack and I immediately headed south, racing along in the Ram down to the Florida Keys. The drive down to the most Southerly point in America was great; island followed bridge followed island as we picked our way across the ocean in our majestic minivan, now christened with her official title of "Her Ramliness".

We arrived in Key West, the final island in the chain. Key West had a rather strange atmosphere; it was fairly small and crowded and had a vaguely Caribbean feel, but it lacked that essential element of Caribbean islands - beaches. Being right by the sea it always felt like we were going to stumble upon a beach, around the next corner, or past the end of the street. But at most we got glimpses of the sea or patches of sand. That big beach never seemed to materialize.

Key West is also pretty gay and very proud of it. Key West has a very prominent gay population, at over 30% of the island. As we walked down the street towards the bars we noticed the rainbow flags hanging from the buildings and the pink taxis. We stopped at a bar, it looked like a beach bar, everyone was in board shorts and flip flops (although the beach was curiously absent again). We played pool and got talking to some people. One chap was keen to play pool with us. He had bleached blonde hair, cut short, with a pretty sharp shirt on but held a rather distant look whenever he was talking to me.

Pretty quickly, he told us his whole back story. He was very wealthy and owned a sailing boat which was moored up in a private marina on the other side of town. He asked if we would like to go sailing the following day and we were happy to accept. As he kept talking his story got stranger, he had served in the US army and had been in Iraq. However, he'd been captured as a prisoner of war.

"That's incredible," I said.

"Yeah tough times, of course that's why I had to leave the army," he said ruefully. He explained that he'd been an interpreter and spoke nine languages and proceeded to name them all.

At one point some bar tough came over and demanded we play pool for money. We weren't keen to play since we weren't very good, and this angered the brute.

"Well what's your problem you pussies?"

"We're just happy to play for fun," we replied, "and we're in the middle of a game."

The man who seemed pretty drunk and unimpressed with the concept of playing for fun continued with his unwanted interruption. "I tell you what I think," he said "I think he's straight," pointing at Jack, "he's gay," pointing at our new friend and "you," he said pointing at me, "well I just don't know about you," he leered in drunkenly.

It was unclear if it was an insult or a question. I decided to call him a British swearword that I was confident he wouldn't understand and returned to the pool game.

As time went on, we learnt more about our new friend. He said that the following day, after our trip on the boat, he might be able to get his friend to take us up in his helicopter. By this point the sheer number of stories were starting to sound a little suspicious.

I waited until he went to the bar and turned to Jack, "I'm not sure about this guy."

"Why not?" he replied.

"Well do you not think it's a bit suspicious? Prisoner of war in Iraq? Seriously?"

"Yeah, but it could have happened, there were prisoners of war there, right?"

"Probably," I said. I was unsurprisingly unable to summon any facts about prisoners of war in Iraq.

"Right then," he declared confidently. "Look, I know about people and this guy seems alright to me. Ok?"

By this time the drunken angry man at the bar was fully immersed in watching our pool game. He was commentating on the shots to no one in particular and most of his comments were not complimentary. At this point the karaoke started setting up and we knew it was time to leave. Our friend didn't want us to go. "Hey guys I'll tell you what, I'll take you somewhere else. Loads of people there - it's a really cool place." Since we didn't have any other plans we were happy to go with him.

We walked down the street and our friend pointed at one of the buildings across the street.

"I own that one," he declared, "and that one," he gestured vaguely. It didn't seem likely, but who were we to argue, if he had a yacht, he probably owned some buildings. After five minutes of walking we arrived in what appeared to be a very empty bar/club.

"Here we are," he declared brightly.

"Where is every one?" I asked tentatively.

"It'll liven up soon, let's get a cocktail."

I held Jack back a second while our friend walked to the bar. "He really doesn't seem legit. Do you honestly think he's telling the truth?"

Jack paused, for the first time wavering in his confidence. "I don't know any more. That stuff about the buildings he owned was pretty weird."

"Yeah, we need to test him. You know, see if we can find some inconsistencies in his story or something," I said.

"Yeah ok, well he's waiting at the bar, so just you know, investigate, but subtly, ok?"

We made our way to the bar, where our friend ordered up three cocktails. We subtly started asking him questions about his story: How many buildings did he own? When was he in Iraq? How long had he been a prisoner for? He didn't seem to mind the questions. Like a lot of people, he was pretty happy talking about himself. He answered all the questions confidently and quickly. Everything matched what he had told us earlier. Either he told these lies a lot, or they were true.

I changed tack. "Which languages did you speak again?"

"French, German, Spanish, Italian, Portuguese, Arabic, Japanese, Greek and English, obviously," he rattled the languages off without effort, like it was something he said a lot.

"Japanese?" I thought to myself, thinking that it was pretty unlikely. "Say, can you speak some Japanese for us?" I asked.

"Sure," he said happily.

"Can you say – we're all in Key West, having a great time in this club?" If you've ever asked someone to speak in a foreign language to demonstrate it, you'll know how hard it is to come up with anything even remotely approaching what a normal human would ever say.

He repeated the phrase pretty quickly in something that sounded like Japanese to my untrained ears. I cursed myself for not knowing

Japanese. At that point, it hit me; I did know some schoolboy Spanish. I'd have to ask him something pretty basic.

"What about Spanish? Can you teach me some Spanish? How would I say Hello, pleased to meet you. My name is Rich."

"Sure," he said, not missing a beat. Then he proceeded to speak. What came out was not Spanish, it was a curious nonsense list of admittedly Spanish sounding words. Some of them rhymed.

"That's not Spanish," I said.

Jack's face flashed thunder as the house of cards of our friend's lies came crashing down. Our friend looked vacant, almost unconcerned, as if unaware he was rumbled.

"What the hell?" Jack demanded. Our friend said nothing. "Why have you been lying to us?" Jack asked.

"I haven't," he said, emotionless, as if the situation was pretty normal.

"You were never a prisoner of war in Iraq, were you?" I said, aware that that wasn't a normal sentence to be saying to a stranger in a bar.

"Yes I was," he answered flatly.

Jack stared at him angrily. "Right, Mister. You are buying us some beers. I have bought you at least two beers you weirdo. Buy us some beers." Jack called the barman over and ordered. It certainly wasn't the most enjoyable beer I've ever had as we sat in frosty silence and glared at each other in the near empty bar. Our friend didn't seem to be unhappy, he appeared to be enjoying his drink. We downed ours.

"We're leaving," we said and walked out.

Outside the bar we discussed the oddness of the situation. Why was he telling those lies? What had he hoped to achieve? Why had we believed him? (I reminded Jack about the glowing reference he'd given him). But since he was lying, why did he happily demonstrate the made-up foreign languages for us without even trying to deflect the request? It was odd.

"I'm going to go in there and give him a piece of my mind," Jack said.

"I'm not sure," I replied.

"No let's do it – I need to find what he was up to."

We walked the few paces back and re-entered the bar/club. We stood at the doorway and saw our friend had left the bar and was on the empty dancefloor, dancing happily to the music, seemingly without a care in the world. It was a strange scene.

"Do you think we should go and talk to him?" I said.

"No." Jack replied. "I think we've learnt a lesson here."

"Yeah, I think so, but I don't know what it is," I said as we backed out of the door watching the strange, dancing, whirling man.

3. Georgia: Sweetness and light

Robyn and I were travelling into Atlanta, one of the biggest cities in the south. Thankfully rid of The Lemon by now, we were travelling in a six year old Hyundai Sonata, a car I liked because on the adverts in the US, the voiceover man finished by shouting the name Hyundai as "Huh-YunDay!!" Then he would shout "Drive your way." The sudden and aggressive way he shouted "Huh-YunDay!!" was how a ninja might say it. Such are the thoughts that enter your head when you have hundreds and hundreds and hundreds of miles to drive.

We entered Atlanta on one of its many massive highways. At one point we counted seven lanes on each side. You would have to be pretty confident that your exit was a good few miles away if you wanted to venture *seven* lanes away from it. It would take a long time to maneouvre all the way across those lanes I thought. Or you could just veer across four of them at once like the man in front was doing. It was a ballsy move I thought, pretty bloody reckless, but ballsy.

Coca-Cola has its headquarters in Atlanta and it also has a very well-branded and troublingly slick exhibit called *The World of Coca-Cola.* It offers regular tours, VIP trips and even a special section for "educators" called a "teacher's toolkit". Now most people like a Coke now and again, but if you're a teacher and you think the best, most educational field trip you can do is to go to a giant Coke advert, you're an idiot.

Nevertheless, since Coke is just about the most popular drink in the world we were happy to head to *The World of Coca-Cola*. To be honest what is more American than Coke? I think the only thing that can make a case for being more American than Coke is possibly America itself, but it's close. Some parts of America don't really look like what you'd expect America to look like, but Coke? It always looks and tastes exactly how you expect. Score one Coke.

We headed downtown and found what looked like Atlanta's walking district. There was a park dedicated to the 1996 Olympics that was held in the city and two plazas at either end. At one end was *The World of Coke* and the Aquarium and at the other was the CNN headquarters. As soon as we entered it felt like being inside a giant advert. The history was interesting though; the drink was originally sold as a medicine in Atlanta pharmacies in 1886.

The genius of Coca-Cola's success though was the branding and the promotion. The Coke logo (that same swirly logo that has existed since the product's creation) was put on lighters, playing cards, matches, pretty much before anything else. The entrepreneur who bought the Coke brand/recipe from the original creator was shrewd. He gave away hundreds of thousands of coupons and within 10 years of its launch a quarter of the US population had tried a Coke, which considering that it was the 1890s and globalisation/homogenisation was unheard of, is kind of astounding. But beyond promotion and advertising, as Coke would have you believe, their product is pretty special too.

Some people will insist that Coke's popularity is down to advertising (it does obviously have a huge advertising budget), but I don't think it's that. I think Coke's real genius is in its branding. In fact according to Interband – Coca-Cola was the world's most valuable brand in 2011. But although Coke is aspirational, like a lot of products it's meant to make you feel good, it's also a great leveller between people, as Andy Warhol once said:

"What's great about this country is that America started the tradition where the richest consumers buy essentially the same things as the poorest. You can be watching TV and see Coca-Cola, and you know that the President drinks Coke, Liz Taylor drinks Coke, and just think, you can drink Coke, too. A Coke is a Coke and no amount of money can get you a better Coke than the one the bum on the corner is drinking. All the Cokes are the same and all the Cokes are good. Liz Taylor knows it, the President knows it, the bum knows it, and you know it."

We proceeded on to the Vault, which was a huge bank-like vault where you are promised that you will learn the secret ingredient of Coke (spoiler: you don't), and the tasting room at the end, where you can try hundreds of Coke's different products from around the world. Think green-tea flavoured soda from Japan, blueberry flavoured soda from Kenya etc.

It was fun but, to be honest, once I'd tasted about fifty different sodas, I could only taste one thing and it was just sweetness, but way too much of it.

The key thing about the South, and Georgia, as much or more so than anywhere else, is the sweetness of the food. It's highly appropriate that the world's favourite sweet drink, or perhaps sweet food/drink of any kind is from Georgia. While we were in Atlanta we also went to Mary Mac's tea room, a traditional Southern restaurant, and everything was really sweet, the sweet potatoes, the sweet tea (called "The Table Wine of the South") and that other Georgian specialty, the Peach Cobbler. It was all great, but we got the shakes afterwards.

Fresh from the sugar high, we were keen to do something enriching for the soul. The city is the birthplace of Martin Luther King (MLK) Junior, the great civil rights campaigner. We took a tour of his childhood home in the Sweet Auburn area of the city (even Atlanta's districts have got that word in their names). The street where he lived, the church and community centre have been preserved, while the MLK centre is a fascinating exhibition about his life and the battle for desegregation and equal rights that he fought so hard for. Overall though, it is a sobering and slightly melancholic place. Despite being an advocate of peaceful protest his untimely death at the hands of an assassin in 1968, aged just 39, loomed large during the visit.

Seeing the neighbourhood where he grew up and hearing the tales of him sliding down the banisters in his family home brought alive his story. More difficult to hear about were the struggles in his life in the deeply segregated and racist South of the 40's and 50's. On his wedding night he was unable to stay in a hotel since the white-owned hotels refused to let the newlywed couple in. Instead they spent the night in a black-owned funeral home. Sad though it was and thinking how unequal a society we still have, it was at least hopeful to think about all that had been achieved by MLK and all that has been achieved since his death.

To finish up Robyn and I decided to go to the largest drive –thru in the world. I'm not really sure what the advantage of the biggest drive-thru in the world is. It was a bit like going to the world's largest bowling alley. At the end of the day, you can still only bowl in one lane. The place, Varsity, located in central Atlanta, was massive though. It looked like a huge truck depot with lane after lane that you could pull into and order up. It was pretty standard fast food, with an emphasis on hot dogs and onion rings which they brought to the window of our car while we waited in the parking lane.

It always feels slightly indulgent and just a little grubby to be eating in the car. In America you can do a lot more things in the car than you can in England, go to a drive-in movie, a drive-thru bank, a drive-thru Starbucks. Call me old-fashioned but I just can't help but see the car as a way to get around, rather than as a mobile restaurant.

* * *

10 years earlier, Jack and I were meandering through Florida, heading for Georgia, and taking in Disneyworld on the way. We were pretty surprised to be fingerprinted in order to enter the theme park. The fingerprint was then linked to your ticket, and then you used your fingerprint to scan in (whilst most people held their actual ticket in their other hand). I asked a couple of the stewards why we had to do this, but none of them could answer why.

"It's our new technology!" one of them responded brightly. The rest of the crowds gave their fingerprint and entered unquestioningly. It seemed particularly odd that we were being treated almost as criminals, since we were the ones who were being robbed blind.

We also took in Gatorworld which was more our type of thing; it wasn't so much an attraction as just a pit of alligators. It consisted of several walkways over the enclosures of gators. There were so many that they were practically piled on top of each other. In a few of the enclosures they were actually crawling over each other. I had a horrible vision of them creating some kind of gator pyramid and reaching the height of the walkway. The whole thing made me feel a little uneasy. If the gators ever launched a planet of the apes-style takeover, then it was clear that it would begin here.

We reached the Florida-Georgia border, where we stayed at a hostel, which for reasons unknown, was pirate-themed. We were considering our next move when the owner of the hostel told us about a hostel located in a forest. It sounded like a hippy commune, but we agreed it sounded pretty unique. The following day we entered Georgia, and a while later turned off the interstate freeway and headed down a country road. Before long, we saw a handwritten sign, it said "Hostel in the Forest" and pointed down a dirt track into the forest. It looked dodgy.

We headed down the dirt track, it was rutted and Her Ramliness bounced around back and forth. Jack was driving.

"She doesn't like it," Jack said. "This is tough going, even for an SUV like her." Jack and I had recently learnt the word SUV (standing for Sports Utility Vehicle). While typically used to describe Jeeps, 4x4s and other rugged vehicles, we happily and willfully misapplied the term to Her Ramliness whenever we described her to anyone we met.

"Part SUV, part motorhome. She's the crossover edition, she can handle it," I said.

"She's feeling more like a motorhome today. I think we run the risk of getting her beached if we carry on with this for much longer," he replied.

Fortunately after another few minutes of bouncing around, we arrived at a clearing. It was an encampment of sorts, although it looked pretty ramshackle. A moment later a rather grubby, dreadlocked, hippy guy shuffled towards us. "Hey guys, welcome to the hostel in the forest," he said enthusiastically. He held out his hand. It didn't look clean and I didn't want to shake it.

"Yes um hello, I'm afraid we don't have a reservation, but we were wondering if perhaps you might have a room for the night?" I said, sounding far too English.

"Reservation? No worries dude. Plenty of space at the hostel. Might even have a treehouse for you." He bumbled off back inside, presumably to check the availability.

"Treehouse?" I turned to Jack. "Is that likely to have an ensuite?" I asked. He shook his head.

Harry the hippy ventured back out from his dwelling. "Actually we've got a really cool room near the lake, but it's a double bed, that's not a problem is it guys?" he inquired. It was unclear why he thought that would not be a problem. Presumably having any kind of bed was pretty luxurious.

"Hmmm..." we looked at each other, eyeing up each other, our potential bedmate for the night. Not ideal I thought.

"It's only $15 each," he said.

We paused, "Fine, we'll take it," we said.

It was a curious set up at the hostel, it covered a wide area in the woods with various clearings, with huts, shacks, treehouses and compost toilets fairly spaced out and hidden amongst the trees. We unpacked our stuff in our hut. There were some badly drawn pictures on the walls and some inspirational hippy-quotes. Most of them were about love, which wasn't really what Jack and I wanted to see, given the awkwardness of our bed-sharing situation. We agreed on sleeping top-to-toe, although as one of us pointed out, that wouldn't make our crotches any further away from each other. We laughed and agreed that it was better if we didn't talk about crotches anymore. We decided to head back to the main clearing.

By this time, the clearing was a scene of activity. A hive of busy hippies buzzed around; I don't think I'd ever seen so many white people with dreadlocks before. A truck had appeared to repair or fix something at the hostel. However, the earth had given way beneath one of the truck's big rear tyres. It was clearly stuck in the ground. Some of them were pushing while the driver tried to reverse, but it wasn't working. The truck was well and truly sunk into the ground.

We asked Harry the Hippy from earlier if we could help.

"Tough times dude! He's stuck," he said. "But hey do you guys have a car?"

"Yes, it's more like an SUV," Jack said unhelpfully, as I thought he was going to ask us to use the Van to shift the massive truck.

"Can you take that dude," gesturing at the driver, "back to the yard to get a tow?"

We agreed and before long we were taking the driver, an old-ish black guy, very southern, (think Morgan Freeman in *The Shawshank Redemption*), back to the nearest town. He was a nice guy and thankful we were helping him. "Good guys those hippies," he said. "They do get into some scrapes though," he chuckled at the thought of it, but didn't add any more. We wondered what other scrapes were in store for us.

After resolving the whole truck in the ground situation, we went and spoke to Harry again. He ran us through some of the rules. There were lots of rules, rules about the compost toilets, several related to washing up, rules about the common area, the chickens, alcohol, the rowboats, the huts and attendance at dinner. It was odd, but man these hippies seemed to love rules.

They also kept their own chickens and were pretty proud of them. Each one was named. This is a genuine description of one of their chickens, from their website.

"I am Andromeda, Keeper of the light and creator of all stars in the sky and I call the Hostel in the Forest home. If you look at my chest, you will see a feathery mosaic of every star that was, and ever will be." So quite a big deal then, for a chicken.

We took a rowboat out on the lake and chatted to some other hostellers on a little pontoon in the middle of the lake. Before long it was dinner time.

We'd been told not to be late and we arrived in time to join other people milling around in a cleared area behind the main buildings. Some benches were arranged around an area where they had previously lit a fire. Harry the hippy came out from the kitchen. "Dinner is about to be served, but first we must form the circle of thanks," he said. Jack and I looked at each other, apprehensive, but most of the rest of the guests and resident hippies seemed to know what to do and began to form a large circle.

Everyone started to hold hands with the person next to them and some grubby urchin of a guy took my hand. The concept was pretty simple, everyone in turn had to say something to the group that they were thankful for. The answers ranged from the simplistic "this beautiful world, man," the overly personal, "my mom and sister have been having troubles recently, and we're pulling together to get through," to the nonsensical, "the lunar phase is deepening my celestial vibrations." Jack and I were nervous but managed to come up with something: "the opportunity to travel and meet new people." Secretly we were thankful for the large case of beer in the boot of the car and the fact we were leaving the following day.

The evening drew on and they lit a fire. A couple of guys brought out guitars and played some peaceful melodic music. It was a warm evening, the fire crackled and the stars shone. I began to appreciate the hippies and their way of life. There was something about being around the campfire that suited the hippies, they begin to sing and didn't seem inhibited at all. We were enjoying ourselves and drinking our beer out of mugs (they didn't allow beer bottles, alcohol was allowed to be drunk but not to be seen, since that encouraged excess drinking they said.) But it was a chilled out night and the hippies seem relaxed. Nevertheless we had places to be and one night of compost toilets and compulsory giving of thanks seemed like enough. Plus we still had that double bed to look forward to.

4. South Carolina: "They started it"

Robyn and I rolled into South Carolina; we were headed to Charleston, one of the grand old dames of the south. South Carolina is the proper South, not this fancy "New South" of megapolises like Atlanta and Dallas, no, the old South: old money, estates, palm trees, old pickup trucks and hunting. It's the type of place where they still go on about the Civil War. A war that finished nearly 150 years ago and one that they lost.

We headed to Charleston which is more about the old money and grand estates, than the other side of the state - the rural side of pickup trucks and billboards for churches, which we saw plenty of as we drove around.

Charleston got very wealthy on the back of slavery and in the early 19th century a lot of the richest people in the US lived in and around Charleston on plantation estates. They lived in luxury while their slaves toiled in the heat. Since slaves were actually pretty expensive to buy and they were property, the majority of wealth in the South was the slaves themselves. The amount of money invested in slaves roughly equalled the total value of all farmland and farm buildings in the South and in 1860, the year before the Civil War broke out, the number of the slaves was still growing steadily, as was the value of each individual slave.

Since the South feared that slavery would eventually be banned (and therefore their source of wealth would disappear – or their livelihood as they saw it) they rebelled. The Civil War actually started in Charleston in 1861. It didn't work out so well for the South, and it could be argued that since South Carolina is still one of the poorer states in the US, it has never fully recovered its glory days.

But why the history lesson? Well as I've learned repeatedly, where there is history, there is unique and interesting food. South Carolina does not disappoint and despite not having one of the more famous cuisines it does boast its own genre of food, in this case "low country food". It is called the low country because this area of marshy coastline is near or below sea level. Because of this, oysters, crabs, shrimp and so on are abundant and the dishes of the cuisine reflect that.

"Low country food" has a lot in common with Southern cuisine more generally, so lots of rice, grits, beans etc. Grits are a controversial topic for any British person that visits the South (and indeed for a lot of Americans from the North). Grits appear to be universally popular across the South and more than 75% of grits that are sold in the US are sold in the South Eastern corner of the country that stretches from Texas to Virginia, the so-called "grits belt." Grits are basically corn kernels that are boiled up, then a generous amount of butter is added. The grits congeal to a porridge-like consistency and are served warm, in a bowl, generally at breakfast time.

I think what confuses British people and other Americans about grits, is that they are so ubiquitous and well-liked in the South. They are served at breakfast buffets in every hotel and tend to feature prominently in diners as well. But the curious thing is that grits are actually very bland. This confuses (and annoys) the Northern Americans. Conversely this seems to make the Southerners love grits all the more. Georgia declared grits their official state food in 2002, while a similar bill in South Carolina decreed "the South has relished its grits, making them a symbol of its diet, its customs, its humor, and its hospitality." A Charleston newspaper in 1952 wrote; "An inexpensive, simple, and thoroughly digestible food, [grits] should be made popular throughout the world." An odd compliment, "thoroughly digestible"? Well in that case, I'll order *two* bowls of them.

We ate in a couple of great restaurants that focus on Southern/low country cuisine, the Hominy Grill and Magnolias, and tried some local specialities. The Hominy Grill is a popular restaurant and hangout spot, selling beers from a window to people milling about at the tables out front on the warm evenings. In fact, it is even named after grits; "Hominy" refers to a type of corn used for making grits. The restaurant is dedicated to serving traditional Southern food but with fresh and interesting twists. So that means the staples of fried chicken, fried fish, beans and rice and so on were at the heart of the menu. I made sure to have their grits (which came in the form of baked cheese and grits). They looked like hash browns and they were a great accompaniment to the meal. We also sampled the shecrab soup – a crab soup made with crab roe, so essentially a crab caviar soup, perloo – a rice dish, a serving of pimento cheese – a Southern speciality, and flounder, a fish which is common in the area.

Charleston is still a very pretty and grand old town. Tourists trot past the colourful houses in horse drawn carriages, while people saunter along the waterfront. We visited Fort Sumter, where the first shots of the American Civil War were fired in 1861. South Carolina declared its independence from the rest of the United States in December 1860 and was quickly joined by several other states, forming the Confederacy. While the political machinery and rhetoric raged it wasn't until April of 1861 when the atmosphere in Charleston reached fever pitch, that the first shots of the War were fired. Fort Sumter, a fortress on a small island that guarded the entrance to Charleston harbour (still under Union military control) was given the option of surrender to the newly-formed Confederacy but chose not to. It was bombarded for 36 hours by Confederate forces before it was finally taken.

Those shots started a four year long war, a war that killed over 620,000 Americans, more than 2% of the population at the time. To put it in perspective, more Americans died in combat in the Civil War than both World Wars, the Vietnam war and the Korean war put together (i.e. the next four most damaging wars). It was a war that destroyed large parts of the South, but nevertheless there is still a certain pride about the War in the South (which they sometimes call the War of Northern Aggression). You can see this pride in the Confederate flags you still see flying all over the rural South, the way the war is spoken about by many Southerners and the tone of some of the Civil War museums and battlefields.

The boat ride out and trip to Fort Sumter was certainly worthwhile and very interesting, but it gave me pause for thought. Obviously Sumter was the starting place of the war, so is rightly preserved and mythologised for its place in history, but it's obviously important to remember what a terrible war it was. I think English people tend to naturally side with the underdog, a trait probably born from our distaste for show-offs and our small island-nation mentality. Sometimes when watching or touring Civil War sites, I found it easy to get caught up and found myself impressed by, or even siding with the South. They were outnumbered, fighting a stronger force, generally on their own land. They believed they were fighting for their way of life (which they were) and scored some really impressive military victories, often against the odds. But then you remember that they were actually just massive racists. And that what they were fighting for, despite what they might say, was slavery, which is clearly one of the biggest evils of recent history. Then it becomes pretty hard to sympathise with them at all.

* * *

10 years before, we continued up the Georgia coast towards South Carolina, Her Ramliness dutifully chugging along. After a day's driving we reached the city of Savannah, located at the border of the two states. We swept through the city streets, it looked very Southern. The oak trees were draped in Spanish moss, it looked a little creepy but atmospheric and authentic. The silvery-grey strands of moss hung from almost every tree.

"This moss is everywhere. It's like straight out of *Gone with the Wind* or something," I said. Or at least I imagined it to be that way, I was only 22 and wasn't cultured enough to have seen the movie, but I was cultured enough to know what it was about i.e. the old South and antebellum buildings and southern belles and things like that.

"Yeah it's weird stuff that moss, it's hanging everywhere," Jack said. He made no reference to the film, clearly he hadn't seen it, the uncultured lout. I continued navigating and we reached the hostel.

At the hostel we were met by one of the employees. Simon was a nervy, twitchy, slightly geeky man. He clearly wasn't a people-person and seemed curiously ill-suited to working at a hostel. He was keen to impress upon us the rules of the hostel. (Yet more rules, we thought). He continued "and finally, there is to be no alcohol in the hostel. You can drink outside the hostel, but no alcohol is to be brought into, or drunk in the hostel." We murmured our assent, but looked at each other quizzically. No alcohol? In a hostel? That didn't seem likely or frankly desirable.

Simon's monologue drew to a close. "It's best if you walk north or west out of the hostel. The centre of the city is in that direction."

"What if you want to walk the other way?" Jack asked.

"Well you should only do that if you like getting murdered," he said matter-of-factly.

I thought it was pretty unlikely that anyone would *like* getting murdered, or that there would be anyway to find that out, since they'd be dead. Simon looked at us and seemed pleased that he'd put an end to our questions.

We had a chilled out day, there wasn't too much to see in the city but it had a good atmosphere, at least where we were, in the zone for people who didn't like getting murdered. It was pleasingly walkable, the architecture was uniformly old and Southern and there was a good vibe to the city. It seemed to have a fairly large student presence and it was nice to be somewhere we could leave the Van for a few days. Being March it was warm out, but it was clear it would be seriously hot in the summer.

The following day was St. Patrick's Day, which we hadn't realised was such a big deal in the US. In England if you happen to be in the pub that evening, you might realise from the solitary banner they've strung up that it was St. Patrick's Day. At that point you may have a Guinness. Satisfied that you've done your Irish bit, you resume normal activities. In the US, it's very different, since their Irish heritage is significant; there's often a parade and everyone makes like the Irish and goes out drinking. If they're feeling particularly Irish then they honour their heritage by drinking even more heavily.

We were in the hostel common room preparing to go out. One of the other guests came in, he was a young guy, American, university age and he had a carrier bag full of beers. He sat down and offered Jack and me and the other two guys in the room a beer.

"I'm not sure we're meant to have beers in here, that Simon guy said so," I hesitated as he held out the beer.

The guy laughed, "Oh I don't think he was being that serious." I recalled Simon's twitching face and the way he stared at us when he was talking about the alcohol rule. I didn't really agree with the beer guy's assessment of the situation. But then I thought, Simon's not here and it is St. Patrick's, screw it. I happily took the beer.

Twenty minutes or so passed and we talked about when we'd head out to the bars for the night. Then the door swung open. There was Simon. It looked like he could *smell* the beer.

"What!?" he shouted. He seemed genuinely surprised at the sight of beer in the hostel, which was surprising to me.

"What the hell are you doing?" he thundered.

Our friend who had brought the beers looked surprised. "Hey chill out man, it's just a few beers," he said, more relaxed than I was. Jack, myself and the other two surreptitiously slipped our beers down the side of the sofas. Simon's face reddened at the outrage of the situation. He looked like he was about to explode. It was like in *Back to the Future* when Marty McFly gets insulted with the word "chicken", or like Superman's reaction to Kryptonite. It didn't really seem proportionate.

Simon paused and then he went for the guy with the beers, "Out!" he screamed, "Out!" He grabbed him by the arm and pulled him up.

"Woah! Chill out man!" The guy said, somewhat more anxious now. Simon wasn't having it and practically chased him from the room. We heard our friend say from down the corridor, "But I've already paid!"

"Out!" we heard Simon shouted again. It was an odd scene. I turned to the others and said.

"So what do you think is up with Simon?" They looked shell-shocked and we grabbed our beers and put them in the bin. It was a strange situation, running a hostel and trying in vain to stop the guests drinking alcohol, even a single beer. It seemed like a pretty tough battle and one he was destined to lose. He was like a modern day Sisyphus, the man from Greek mythology whose punishment was to roll an immense boulder up a hill repeatedly, only to get to the top and have it roll to the bottom again. For eternity. I doubted Simon would appreciate the comparison.

We headed out to the bars. They were heaving along the waterfront. Some of the banners boasted that Savannah had the biggest St Patrick's Day celebrations in the South. A lot of the bars were in buildings several stories high. Most of these bars seemed to have floors on all the levels and they were uniformly busy, mostly of college-age students. It was our first real introduction to the college-age American male. We got talking to some guys from Iowa who were on a break since it was St. Patrick's Day.

"So you guys are here? From England?" one of them asked.

"That's right, we're travelling across the country."

"But you're here in Savannah for tonight, for St. Patrick's Day?" he said incredulously.

"Umm yeah." It wasn't clear if that needed answering, since it was patently obvious.

"But here? Of all the places. That is un-believable," stressing the word like it genuinely was unbelievable, rather than the small coincidence that it actually was, since we had to be somewhere.

We got talking to another guy, who seemed to think he was pretty smooth. He was wearing a deliberately jaunty-looking hat. Again he was impressed that we were from England. It was pretty easy to impress the college students in Savannah. Suddenly distracted, he pointed towards the window. "Look at that sweet piece of ass," he said excitedly.

"I'm sorry?" I said looking over, to where a woman was leaning out of the window, shouting to presumably a friend on the street below.

"Hey! Hey!" he shouted trying to get the attention of a different guy standing closer to the woman. The guy turned round and the smooth guy shouted again.

"Grab it! Grab it!" gesturing towards the woman. It wasn't clear if they knew each other, which was troubling. The other guy looked at him, saw what he was pointing at, laughed, but waved him away.

The smooth guy turned to me and Jack, "Let's go over." We followed him and he struck up a conversation with the window girl. "These guys are from England" she looked up, but didn't have anything to say about the unarguable fact that we were indeed from England. "Where you from?" he asked.

"Tennessee, from Nashville," she replied.

"Wow you got a real cool Southern accent, really classy," he said. "See I'm from the Midwest, so I've got one of those accents like the movie stars." It was nonsense. The ridiculous statement needed challenging or he needed slapping. Unfortunately she did neither. She just smiled happily and he continued with some of the most cheesy lines I'd ever heard. We drifted away and looked round the packed bar. Another college age guy came up to us.

"Hey guys, what's going on? Oh my god, it's so hot in here, it smells terrible, like ass." Jack and I looked at each other. There it was, good or bad, it all came back to the ass with these guys.

5. North Carolina: The wolfpack

We arrived in Raleigh, a medium-sized city in the middle of the state. Raleigh is perhaps not the best showcase of North Carolina, a state that boasts some fantastic sandy islands (the Outer Banks) on its Eastern coast and the Blue Ridge Mountains to the west of the state. The middle of North Carolina is where the majority of people actually live though; Raleigh, Durham, Charlotte etc. This central area is also where North Carolina has its strongest food traditions.

North Carolina is a mixed bag in terms of its identity. It's Southern, but not that Southern, it's kind of urban, but doesn't really have any truly noteworthy cities. It's got some notable universities, but not the really elite universities, and I think that blurred identity extends to its cuisine as well. There's some interesting-ish food - North Carolina has a lot of barbecue - but there are places that are far better known for barbecue. It's got some down-home Southern cooking, but nothing as notable as that found in South Carolina or Georgia, and it doesn't really have strong immigrant food traditions, like Italian, German or Mexican to draw on either.

North Carolina barbecue is pretty distinctive though. Typical (East) North Carolina barbecue is pulled pork with a vinegary sauce (as opposed to the smoky or sweet sauce, or having it dry). It tends to be pulled pork rather than the ribs used in barbecue in other states. The other thing that typifies North

Carolina barbecue is it being "Whole Hog" style. I kid you not. In some of the downscale establishments you actually see them carving directly from the pig. We went to a place called "The Pit" which is definitely a great name for an eating establishment. Ironically, despite its name "The Pit" is one of the more upscale establishments (go figure). I can only presume the downscale ones are called things like "The Hole", "The Dump" and "The Crapheap" to make the distinction perfectly clear.

Anyway The Pit was great, and the pulled pork was unique and delicious. It came smoked and freshly pulled from the bone. The pulled pork is achieved by using a fork like implement, which literally pulls it off the bone in that stringy style. It's then lumped together into a pile of tasty separated pork and then sauced to your liking. We also got some good down-home Southern sides: collard greens, mash potatoes and gravy and mac and cheese. The tangy, vinegary pulled pork was tender with just a bit of chew to it and paired well with the crunch of the greens and creamy macaroni cheese. Delicious stuff.

As well as *Eastern* North Carolina barbecue, there is also *Western* North Carolina barbecue, which is made from pork shoulder (rather than whole hog) and is generally coated in a sweeter sauce than its eastern counterpart.

We were also keen to visit another Raleigh food institution, the type of place that thrives on word-of-mouth and seems to be a relic from a bygone age.

"The Roast Grill" is a tiny hotdog shop which seats about 14 people, and is one of those places that proudly states things like, "No credit cards", "No Mayo", "No Ketchup", as though they are selling points. In fact its website declares "Limited Options, Limited Toppings, No Menus." I've visited a lot of these types of places and more and more I realize that pretty much every business owner would love to be as obstinate and unhelpful as possible, if only their business was popular enough. These places they seem to always have a queue out of the door at any time of the day and so the owner's response is always, "Great! Now I don't have to take credit cards!"

It was a weird place; it looked like the only thing that had changed since the 70's were the prices. Coke is the only drink and it came in those little glass bottles and the food options were strictly limited. At the end of the day though, the hot dogs or "weiners" were what was important, and they were good. They were cooked up fresh in front of us, I had one with onions and with chili, and they were really tasty; *eat them in twenty seconds tasty*. Hot dogs, rather like kebabs, get a bad rep, not because they are bad, but because they're always cooked so badly, or being eaten by bad people in a bad place (e.g. British people falling out of a nightclub at 3am). If you actually have a good hotdog or a good kebab you realize they can be truly great. These were great and like most people in there, we ordered up a second round of them.

In Raleigh we also went to a college basketball game. America loves college (university) sports, in some ways even more than their professional sports. College football, (American football), seems to be just as popular as professional football and many people will often support a college team instead of a professional team. There are a lot of reasons, including tradition, a feel that it's more authentic and that there is more passion and conviction amongst the student players.

Fun fact – 9 of the 10 biggest stadiums in the US are not home to professional teams but to college football teams. That's right, stadiums built for teams of amateur student athletes. 7 of these stadiums have a capacity of over 100,000 people! That's larger than Wembley, the biggest stadium in England. The players are often stars in their own right and go on to become professional but, even so, technically they're still just students. Whereas in the UK it's the opposite, nobody watches or cares about university sports. In fact the only way you could identify a player on the university rugby team is the fact they would be downing 10 pints of beer, chanting "Rugby! Rugby!" before collapsing in a drunken obnoxious heap.

We went to see the NC State basketball team for a midweek game. College basketball tends to be a little out of the limelight until the finals – "March Madness" - comes around. At that point everyone seems obsessed with college basketball and it can be quite entertaining. While watching the NBA (the professional league) is a bit like watching a bunch of 8 foot-tall mutants lolloping around the court before going on tiptoes to "slam dunk" the ball, college basketball is something different. For one, the kids are not 8 foot tall; instead they tend to be gutsy 19 year-olds trying long 3 point shots on a hope and a prayer. There's often an underdog team going all the way to final and there are always big upsets. Sometimes the match-ups are bizarre, like when a college of exclusively pasty-faced Mormon students takes on some all African-American urban college. It feels a bit like watching West Side Story on a basketball court.

Seeing NC State was fun, the place was packed to the rafters. It's not just the college kids who were there to see the team, there seemed to be a good mix of all sorts. Everyone was wrapped up in their traditional red colours. The team is nicknamed the Wolfpack, which was good because they had an amusing wolf mascot who danced around and because they had a chant that was literally the crowd attempting to howl like wolves. Not a chant about being the best team the world had ever seen, or about beating the other team, just everyone howling like wolves (unconvincingly). Strange but entertaining.

* * *

Jack and I had some distance to make up. Her Ramliness was due to be returned in New York in a couple of weeks. We decided to spend the night in Charleston before heading into North Carolina. We'd been on the road for a good few weeks, and by now we were rather devil-may-care about our accommodation. We noted in the guidebook that there were two hostels in Charleston and we thought that we could just rock up and get a room for the night. We arrived at the hostel, which was a traditional white clapboard building, with a large porch. It had a vaguely menacing air, there was an abandoned car in the drive, slowly rusting.

We got out and took in the scene. There were four guys sitting out on the porch. Two of whom were wearing string vests. They didn't look friendly.

"What are you thinking Jack?" I asked.

"Well they don't look like your typical backpackers," he replied. I eyed one of the men on the porch. He looked grizzled and half cut even though it was early afternoon.

"It's got more of a *just out on parole* feel to the place than your average hostel," I said uncertainly.

"Well let's at least go in and see what the situation is," he said.

We proceeded inside and saw a woman behind a table. She was smoking a cigarette and looked like she was manning a particularly messy table at a jumble sale.

"Hello, we were wondering if you had a room, or two beds in a dorm?"

She looked down at her logbook, "Ummm, double bed ok?"

"What?" I said. Jack and I looked at each other. I was annoyed, he looked confused. He was thinking the same thing as me: *Just what kind of signals were we giving off?*

"Huh?" she said looking up from her notebook, "I mean will you take a double bed, it's just we're quite busy, we ain't got no dorms available," she paused. "Actually even the private rooms are taken."

"Really?" I was taken aback, since we hadn't really had any problems with availability up until that point.

"Well we got a lot of long-stayers darling," she said ending the conversation. We retreated from the house, passing by some of the semi-comatose guys on the porch. Presumably they were the *long-stayers*.

We called the other hostel and they were full too, it was unclear whether with actual travellers or other recently-released convicts. We headed into town and decided to ask around to see if anyone could recommend us a place. We pulled up in the centre of Charleston at a large park. People lolled about in the sunshine, bunting and streamers crisscrossed above, tied between the poles and lampposts. We approached a young couple, they looked college-age and like they might know somewhere to stay.

"Hi chaps, just wondering if we could ask you something," I said. They looked confused, we were being too English again. "We were just wondering if you knew anywhere to stay?"

"What?" the guy said, he didn't look too with it.

"Well we tried the hostels and they were both full," I explained.

"Hostel?" he looked concerned and slightly confused. It was only later that we learnt that the concept of hostels was not always well-understood in America, where the tradition of backpacking is not as common. Sometimes hostel is understood to mean a halfway house, a refuge or even a place for homeless people to spend the night. God knows what he thought was happening, or why two possibly homeless Englishmen were asking him for a place to sleep. Inexplicably he said, "Well I don't have a spare room, but Steve might. Steve's that guy over there." He pointed to a guy about 100 metres away on the grass who looked he was sleeping.

"Umm thanks," we said and walked away.

It was clear it wasn't working. "Do you really want to go and approach *Steve*?" Jack said.

"Not really," I replied. "What are we going to say? *Hi Steve, we don't have anywhere to sleep but guy over there, whose name we don't know, said we could stay at yours. Can we?*"

"Yeah I don't know Steve or anything, but I just don't think he's going to go for it," Jack paused, "You know what we should do, we should just bed down in the Ram again."

It was an unappetising concept. We'd slept in the Ram before, down in Florida, we'd arrived at a hostel but it was more expensive than we'd bargained for. It was already really late and we reasoned we could just park in their car park, sleep in the Ram and shower in the hostel. It was ok but not comfortable. I was unsure.

Jack was sure, "It'll be fine, we'll just find an empty car park, go out and get battered and then we'll get to sleep, no trouble."

We drove around until we found a large car park, which was down by the aquarium. It was spacious and it was already clearing out. We parked up.

"Do you just want to head straight out?" Jack said.

"Well I don't see much reason to stick around in the hotel room," I said, looking around the Ram, our abode for the night.

"Yeah the minibar sucks," said Jack, rummaging about in the glove box and finding some empty frappucino drinks bottles. "Oh how ghastly, someone's left litter in here!" he said, smiling at me. *He'd* left the litter in there and he knew it annoyed me. I stared at him. He looked pleased with himself. "Empty frapp?" he inquired, proffering a bottle of one of the frappucino drinks which he drank incessantly. I took it and threw it at him.

"Right let's go and have some booze," and with that we opened the doors and headed into the night.

We went out amongst the lively bar scene of Charleston and proceeded to drink a fair amount. The first two stages of Jack's plan were working perfectly. After several hours we walked back to the car park on the edge of the city centre. By now it was deserted, the Ram stood proud but alone in the empty dark car park.

"Hmmm, not so sure about this Jack," I said.

"Yeah it's almost a little *too* quiet," he replied watchfully. "But we'll be fine in the Ram."

"I can just see the headlines now. *Two young would-be hostellers found dead in van. Selfish Steve to blame.*"

We bedded down in the Ram, which involved getting into our sleeping bags fully clothed and reclining the two front seats as far back as they would go, which was pretty far. It was like sleeping in an aeroplane, except with absolutely no ability to get up and move about. I seriously did not want to get the call of nature in the night. We turned the internal light off and Jack listened to his podcasts, snickering and sniggering away until I hit him. Fortunately because we were both sleeping in the two front seats he was within easy punching distance. Unlike in Florida where we had basked in the tropical temperatures and the warm nights, we were by now at least 700 miles north and the night was cold. It kept getting colder and it began to feel less like sleeping in a plane and more like sleeping on a mountainside. As the cold began to bite I eventually fell asleep.

Morning broke as the light streamed into the front window. Jack spoke, "Boss, are you awake?"

"Well I am now," I croaked, still huddled in the sleeping bag. My toes and fingers felt cold.

"Shall we wind the seats back up?" he asked.
We both began winding the wheel at the side of the

seat and slowly began to pull ourselves up from the reclined position towards upright.

"Can you imagine someone watching this? Us just slowly winching ourselves up in tandem, like a pair of morons?" I asked. I looked at Jack. He could see that I was annoyed with the stupidity of the situation. He found that funny and laughed. We both started laughing and continued to winch until we reached the upright position.

"What now?" I said. I looked over and Jack was in the driving position, he leaned forward and put the key in the ignition. He turned the key and we laughed again at our idiocy.

"Well at least it's efficient. Let's drive."

We had a long drive ahead of us, all the way to the Outer Banks in North Carolina. It was 500 miles and at least 8 hours via the interstate. It was the longest drive yet. Despite this we thought the coastal route would be more scenic and interesting. It was a mistake, it was slow going. 10 hours into the journey we were still more than 50 miles away from the hostel. It was approaching the time when their reception was closing. We called them and spoke to a happy sounding guy who said he'd be happy to hang around to let us in.

Another hour and a half later and about 12 hours after we'd winched ourselves into the driving position in Charleston we arrived in Kitty Hawk, North Carolina. The friendly man on the phone came out to meet us. He was mid-forties, black, with a big frame and a big smile. It was clear he was large and in charge. "Hiya folks, glad you made it!"

"Yeah it was a long drive, we came from Charleston, guess we underestimated it."

"I love Charleston!" he boomed.

"Yeah it's pretty cool down there," we said exhausted, hoping that he would hand us the key to the room.

"Great soup they got down there," he beamed.

"Oh yeah?" I said, "I don't think we tried the soup," I said wearily.

"Well you should have! It's fantastic, I used to go down there, just for the soup."

Jack and I looked at each other: *What the heck did he just say? We've just driven 500 miles, the longest drive we'd ever done and we're exhausted. Is he messing with us?*

"For the soup?" I said.

"Yes siree, sometimes for the weekend, I went for the day once," he said.

"For the soup?" I was unable to say anything else. I hadn't showered in two days and I was as tired as I'd been on the trip. I wanted to resist. I wanted to grab him, I wanted to shake him and say, "What. Are. You. Talking. About. You are mad. It's too far. It's too far for soup." But I didn't say any of that.

"Yes sir, fantastic soup," he said wistfully, vividly remembering the soup. We took the key and left the man, who we nicknamed Soup, to dream about Charleston and its fantastic soup.

6. Virginia: Sing-a-long

Virginia is an interesting state; it's Southern in character, mountainous on its western border, full of farmyards and vineyards in the middle and has the Atlantic coast on its eastern edge. It's historic, we saw lots of pretty villages full of picturesque clapboard houses. The character of the state seems to vary enormously from the rural south (pickup trucks and Confederate flags flying) to the urban north where it borders Washington DC (with its massive 10 lane "beltway" or ringroad).

We visited the more rural part, we wanted to take in the more traditional, authentic, old Virginia. We'd heard of a couple of diners that were meant to be especially good. In some ways I think diners have the same cultural significance for the US as the pub does for the UK. In movies, TV shows (at least in the old days) they seemed to be at the heart of the community. Diners have long occupied a special place in the idea of America. It seems that the diner is probably in decline in the US, being under threat from chain restaurants, drive-thru fast food and the increasing popularity of "upscale eateries". Perhaps their decline is linked to the decline, or at least perceived decline, in communities themselves. Modern society's lack of "community" is often what is blamed for the decline of the local pub in the UK, or at least the decline in the number of pubs.

Diners are often independent places, a category oddly referred to as "Mom and Pop" places in the US

(I've been in dozens and never noticed one being run by two parents). These places have not done well under the onslaught of the mega-brands. The chain restaurants and chain diners, with their huge advertising budgets, brand recognition and ability to undercut prices have marginalised the old-fashioned diner. However, I think that the further south you go the more of these old places manage to survive.

We went to Dot's Back Inn, in Richmond. I don't know if that is a pun. I presume it is, which is disappointing. Although we can all appreciate a pun now and again it just does not seem like a good idea for a business name. At best it will make us laugh momentarily, it may make us groan, we may even take umbrage at the sheer terribleness of the pun and forever hold it against the business. All we can say for certain is that whoever owns that place has to look at that name everyday, perhaps even saying it dozens of times a day when answering the telephone. That joke must wear extremely thin, to the point where it is surely no longer funny. Surely even the most well-crafted pun cannot amuse the owner day in, day out? Perhaps it does wear thin, but by that time, the signs are up and the leaflets are handed out and they're stuck with it. And what if the business ran into difficulty and the liquidators moved in? Surely by that point, amongst the unpaid bills and the dread of hearing the bailiff's knock, the pun would start to particularly grate.

But people love puns and wacky names. Where I used to live, there were two barbers and both of them were called "Sweeney Todd the barber". They were completely independent from each other, yet had exactly the same stupid, wacky name. This is problematic on so many levels. Firstly, it is very confusing for the residents of the area. Imagine recommending it to someone new to the area. It simply invites a completely unnecessary level of confusion. Secondly the original Sweeney Todd was famous for murdering his clients, which doesn't seem to be a strong selling point. Finally, one of them must have been called Sweeney Todd first, so how the heck did the second one decide to choose that name? And since then, why had neither changed it? They were locked in a battle of wills to keep hold of the terrible wacky name.

If there is any further need to drive the point home, then I ask, what really successful multinational company has a pun for a name? Or even just a really wacky name? None that I can think of. So if a friend of yours tells you, "I'm opening a flower shop, it's going to be huge," and they tell you it's called "Florist Gump," tell them to stop immediately.

Dot's Back Inn was a proper neighbourhood diner, tucked away down a fairly anonymous street. It was not the type of place that's going to attract any passing trade, so it was testament to the quality of the place that it was nearly full when we arrived on a Saturday lunchtime. It seemed like a good mix of a diner (tasty, hearty food) and that type of coffee shop that exists only on TV shows, where people sit around for hours, and where you always get your favourite booth. There were plenty of people just reading the newspaper or just chilling out (unlike say a Starbucks where people always seem to be either blankly staring at laptops or having coffee in a suit in the middle of the day, despite the fact they look like they should be at work.)

The food was good without being amazing, we had huevos rancheros and corned beef hash between us. It was inexpensive, quick and the type of food that's being eliminated from a lot of places as they move upscale.

Mainly I liked Dot's for the atmosphere. It was the type of place where the owner walked round the bar and saw one of the two TVs wasn't showing Richmond's college football team but instead was showing some other teams. This seemed to bother him, so in an annoyed manner he scrolled the channels till he found the Richmond game, and then seemed quite pleased. You wouldn't see that at a Denny's (a big chain of diners) where all policy is probably dictated from some central board. It reinforced a sense of individuality and community to the place.

We also went to The Southern Kitchen in New Market. I wanted to try one of the local specialities of Virginia which is peanut soup. I also wanted to try some Virginia ham, which is probably the most well-known food speciality of Virginia. However, for the most part, Virginia ham is more commonly sold in grocery stores rather than as a dish at a cafe or restaurant. But the Southern Kitchen delivered on both dishes. It was more of a roadside diner and had a real look of the early 60's, not because it was retro-styled, but just because that's the way it was. There weren't many people there, so it felt a bit like that atmospheric Edward Hopper painting of a lonely night-time diner.

Peanuts have long been grown in Virginia, so there's a fine tradition of peanut-based dishes in the state, including peanut cake, which is like pecan cake and the peanut soup I mentioned earlier. Even though peanuts are savoury I tend to associate them with sweetness, perhaps because of peanut butter. The peanut soup was served as a regular starter, and wasn't really sweet at all. It was creamy, not thick, kind of light really, and had a hint of onion to it. It was better than it sounds. The Virginia ham was a good piece of meat but it was really pretty salty. There's not that many places just serving up ham and veg any more so perhaps it's not surprising that it is a little tricky to find the ham in Virginia restaurants. It is after all just a big slice of ham. It's hard to dress it up as fancy dining, but it was exactly what we'd come to a traditional diner for.

I'm not sure what the future is for the diner in the US. In the UK, pubs have had to modernise and the majority now serve food, but diners already serve food....maybe they could serve alcohol?! I imagine that good quality diners will survive although

Americans don't seem to be quite as nostalgic about the past as the average Brit is, and I don't really think people feel much obligation to keep something going just because it's existed for a long time. Maybe in the way that British pubs have reinvented traditional British food, with the concept of the gastro pub, a similar thing could happen, but going "upscale", as they say, would be probably be a direct contradiction to the diner's everyman ethos and appeal. Who knows? For the meantime there are still plenty of good independent diners out there, if you're willing to look.

* * *

Jack and I headed out of the Outer Banks. We stopped at Kill Devil Hills which is the site of the first ever powered flight. The Wright Brothers developed and built the first powered aeroplane and did the test flights in the area. They wanted a clear spot with the right elevation, brisk breezes and soft landings. The sandy, grassy terrain of the Outer Banks was perfect for them. In December 1903 they made the first of three successful flights, the first being 37 metres (120 feet), then 53 metres, then 61 metres. They were only about 10 feet (4 metres) off the ground and the brother who wasn't flying, Wilbur, was able to run alongside, since they were flying at only 7 miles per hour. It's endearing to think of, given what planes are capable of now, only a little over a century later.

The whole visit was extremely inspiring, the site and visitor centre (like so many attractions in the US) were extremely well done. It was exciting to stand in the first place that anyone ever flew an aeroplane and it was heartening to watch the kids run along the line that marked out the distances of the first ever flights. The thing that I found so inspiring about their story was that it was these two individuals themselves that truly pioneered powered flight. The plane was their invention through and through. It took incredible innovation and persistence. A lot of the concepts and principles they invented are still in use today (mainly around the wing aerodynamics).

We carried on and made the short trip over the border to Virginia. We were going to see a concert by one of our favourite bands; Interpol. Interpol play a particularly gloomy brand of rock music. It's not heavy, but it's kind of dark. They wear black and they look moody. It's clearly a look but they are a *serious* band. They sing about love, heartbreak and all the usual things but seem to deliberately avoid any kind of humour or levity to their songs, perhaps in order to give them an epic and atmospheric resonance. Or maybe the Joy Division album just got stuck in the lead singer's tape deck when he was growing up.

The venue was full and held a couple of thousand people, all standing, with a large floor area and a balcony area. We went upstairs to get a good view. The lights went out and the band came on stage. They were dressed in black and looked gloomy.

There was no banter in between songs, just four figures looming out of the darkness playing their songs of melancholy and heartache. Before long the bassist, who looked particularly moody, kept pointing to his bass and his monitor in front of him and then pointing up. Clearly he wanted his bass louder and higher in the mix. The soundman obliged. Two songs later, the bassist repeated the motion and the bass went up again. Before long the bass drowned out the rest of the music. He didn't look any happier.

It was odd and made me wonder about what it was like to be in a band and be having a bad day or be in a mood. It must happen, you play gigs night after night, clearly you're going to have a bad day sometimes. The situation is probably made worse by having a permanent hangover. Whatever the reason, the bassist had been in a bad mood, he wasn't happy with the sound, perhaps he hadn't slept well, maybe he was just annoyed because he never got to sing. Maybe he thought he could do a better job; the singer of the band wasn't your average rock singer, he sung in a kind of baritone, which sounds odd, but gave a strange gravitas to the band's songs, particularly when paired with their cryptic and melancholy lyrics, *"oh you put the weights into my little heart"*.

The following day we were driving again, through Virginia's national park, Shenandoah and towards Washington DC. By this time all barriers of normal car protocol had broken down in Her Ramliness. Littering had become commonplace. Sometimes I would go into the back seats while Jack drove, just for the sheer variety of it. One thing that began around this time was the singing. It began innocently enough, a song came on that we both liked and perhaps one of us started humming, or a particularly catchy line escaped from one of our mouths. Before long singing was perfectly acceptable behaviour. Soon, singing as loud as you wanted, whether music was playing or not, was a regular feature of the journeys.

The day after the concert, we were driving and Jack spoke, "You know Interpol, do you think the singer ever sings other stuff, like other people's songs?"

"Well yeah, he's a singer isn't he?" I replied.

"But I mean, like at Christmas time, maybe the family is having a sing-song and it's some upbeat festive ditty, do you think he sings that?"

It was an odd thought, he had such a distinctive, baritone, deep and serious singing voice, that it seemed incongruous, "I don't know, it doesn't really seem like it would suit him."

Jack turned to me. I knew what was coming. He cleared his throat and started singing, loudly, imitating the deep and melancholy baritone, *"Rocking around the Christmas Tree! Voices singing, let's be jolly, deck the halls with boughs of holly."* It was amusing. We laughed. He sung it again.

Soon it wasn't funny, but it didn't stop. While singing in the car could be fun, it could also be a rather dangerous thing, because if one person was not in the mood for singing and the other one was, then it was a rather toxic combination. Several hours later, with a couple of hours still to go I snapped, "Jack."

"What?" He stopped singing.

"You need to stop singing." He looked surprised.

"Why?"

"It's annoying. I'm getting increasingly annoyed."

"What? It's funny."

"It was funny."

"I can't help it if you're annoyed," he said, slightly hurt.

"Yes but you can. You *can* stop annoying me. I can't stop being annoyed, but you can stop annoying me." It was a revelation and it flummoxed Jack. I continued more gently, "So if you you're the one being annoying, you can choose to stop doing it. Right?"

He conceded the point then paused for a moment before speaking again, "But I'm not the only one who's annoying," he said matter-of-factly and it turned out that I too could be annoying. We continued to drive.

7. Washington DC – Car trouble

Washington DC is not a state, but a district. The nation's capital is an unusual city. At the risk of sounding obvious, it's very political. It has a reason for being and that reason is government. It's a planned city with its magnificent grassy, tree-lined mall and the extravagant sweep of the diagonal avenues that radiate out from the Capitol building, home of the Senate and Congress. At its centre it is grand and impressive. Rather like the cathedrals of medieval Europe which were imposing, huge and looming large, built to inspire awe amongst the peasantry, DC too is built on a grand scale, in such a way that any visitor could not help but be impressed by the magnificence, wealth and importance of this city and therefore this country. So that's what I felt like in DC, like a modern day medieval peasant, awed and wowed by the splendour and scale of it all.

As you walk around the centre, you can't help but marvel. The government buildings are clustered around the mall and the blocks surrounding it. It feels like every building is at least a block big. We walked along the mall and saw the large Smithsonian museums lined up, one after another. The mall stretches from the capitol building at one end, past the Washington monument in the middle (a very tall spire-like stone construction) and on to the Lincoln memorial at the far end. Almost all the other tourists were trying to do this 2 mile walk. It seemed like it could be very pleasant but that day, in the summer, when the temperature was 35C (95F), it was no mean feat. We saw the fallen strewn along the benches and under the trees all along the mall. Wheezing and sweating: the foolhardy, the underprepared and the morbidly obese in their lurid t-shirts and inappropriate shorts, unable to complete the walk - all having bitten off more than they could chew. Which ironically, in the case of the morbidly obese, is also the reason why they were never going to be able to make it in the first place.

One thing I liked about Washington is the slogan that they've chosen for their number plates. When we visited the US on family holidays, I always liked looking at the different mottos on the number plates. They're normally fairly generic and highlight one interesting thing about the state, e.g. Wisconsin – America's Dairyland, or Minnesota – 10,000 lakes. Sometimes they're even a little stupid e.g. Idaho – Famous potatoes.....However, I think Washington's is the best, being, as it is, an angry remark, an accusation even: "Taxation Without Representation."

As Washington is in no single state (and was planned that way, so as to be a neutral capital of all the states) it is actually governed differently. For instance it has no senators (every other state gets two senators), which means that the people of Washington are essentially denied this one element of democracy. Given that around 700,000 people live in DC, which is more than two of the "proper" states (Vermont and Wyoming), that's a lot of people who are being democratically disadvantaged.

What was it that the colonists in the Americas who rebelled against the British were annoyed about in 1776? Wasn't it exactly this issue? Didn't they even use that same slogan? It's pretty ironic that a country should fight a war of independence over an issue, then perpetrate the same offence against the people of its capital. It would probably be more ironic if the people of Washington then fought a war for independence from the country it governs. We'd have to call it the war of ironic independence. If that war ever happens, I'm claiming that name. The rest of the US can't say they weren't warned – the residents of DC have put it right there on the licence plate.

The one speciality dish we wanted to track down in DC is the half smoke. The half smoke isn't too different from a hotdog, although it's kind of more like a polish sausage. It's meatier, coarser and thicker than a hotdog. There is a disputed history to the name; some say it's because the sausage is half beef/half pork, some say it's because the sausage is cut in half and grilled split open. However, the half smoke is not always smoked, so there is some debate around the recipe and how it's served. Nevertheless it seemed the quintessential place to get a half smoke is Ben's Chili Bowl, which is where we headed.

Ben's Chili Bowl is a great place, with loads of atmosphere, and plenty of hustle and bustle inside. It's also got a fine history, having been there since 1958. It's housed in a former silent movie theatre (Washington's first) and is a DC institution. Chili (as they spell it) is a speciality that can be added on top of any of the staples (burgers, fries and half smokes). So we had half smokes with chili and, then since a lot of things seem to get smothered with gloopy cheese there we also got the fries covered in the bright yellow cheesy sauce.

The food looked messy but it was still a tasty treat. The hotdog came covered in chili or cheese so it didn't look that appetising, but each dish was in its own little red plastic basket, lined with paper, as is common in American fast food places, which was quite appealing. It was a messy feast as we tucked in to the multitude of little baskets that covered the table. The half smoke was actually a decent meaty sausage – something not always commonly available in the US. While the frankfurter is readily available, and speciality sausages (particularly German and Polish) abound, the truly meaty style, with the crispy skin, is not that common. So there you go, Washington may not have any senators, but they do have decent sausages.

* * *

Jack and I arrived in Washington following our long drive through the mountains of Virginia's Shenandoah National Park. We hadn't been in a city for a while and our beloved Ram had now become a hindrance in this new urban environment. We wanted to book into a hostel in the centre of the city but we were told that it would be very problematic to park the Van. Instead we chose a hostel in the northern suburbs of the city, where we figured it would be easier to park on the street.

City parking is one of the perplexing and slightly frustrating things about the US. Clearly Americans love their cars. Practically every adult has a car; if you don't have a car or even worse can't drive, then you are basically subhuman. There are a few pockets of resistance, such as people living in the middle of the biggest (and oldest) cities e.g. New York or Chicago, or those hip young people on the West Coast living in green-minded cities that have decent public transport, like Portland or San Francisco. In general though, everyone has a car, whether they can afford it not, whether they're terrible at driving or not. People don't even tend to share cars with their partners, everyone's got their own. If you are American and said that you didn't want to learn to drive, it would be unthinkable. It would be as bad as saying that you didn't like America.

Cars are integral to the American psyche and lifestyle and are fundamental to American life. They symbolise freedom and aspiration. On the other hand, what is more restrictive and symbolic of failure than having to use a bus? It's anathema to a lot of Americans. That said, just because everyone wants to use a car, even in most cities, that doesn't actually mean there's any parking. To our surprise and annoyance, it was not easy to find parking in most American cities, it was either very limited, subject to a lot of restrictions, or prohibitively expensive, or all three.

In DC we eventually found some on-street parking, parked up and came back the next morning to find that we had been given a parking ticket. We were vexed. We had obeyed the timing restrictions, we had obeyed the zoning restrictions, we had kept clear of the 'keep clears'. We were at a loss, "It says here Jack that we were parked facing oncoming traffic."

"Right," said Jack agreeing.

"That's an offence here, apparently."

"What the hell? Where has it said that anywhere? Why would that be an offence?"

We looked around and saw all the vehicles on our side were parked in the direction of the traffic and on the other side were parked in the opposite direction. Her Ramliness was the odd one out.

"Ah crap," said Jack succinctly.

"Why would that be a rule? When you think of victimless crimes, this one would be right up there, wouldn't it?" I said.

"This makes no sense!" said Jack exasperated. "The only people who would commit this offence are people that don't know this is an offence. Aren't they? What possible advantage would you be gaining by parking facing the traffic? It's not like speeding is it, where you can see why someone would do it, even if they knew the bloody rule? The only people they are catching doing this are people who don't know about it and maybe... the chronically lazy."

Jack's ranting was correct, but the police department wanted $40 anyway.

We decided to move the Van and spotted a building that was labelled as a religious meeting place, it looked like it had a big car park. We ventured in. As well as the car park at the front it appeared to have a car park around the back, so we drove round, so as to put the Van out of sight. It was a decent size car park and had only one other car in it. We decided we couldn't take any more risks on the many rules (known and unknown) that governed the street parking and left the Ram there.

We had a good time in Washington DC, spending a couple of days exploring the city and taking in some of the museums and pleasant neighbourhoods. On our final day we returned to the Ram, it was Sunday morning, perhaps not the best time to try and inconspicuously pick up an illegally parked minivan from a building hosting religious gatherings. Unsurprisingly it seemed a lot busier than on the Friday when we'd left it there.

We walked towards the building. "Heads high, just act confident, like we've got every right to be here," I said.

"The backpacks might just be a giveaway," Jack replied perceptively.

We continued walking to the building, a few of the middle-aged people, bustling at the front of the building looked at us, but we kept walking. We headed around the side of the building and to the back. The car park was a lot fuller now and we crossed no man's land, walking towards the Ram.

Jack saw it first and he stopped. I tried to see what he was looking at and then I saw it. The Ram was injured, her left rear tyre was flat or on the way to going flat.

"Ah crap," Jack said, not for the first time.

"Don is not going to be pleased about this." I said, referencing the mysterious German owner of the Ram. Since our first and only contact with Don (on the phone) when we were negotiating rental of the Ram, Don had been a looming omniscient presence in our lives. We didn't know much about him, but he seemed to a) be a bit of a shyster and b) not suffer fools gladly.

Don fascinated us and throughout the journey we'd often imagine fictitious scenarios, which would result in us having to call up Don and explain the increasingly bizarre predicaments that we had got ourselves in. They started off reasonably mundane, but eventually they became more peculiar. They would go something along the lines of:

"Don! Don! We've been sleeping in the Ram and Jack's sleeping bag won't come unzipped and he's stuck in it. What are we going to do?"

To the more urgent:

Don! Don! We went into a car wash and the car wash is broken and we're stuck inside. The windows won't open, and we think the oxygen is running out. Come quickly!"

Or even more sinister:

"Don! Don! Jack killed a man! It was an accident, but he's in the boot of the Ram now, you need to help us bury the body, otherwise we're all going down!"

But now we had a real predicament, a puncture, and Don wasn't there to help us.

We approached the Ram, tentatively, as if the tyre situation might change, as though it might have been a mirage. But it didn't and it wasn't.

"Well it's not totally flat," Jack opened with.

"Yeah, I wonder if we could drive it to a garage?"

"Do we have breakdown cover?" We looked at each and both knew that that was highly improbable. We'd been given very little documentation or instruction at the second hand dealership where we'd picked up the Van.

"Well let's get out of here, I think we're a bit conspicuous. It looks like they're setting up for church. Let's just drive, I'm sure we'll see a garage before long."

We got in the Van and it didn't feel right, it listed slightly and as soon as Jack put it into reverse, it listed even more. Whatever air was left in the tyre must have started leaking out as soon as the wheel started turning.

"This isn't working," Jack said obviously.

"Look, we don't want a puncture *and* a big fine for parking in a private car park on top."

We pulled forward to head round the side of the building and back out the front. The wheel was making a funny noise and the people started looking at us. Some of them were really staring. They were almost certainly thinking, *"Do those two not know they're driving on a flat tyre?"*

"This isn't going well," Jack said, as he drove the Van forward very slowly.

One man started gesticulating at the side of the Van with the flat tyre. I waved at him, he continued gesturing towards the flat tyre, increasingly vigorously. I didn't know what to do, so I gave him the thumbs up and grinned at him stupidly.

We rounded the corner and pulled to the junction. Jack turned right on to the road, the Ram listed again. "I reckon I must be running on the rim. I'm pulling in. You never know, there might be a spare tyre and a jack somewhere."

So as we pulled out of the turn-in for the church, Jack indicated and pulled immediately in to the next turn-in, alongside three low buildings which included a convenience store. We were right next to the religious building and some of the people out the front who'd watched us drive out and then immediately back in, looked at us bemused.

We got out, the tyre was completely flat, the Ram wasn't going anywhere. We found the spare tyre quickly but in the middle where the jack was supposed to be, there was just a hole. It wasn't really clear how we were meant to put the tyre on and we stood there looking confused. Then we realised, now we did actually have to call Don. Despite having pretended to call Don on dozens of occasions neither of us really wanted to do it now, now that we had an issue to own up to.

"Fine, I'll do it," I said and called the number.

"Hello," a German voice answered.

"Ah Don! It's Rich here, with the Ram minivan."

"Who?" he asked. *Did we really mean that little to him?*

"Rich and Jack, we've rented the Ram from Florida and are bringing it to you in New York."

"Ok." He didn't seem interested and clearly didn't want to deal with any of our problems. *He's getting off lightly* I thought, *Jack could have killed a man*.

"We've got a puncture, we've found the spare, but there's no jack. Where is it?"

"I took it out."

"What?" I didn't understand. *Was Don working against us?*

"Yes the Van is too heavy for you to jack up, you need a professional to do it for you."

"Ok well then what's the number for the breakdown service?'

"There is no breakdown cover. Go to a garage. Ok thanks." He hung up. Clearly Don wasn't some benevolent protector figure, guiding us to him in New York. He was just a dick.

Jack and I discussed our predicament. We seemed to be out of options, since we couldn't even drive the Ram to a garage. At this point a man ambled by and saw us looking forlornly at the flat tyre. Middle-aged, black, slightly scruffy looking, but friendly, he asked us if he could help and before long came back to the same issue that we identified.

"You boys need a jack."

"We certainly do, but we don't really want to pay a call-out fee and a repair fee. The problem is Don said it was too heavy to jack it ourselves."

Our friend didn't think too much of Don's opinion, which we liked. "I'll tell you what. I know a garage up the road. I can go and get a heavy duty jack and a crowbar. You just buy me some beers and I'll sort you out."

We were happy, the terms seemed favourable and paying for work with beer, as though we had entered some kind of beer-based economy, was perfect. The man disappeared up the road and we went to the very convenient convenience store behind us. An hour later we were on the road, but this time with a score to settle.

8. Maryland: Ahoy pirates!

Maryland is dominated by three things, firstly DC to the south, a lot of DC's suburbs spill over into Maryland and a lot of Marylanders work in the capital. Secondly Baltimore, which is the biggest city in the state, and still one of the biggest in the US. For a long time Baltimore was the most obvious American example of urban decay, white flight and industrial decline, but it has been resurgent in the last twenty years. Finally the third element to understanding Maryland is the Chesapeake Bay – which is really the heart of the state. The estuary is the largest in the US, more than 150 rivers drain into it and the total shoreline of the bay and its tributaries is over 11,000 miles. It practically covers the eastern side of the state and it is the dominant feature, both geographically and culturally. The slogan "save the Chesapeake" can be seen on drains, bumper stickers and some number plates (unfortunately the bay is at risk of chronic pollution). The Bay is also responsible for the sailing culture which is deeply embedded throughout Maryland. Many Marylanders sail and/or own a boat. Maryland's own capital city (states have their own capitals), Annapolis, calls itself the sailing capital of America and is home to the US Naval Academy.

Fittingly, the cuisine of Maryland is also heavily influenced by the Bay, or more specifically what lives there. Marylanders are obsessed with crabs and the particular type of seasoning that goes with them, Old

Bay. There are dozens of crab-based dishes: crab cakes, crab imperial, crab dip, crab soup, whole crabs, softshell crabs etc. They love all of them, many of which they invented. Therefore you might conclude that the Bay must be the home of an abundance of crabs. Unfortunately not, due to overfishing, the native blue crab is actually somewhat scarce, and the majority of crab now eaten in Maryland is shipped from the Gulf of Mexico. Nevertheless Marylanders have retained their taste for crab and their expertise in preparing and eating it.

Robyn and I visited Baltimore, which is something most tourists do with both excitement and a fair degree of trepidation. If you've ever seen the TV show *The Wire* you'll know Baltimore for its reputation as a drug-riddled jungle of cornerboys and crack dens. That isn't fair; Baltimore is so much more than that! Baltimore certainly does have those ghettos and 'hoods that you probably wouldn't want to walk around in on your own or even drive through at night, but it also has some nice neighbourhoods, especially immediately surrounding the centre. Most tourists head to the very centre, the Inner Harbor, which is like the Green Zone of Baltimore. You know you are going to be safe there. However, if you do walk 15 minutes in the wrong direction (especially West past the stadiums) then you can find yourself in hostile territory.

Baltimore was a city built on the fortunes of its docks. In the 18th century when sugar and other goods were being produced in the Caribbean and shipped to the US, the merchants realised it was a lot quicker to sail up the Chesapeake and dock in Baltimore rather than sailing all the way up to New York in the north. Baltimore prospered and it became one of the North East's biggest cities. Post World-War 2 many Baltimoreans (like many Americans) decided that they wanted to live in the suburbs in bigger homes with big gardens and picket fences. The wealthy (largely white) middle classes rapidly decanted to the suburbs, the city started to die from the inside out, as the docks started to decline and the industry closed. Baltimore gained a reputation for violence and crime and more people left.

In the late 1970s at the nadir of this, the city decided to embark on an ambitious project to revitalise the city from its decrepit centre. The Inner Harbor, largely an industrial wasteland of piers and warehouses, was cleared out and remodelled, making imaginative use of the piers and the waterfront area. The Maryland Science Center and the Convention Center were opened. In the early 80s they attracted the prestigious National Aquarium to build its new base there and following that they built two new stadiums for their American Football and Baseball teams (Ravens and Orioles respectively) right at the edge of the harbour area. When we visited it was game day and it made for a lively atmosphere with fans drifting back and forth from the Inner Harbor.

The Inner Harbor project has been so successful that it now attracts significant numbers of tourists (unthinkable thirty years ago) and other cities study it as a fine example of urban regeneration. That said, the fact the Inner Harbor is so pleasant and safe only underscores how different it is to a lot of the impoverished neighbourhoods and ghettoes which still exist. The city, as much as any in the US, feels like a real patchwork.

Robyn and I decided to spend the day in Baltimore, and headed for the hip Fells Point neighbourhood just next to the Inner Harbor. Fells Point has cobbled streets, old buildings and a distinctly maritime air. The old pubs open right on to the waterfront and I could imagine ships docking here in centuries gone by. But we were here to board another type of ship entirely, a pirate ship cruise run by the so-called Urban Pirates. An unusual cruise to say the least: we were encouraged to dress up as pirates for our sail around the Inner Harbor while drinking and generally acting like pirates.

We'd made a few friends as were lining up for the "Bring Your Own Grog" cruise. Some of them had taken the trouble to dress up as pirates beforehand. I was confident that I would find some suitable clothing in the costume chest. We boarded the ship and the pirate impressions started immediately, and not just from our small group of friends. Random strangers were more than happy to engage in Pirate-related banter, "Ahoy matey! Where are you hailing from?"

"England."

"Well shiver me timbers!"

I rummaged through the costume chest and found an extremely ill-fitting waistcoat, a ridiculous blue sash, an eye patch and a hat that looked like it had been sat on by a particularly fat pirate. Robyn had picked out a nice looking sash and a colourful jolly hat. I thought that I had looted a fine costume, "Arrrrghh, 'tis some fine booty I have captured! How do I look?"

She raised an eyebrow and then scrunched her face, "You look like a bit of a fool."

"Aye." I had to agree. "But you're married to me, so who's the real fool eh?" It was a zinger.

She'd been zinged and she knew it.

"I guess we both are."

Dammit.

The rest of the pirate cruise passed in a blur of games of limbo, conga lines, singing of pirate shanties and drinking rum. At one point we closed in on the harbour and the tourists milling around. We were instructed to man the guns (water cannons on the side of the ship). Aha! This was our chance to finally mount an attack on the landlubbers. We rushed to the cannon and opened fire. Unfortunately the jets of water only reached about halfway to shore before petering out, lamely dribbling into the harbour water. The tourists on shore could see what we had attempted and started laughing at us. How dare they? We were the pirates! Yes we were adults dressed up in ridiculous costumes, at 6pm, on a pretend pirate ship, but even so, we were still pirates!

Our friend who had consumed considerably more rum than us began waving his plastic cutlass in an agitated fashion. "Avast ye landlubbers! I'll put you in Davy Jones' Locker, you muthaf****s!"

We laughed, "That's a bit strong isn't it?" I asked.

"Yeah I just thought, you know, it is Baltimore isn't it?"

We followed our friends to a bar in the trendy Federal Hill neighbourhood just to the south of the centre. It was a magic bar. This wasn't something I'd come across before but I was intrigued, "So it's a bar, but how is it magic?"

"There's also a magic show," said our new friend matter-of-factly.

"At the bar?"

"Kind of, it's actually on the bar," she replied.

"Like someone pulling a rabbit out of a hat or card tricks or something?"

"Oh no," she replied, "it's a full magic show. Just wait and see."

By now I was imagining lions, a man jumping through a flaming ring or at the very least a woman being sawn in half.

It looked like a regular bar, it had a fairly orderly set of tables in the front and a very long bar, with mirrors behind it. After an hour or so of waiting, the magic show began and it was indeed a full magic show. The magician performed some complex sleight of hand stuff, some remarkable illusions and a very impressive finale involving the magician tied up in a straitjacket being suspended from the ceiling over the bar. He finished and the audience erupted into applause.

"Wow," I said to our friend, "that was impressive, how many times have you been?"

"This is the third time," she said, still in wonder at the show.

"Incredible, and what were the other shows like?" I asked.

"Oh they were exactly the same," she said as she finished clapping.

I turned to Robyn and whispered, "What? Exactly the same? Did you hear that? It doesn't change at all?"

"Well, if people enjoy it," she said, justifying it.

"That's mental. I mean literally mental. It's a good show but can you imagine saying next Friday night, oh it's Friday again, shall we pop down to the magic bar? It just gets better and better doesn't it? That same bloody show," I said.

"It was a good show," she said, signalling it was time for me to stop complaining.

At this point our thoughts turned to the food. Now people from other states will most likely identify the crab cake as the number one crab dish (and a crab cake is indeed a wonder to behold). The best ones have as much lump crab meat in as possible, and are mixed through with breadcrumbs, milk, mayo and eggs, along with the spicy Old Bay seasoning. Typically these will be fried or broiled (grilled) and often put in a sandwich. Unlike a lot of other fish cakes you won't tend to find potato in there, so it's really meaty in comparison. Unfortunately since crab meat is kind of pricey, crab cakes can be a bit on the small side and it's normally worth paying the extra to get a proper jumbo crab cake. Delicious, undoubtedly, but there is another experience that is even more authentic than the crab cake and definitely more specific to Maryland.

We visited one of the premier places, Bo Brooks, on the waterfront, which announced itself with the tagline "Baltimore's best crabs". As well as the multitude of other crab dishes that I mentioned earlier, they're also particularly well known for their steamed crabs. We arrived and they covered our table in a huge roll of brown paper, because it was about to get messy. They took our order (crabs come by the dozen or half dozen) although they advised us three or four crabs sufficient per person was about right.

The process they follow is to get the live crabs, stun them, boil them up, dip them in a quick ice bath (to prevent the crab meat overcooking) absolutely cover them in Old Bay seasoning and then dump the whole crabs on the table. We were given a mallet, a leg cracker device, a bucket to chuck crab bits in, and even bibs. It's was a bit bewildering being confronted with our first crab. Because they were whole and covered in a very hard shell, it was quite tricky to work out how to get into it. It's a little bit like the restaurant equivalent of unpacking an Ikea shelving unit and wondering where the hell you start.

Fortunately the restaurant staff were happy to give a quick crab-cracking masterclass. The normal method is to start by cracking the legs off, and put them to the side. Then you take the body, turn it over and pull a piece of the shell that looks like a tab. This allows you to split the round body in half and this makes it easy to just pop the top shell off. You then have to remove the lungs/gills and then finally you can get at the meat. The meat right in the centre is some of the best. When you've finished with that and dispensed with all the other bits, you can return to the legs. You use the leg-cracker implement (it looks a little like a pair of pliers) to break them open and take out the tasty leg meat. Sounds a bit complicated but plenty of people around us were making the whole process look quite elegant.

What is much more likely to happen and what happened to us, is that it was hard to get into the crab, so we started breaking pieces of shell off roughly rather than the nice orderly way it was meant to happen (so exactly like wrestling with Ikea furniture). Sooner or later, in desperation to get to the tasty meat inside, the use of the mallet became completely indiscriminate and increasingly forceful. Then disaster struck – I cut a finger on the spiky edge of the crab. My hands were covered in the spicy Old Bay powder and as it entered the newly formed cut on my finger, it really was a special kind of pain. At that point I thought a crab cake wouldn't have been such a bad idea after all.

* * *

"I just don't want to go," Jack protested.
"Why not?"
"You know why."

Jack and I were debating whether we should go and visit someone who we had met earlier in the trip. We were on the road, having left Washington DC. We were driving straight through the next two states (Maryland and Delaware) to get to Philadelphia. We only had about five more days before we had to hand our beloved Ram to the evil Don in New York.

While we were down in Florida, we had met a girl who had taken a shine to Jack. The feeling was not mutual. She was an odd-looking girl with frizzy, ginger hair. It was big hair. Too big. She was tall, stick-thin and wore braces. She was the complete package. But she was not without confidence; she was loud, mouthy and opinionated with it. She cackled madly at the slightest excuse and it wasn't a pleasant sight. Perhaps it was the cackle or perhaps it was the feeling that she would have quite happily put a curse on Jack to make him fall in love with her, but for whatever reason we called her "the Crone."

"I don't want to see the Crone again."
"What? She was nice," I said innocently.

"She wasn't, she was awful," said Jack, agitated. He seemed to shift around uncomfortably in the driver's seat at the thought of her.

"She had a certain charm," I said picturing her throwing her head back in her mad cackle and inching in ever closer to Jack as she sat next to him on the bench.

"You're such a bastard," he said, accurately.

We had been staying at a hostel in Orlando, before our trip to Disneyworld and Gatorworld and all the other worlds that exist in that corner of Florida. The Crone had been working somewhere near there during her holidays, in between studying at a university in New Jersey. She had no money as she would repeatedly say, as though it was some kind of motto. "No Money. *No. Money.*" Then she would draw a horizontal line through the air. I didn't really know what it meant, but it was annoying, like almost everything she said.

There was an eclectic group of people at the hostel, including a man who was living there who would only call himself New York. He was in his early 50's and retired from the police. He was remarkably upbeat for a man who lived in a dorm room in a hostel. However, hostel life was dominated by the Crone. Her shriek pierced the warm evening air as we sat around the courtyard. She introduced herself to us on the first evening and was clearly aiming to come across as "feisty". However, we did not take kindly to her mocking of our precious Ram or scepticism of it being an appropriate vehicle for two backpackers undertaking long distance travel.

Sooner or later though, in between the stories of her job, the stories of her stay in the hostel, the story about some up and coming country and western singer she had met, her lack of money and the fact she was going to be a big deal, it became apparent she liked Jack. She finally asked us some questions about our travels. "What's the deal with you two? Ya gay or something?! Hahahah," she cackled madly.

"Just because we're two guys travelling around together doesn't mean we're gay," I said matter-of-factly.

This piqued her interest and her gaze lingered on Jack for a moment too long, "Well are you coming through New Jersey?"

"I don't know about that," said Jack quickly.

"Well you are you if you're heading to New York, ya pair of douchebags. Hahahah." She made herself laugh again. "You guys are welcome to stay the night at my place," she said and squeezed Jack's knee.

He didn't seem to like it.

Back in the Ram I continued to make the case for a visit to the Crone, "Look, it's a free night's accommodation. We spend a few nights in Philadelphia, one night with the Crone and then drop the Ram off."

"I don't want to."

"Jack, be reasonable, it will be interesting, we'll get to see an American university. I'm telling you, it'll be interesting."

"She might try something."

"She's not going to try anything. You big wimp."

"I don't want to go."

We drove straight out of Maryland and entered Delaware, continuing towards Philadelphia.

9. Delaware: The Taxman

Delaware has a date on its flag, December 7, 1787, the date at which Delaware ratified the constitution, the first state to do so, giving rise to its official nickname "The First State". What actually gave rise to the name, according to the Delaware government homepage, is this: '"The First State" became the official State nickname on May 23, 2002 following a request by Mrs. Anabelle O'Malley's First Grade Class at Mt. Pleasant Elementary School.' Any state that is willing to enact legislative change on the basis of a letter from a class of 6-year olds is alright by me.

Many years ago, I was intrigued by Delaware. I'd heard of it as a state, but had no real conception of what it contained. We all know something about New York, Texas or California; even those states we know little about such as Kansas or Iowa, we at least have an idea that they're in the middle of the country and have a lot of farmland (correct).

But what of Delaware? What does it contain? What's it all about? I knew it was small (the second smallest of the states in fact). I am always attracted to the idea of small countries and islands. There is something infinitely appealing and slightly mysterious about an island or small country to me. Conversely the idea of a big place like Germany, Poland or a big state like Nebraska just doesn't have the same appeal. When I was backpacking the idea of visiting small, mysterious islands in the South Pacific intrigued me much more than say Australia. At one point I had the idea I'd like to write a book about travels to such places, the types of mysterious, often small places you'd heard of, but didn't know anything about, entitled "You went where?"

The reality of visiting these places is that they're often not as interesting as they promise (although sometimes of course they can be). I feel there must be a lot of people out there like me, fascinated by the idea of certain places. For instance, take San Marino, this tiny nation or "enclaved microstate" as wikipedia calls it, gets 3 million visitors per year! So there's either a lot of people like me, or a lot of box-tickers out there who just want to tick off as many countries as they can, because what the heck is attracting 3 million people to San Marino? As Lonely Planet describes it: "It's all very toy-town, and the packed streets and kitsch souvenir shops are not everyone's cup of tea. But the novelty value of this enclave cannot be overestimated". So the main attraction is novelty value then. In fact Lonely Planet lists the top thing to do as "Revel in pure unadulterated kitsch in San Marino's overdose of souvenir shops." Really? But enough of San Marino. For the second time, what of Delaware?

Well, while Delaware is not a total write-off, it's also perhaps not the most interesting of states. Delaware is the only state to have no national park, national monument or national battlefield. Even Guam (not even a state, but a small American island in the middle of Pacific) has a national park. Delaware also has no major professional sports teams, no commercial airport and contains the fewest counties of any US state (3). So what does Delaware have? Well it's got Obama's Vice President, and long-time Delaware senator, Joe Biden. I mean he wasn't born there and since he became Vice-President he obviously doesn't live there either. So maybe he's not the best example. It's not easy finding things that Delaware is famous for.

Even if you asked most Americans about Delaware, I doubt they'd be able to tell you much about it. I think their overriding reaction would be nonplussed, turning towards irritation the nearer they lived to Delaware (it seems to inspire a kind of vague dislike). Delaware is pretty non-descript. You might try and put this down to its small size (but Rhode Island is smaller and is known for a few things, mansions and sailing to name but two), Delaware is the fifth smallest state by population, but those smaller than it in this respect, also seem to loom much larger in the US imagination (e.g. Wyoming – known for Cowboys and Alaska – bears and snow).

For those that live in the North East/Mid-Atlantic region, they are more likely to have an opinion on Delaware, although this can often be fairly negative. Some people perceive Delaware to be a bit of a naughty neighbour. It positions itself as a bit of an offshore tax haven, which is a little bit odd, since it's mostly definitely onshore and one of the regular 50 states. There's no sales tax in Delaware (only 5 of the

50 don't levy this tax). The sales tax is typically 5-10% on top of the price of any goods and services. In Europe this tax is normally already factored into the price of goods, so the price you see is the price you pay. Not so in the US – if it's $9.99 and you're in a state with sales tax then don't go to the till with an outstretched $10 bill and a smile on your face, because it's going to be rung up as $9.99 plus the tax, and you'll look a little silly.

I've always thought the approach to sales tax tells you a little bit about the American approach to tax and the government. It's like the stores are saying, *look if it was up to us, it'd only be $9.99! That extra 70¢? That's not for us - blame the government for that!* It makes Americans very resentful of sales tax, because it's very obvious whenever you buy anything. The irony is that throughout Europe and most of the rest of the developed world, the sales tax is 15-20%, at least double the average in the US - but because you don't see it, you don't notice it or resent it in the same way.

Americans really don't like tax. I mean no one *likes* tax, but Americans really resent taxes. The country partly came into being because the colonists resented the tax regime of the imperialist British. I once had a conversation with someone who genuinely believed there should be no income taxes whatsoever. She put it like this, in all seriousness "What gives the government the right to come to your house and point a gun at you and say that they are taking your money through income tax, whether you like it or not?"

While I thought that taxes generally got taken straight out of the pay packet, rather than at gunpoint, it was still an interesting viewpoint and one that seemed very American in its ideology. All tax is bad and the government is essentially stealing from you. Ultimately it comes from a distrust of the government and a view that they cannot be trusted to spend your money. This is essentially libertarianism, which says societies work best when government is reduced to an absolute bare minimum and individuals are left to look after themselves.

So if tax is bad and Delaware is a low tax state, why can it inspire hostility amongst those who live near it? It's because Delaware doesn't want the people who actually live there to pay any tax (e.g. lack of sales tax and it's extremely low rate of taxes on businesses), but if you're passing through, well then Delaware has $$ signs in her eyes. Delaware is strategically placed on the main interstate on that runs up the East Coast of the US – I-95 - and Delaware, like some modern day highway robber, knows this very well. Despite the fact that the I-95 section that cuts through Delaware is pretty short – about 20 miles, they manage to toll you twice, in both directions. There's over 300 miles of the same interstate in Florida and there are no tolls, so Delaware is really taking the piss. There aren't even any bridges or tunnels, which are kind of gimmes for tolls. Ok so you built a big bridge and now you want a few bucks. Fine. But for a normal road?

No wonder Delaware gets a bit of a bad rap. The fact that it doesn't have a sales tax naturally attracts people from neighbouring states to do their shopping there and Delaware does have an absurdly large number of shopping malls taking advantage of this. Many of them are located conveniently just off the interstate. However, I'm not sure it's that cost effective, if you are from out of state you would have to drive a fair distance to get to Delaware and pay the associated fuel (gas) costs. Plus as soon as you got there, they'll toll you immediately anyway. The state border sign may as well say *"Welcome to Delaware! $5 please."*

Of course on a personal level, avoiding the sales tax is a great move, but every state needs those tax dollars for the roads and the schools etc so they'll probably only raise some other taxes that the residents can't avoid, like property taxes. But there are a lot of Americans who would rather pay the fuel costs and tolls than pay sales tax; taxes are there to be avoided if at all possible. There's just something psychological about taxes that Americans particularly don't like. Maybe taxes can be added to our list of *Un-American things.*

So what else do we need to know about Delaware? The food! Well unfortunately (but perhaps not surprisingly) Delaware does not have a state food. It does have an official state beverage – milk. But I don't think there would be an awful lot to say about that. *So I drank some milk in Delaware....tastes the same as drinking it anywhere else.*

So what does it have? Well there is actually a Delaware-only chain of burger restaurants called "The Charcoal Pit" whose website invites you to: "Be a part of a true Delaware tradition!" To be fair to the Charcoal Pit, they do provide a twist on burgers, they cook them over charcoal rather than grill them and they've been doing it this way for over 50 years. So we decided to stop at the original Charcoal Pit in Wilmington.

I imagine the restaurant looks as it did when it opened in 1956. It looked seriously 50's. Outside *The Charcoal Pit* is written in these massive neon bubble letters that brought to mind The Jetsons. You can just imagine those old Chevys and Cadillacs with the big tail fins and circular red taillights parked out the front. In fact walking up to the entrance and into the foyer felt a bit like being Marty McFly in the original *Back to the Future*.

The look is definitely immediately identifiable with that classic 50's era we know from the movies when High School students went to the diner to hang out, ordering endless milkshakes and burgers. Unfortunately not that many of these establishments still exist, having been ruthlessly exterminated by the shift to drive-thru and the price-cutting tactics of McDonalds and Burger King. However, a few stick around, if only out of nostalgia and loyalty.

The Pit is also pleasingly retro on the inside, not in a clean, calculated way like the chains Johnny Rockets or Fuddruckers (which bemusingly try to recreate the retro look, even though hundreds of the real 50's diners must have died out through lack of popularity). There is nothing contrived about the look of The Charcoal Pit. The 50's touches are there in a genuine "we never thought to replace this stuff" kind of a way. The place has personality, and mini jukeboxes on every table.

It also had a pleasingly simple menu, not one of these fancy places with a variety of options. On the hamburger front, you could get it plain, with cheese, "Deluxe" (with lettuce and dressing) or "Special" (with fries). I kid you not.

I ordered a special and a milkshake (classic choice, well actually one of the only choices), and I must say the burger was perfectly respectable, decent, if nothing spectacular. The milkshake though was a delight; thick, tasty and served as they often do in the US accompanied by the silver mixing shaker, icy to the touch on the outside and a big spoon left in the remainder of the milkshake that was still in the shaker. Luscious.

So maybe Delaware doesn't have any national parks or sports teams or airports or major cities but so what? It's a slice of America just the same, and it's got some nice beaches and pretty towns. Plus it's got diners with burgers and milkshakes. Oh and I saved $30 in sales taxes when I bought my new iPad there.

* * *

"Ok fine. Fine. We'll go." Jack had relented. We were going to see the Crone.

10. Pennsylvania: Independence

Robyn and I carried on to Philadelphia, a city with a rich history and home of the Philly cheesesteak. We arrived hungry and set off to get ourselves some cheesesteaks. A cheesesteak is a sub roll containing thinly sliced up steak which is fried up on a lightly oiled griddle. Melted cheese is compulsory and onions tend to be added as well. We went to Jim's on South Street, which had an interesting art-deco-meets-futuristic-chrome look and is renowned for its cheesesteaks.

Two cheesesteaks were duly served up but I couldn't help but feel that they were a bit light on the cheese and despite the addition of onions it tasted only of the steak. I had ordered mine "wit whiz" (not in any particular "street" voice or anything, that's just how you have to do it). This means with Cheez Whiz, which is a kind of orange, gloopy, ready-cheese. This is the quintessential way to have the cheesesteak, although "American cheese" is also an option.

I've never really figured out what American cheese is exactly. It seems to just be cheese, but the plainest, blandest, pale yellow cheese you could imagine. Not too hard, not soft, very little taste, it should just be called cheese. I think Americans sometimes have a habit of sticking "American" on the front of stuff when they can't think of any other suitable descriptive word. For example, the TV show about making a new pop star is called *American Idol* (it's called *Pop Idol* in the UK), and a horror TV series was called *American Horror Story*. Presumably calling it just *Horror Story* was too plain. So when I see American cheese, I just think ok, so you mean just cheese then, and boring cheese at that.

The alternative to American cheese is the Cheez Whiz, which has got a very tenuous relationship with actual cheese. There are two key giveaways, firstly it comes in a jar or squeezy bottle, which is not the usual container for cheese, secondly, it's basically just gloop. Interestingly even though Cheez Whiz appeared in 1952, a good 20 years after the original cheesesteak in 1930, "wit whiz" is now the way to go. Frank Olivieri, the nephew of the inventor of original cheesesteak said that he always used "the processed cheese spread familiar to millions of parents who prize speed and ease in fixing the children's lunch, for the same reason, because it is fast."'

The Philadelphia (Philly) cheesesteak is synonymous with the city (and famous across the US) so we had literally dozens of places in Philadelphia to choose from. These famous dishes tend to attract multiple restaurants who realise it's good business if they can lay claim to having "The very best" one in the city. There were several who'd awarded themselves that title. Even better if they can claim to be "The original", even if it was just that the inventor's cousin worked washing pots in their place 15 years after the original guy invented it somewhere else. The imposter-place then normally comes up with some hokum about how the potwashing cousin brought the secret recipe with them and made some important modification so that their restaurant is, in fact, the home of the "true original." Such are the minefields to be navigated in a quest like ours.

The upside of having so many different competing places claiming to have the best cheesesteak is it meant there were plenty more options for us to try. Later that day we headed down to the Italian Market, where Central Philadelphia meets South Philadelphia. The Italian Market is great; it's a very authentic few blocks of Italian-produce shops and dates back to the beginning of the 20th century. There is also a huge and striking mural at the start of the Italian Market, depicting Philadelphia's Italian-American Mayor, Frank Rizzo. Philadelphia seems to specialise in these street murals. They are normally found on the end walls of buildings and the one in the Italian Market was particularly impressive.

People often associate the waves of Italian immigration to the US with New York City, but I think Philadelphia is as heavily influenced by Italian culture as New York. The Italian Market is a fascinating place. I felt like I could be in Sicily given all the amazing produce we could see bursting from every shop front. Dozens of delis and grocers packed together along the three block stretch, all of them stuffed to the brim with fantastic smelling and looking food. Hams and pork joints were hanging from the rafters of one place, wheels of cheese spilled from another. Exotic packets with Italian labels were everywhere to be seen. Pasta, bottles of olive oil and balsamic vinegar shipped fresh from Italy lined the shelves everywhere we looked.

Dotted along the streets of the Italian Market were a few places making the familiar claim to serve the best cheesesteaks, so we duly indulged. We went to Lorenzo's, a pizza and cheesesteak place which didn't seem nearly as popular as Jim's but would get my vote. The one at Jim's tasted rather plain, and of just straightforward steak, whereas the one from Lorenzo's was a great mix of steak and cheese, and $2 cheaper as well. It was also a very generous serving. The sandwich, cut in half already, easily fed the two of us. Plus, being full up from the cheesesteak made it a lot easier to walk around the rest of the Italian Market and resist the temptation of buying all that great-looking food.

We also hoped to get some pretzels and other Amish food from the stalls in Reading Terminal Market, which is a covered market in Central Philadelphia. The Amish are a very traditionalist religious group, who live in Pennsylvania and are known for producing a variety of foodstuffs, including pretzels. Robyn and I headed into the market.

"I'm seriously looking forward to this, I love the soft doughy type of pretzels," I said, thinking happily of the tasty goodness heading my way.

"Are you actually looking forward to the pretzel or to the butter?"

I have a serious weakness for butter and it's true that while I did look forward to the pretzel, it was mainly as a vehicle for the delicious melted butter

that it would be covered in, "Ummm both, I suppose."
We approached the Amish stall but it was closed.

"Ah no, why is it closed!?" I was genuinely disappointed. The dream of the hot doughy pretzel, covered in a delicious buttery glaze evaporated.

"I guess," she paused, "that the Amish don't work on Sundays."

"Hmmm," I said. "Well I guess we could have figured that out ahead of time."

Following our stay in Philadelphia we decided to visit the Amish in their traditional home, Lancaster County, Pennsylvania. They wouldn't be keeping their tasty pretzels away from us any longer I thought, as we drove over the border into Amish country. As soon as we did drive over the county line into the area where a lot of the Amish live, they were immediately very noticeable.

The Amish are a religious community of extremely traditionalist Christians, renowned for their simple living and unusual attitude to modern life. They are descended from Swiss and German Baptists who came to the US in the early 18th century to be able to live without interference from their own governments. Their teachings instruct them to live separately from the rest of society, eschewing much (but not all) technology, convenience and what they perceive as materialism. This means that they are a very distinct group, both in appearance and lifestyle. They don't drive cars, instead using horse-drawn buggies to get around. They tend to live a simple, mostly self-sustaining life, so a lot of Amish work in the fields, favouring horse-drawn ploughs instead of any modern machinery.

They do interact with the rest of American society (they sell a lot of their produce at markets – although not on Sundays obviously). But don't participate in social security, join the army, or send their children to public schools. Most still speak "Pennsylvania Dutch" (actually a dialect of German) in the home and community. However, they will also learn English in order to converse with the "Englishers," which is what they call the Americans. They are a not tiny group by any means. There are estimated to be nearly a quarter of a million Amish, mostly spread across three states, Pennsylvania, Ohio and Indiana. There are various divisions within the Amish community, with different denominations and orders. Each community lives according to their own "ordnung" (set of rules). They take their religious and civil rules very seriously and many of them are based on their own doctrinal interpretations of the bible. One group, the Troyer Amish, separated from the other Amish in the 20th century because of a dispute about the width of hat-brims. I kid you not.

The Amish (in Pennsylvania at least) do get their fair share of tourists. They tend to welcome these tourists as they have a lot of shops and markets selling crafts and produce. However, there is a small element of the tourists that can be a bit insensitive and disrespectful. These people act like they are in a human safari park, gawking, pointing and taking intrusive photos of the Amish who are just trying to go about their daily lives. For the most part though the tourists and locals in the area seem to get along fine with the Amish; they pull out widely when overtaking the horse-drawn buggies and a lot of the tourists seemed respectfully interested in the Amish way of life when asking questions about their lifestyle.

We took a pleasant drive around the country roads of Lancaster County and stopped at a couple of the amusingly named Amish villages: "Bird-in-hand" and "Intercourse" being two of the top ones (Intercourse is so named because it is at the crossing of two roads, so get your filthy mind out of the gutter!) The sun was out, bathing the golden fields and we could see plenty of Amish working by hand, dressed in their distinctive woollen clothes, all the men with wide-brimmed straw hats and distinctive beards. We stopped in at one place that offered horse-drawn buggy rides. It seemed like a very touristy thing to do, but being tourists, that didn't seem to be a problem.

The carriage took a leisurely meander around the back roads in the bucolic scenery. The guide was an engaging Amish guy in his early 30's. He had left the Amish for a few years in his early twenties (which is not uncommon) but had returned. He told us about the Amish way of life and was more than happy to answer any questions we had for him.

We learnt that while mains electricity is universally banned amongst the Amish, depending on the specific denomination some do allow some forms of electricity. Some groups permit it when it's derived from solar-power or from a generator in the home, just never from the mains. There were lots of intriguing rules, so many in fact that it seemed like it might be tricky to keep on top of them all if you were Amish. Many seemed completely contradictory. For instance, beards are compulsory but moustaches are forbidden. Trousers compulsory, belts forbidden. Driving a car forbidden, but being driven by a non-Amish person in a car, strangely ok. Some of it seemed totally mad.

He told us there was even a trend now amongst young Amish guys in their horse-drawn buggies to hook up a solar-powered speaker system in order to blast out the tunes. The whole thing reminded me of when you avoid stepping on the cracks on the pavement, just because, and then you try and do it all the way home. Being Amish would be like taking the whole pavement crack thing, then inventing hundreds more of these arbitrary rules, then just seeing what happens, and then doing it for the rest of your life. Oh and then shunning anyone who deliberately broke any of these rules (which is what they do – the shunning is a form of punishment). Whoever was making all this stuff up was clearly just a man with massive OCD. *Beards - yes! Moustaches - no!* But why? *Because I say so!*

Another highlight was visiting the home of an Amish family for dinner. Our Bed and Breakfast offered us the opportunity, saying that the family often invited up a small group of tourists to their house for a family style dinner. It was only $15 each and sounded very authentic so we jumped at the chance. We arrived about half an hour before dinner and were shown around the home and gardens by one of the children. The family had about six children (which is fairly typical for the Amish), the grounds were pretty extensive, a big garden, a stable and a couple of fields out the back. The children ran around happily, unsupervised, even the little boy, who looked about three, with a funny bowl cut and wearing a mini version of the adult Amish attire. They played games and the eldest child proudly showed us her horse in the stable.

Robyn was impressed, "Whoa. I'd love to have a horse!"

"Would you like to be an Amish child? Because it seems like horses are part of the package."

"It seems like a good deal to me!" she said happily.

We were called in for dinner and had a look at the kitchen and front room. It was interesting to see inside their house. It looked like a house from 100 years ago, preserved or recreated, especially in the living room. Obviously there were no electrical appliances, like a TV or any modern conveniences such as radiators. Interestingly there were no family photos. The wife, who was doing the cooking, told us over dinner that the Amish don't have photos. They think that it encourages vanity and prevents them from being humble in front of God (strict Muslims take the same approach, forbidding photography and images of people). While I respected their choice, it seemed a shame to think they wouldn't have any photos of their adorable children. It brought home how austere and devoted the Amish really are.

The meal was great: simple traditional food and lots of it. There were delicious red potatoes and other vegetables they'd grown themselves, chicken, a casserole and homemade bread. The highlight was probably the desserts, a choice of several pies, including the shoofly pie, made with treacle. This is a traditional Amish dish, which got its name because the sticky-sweet filling used to attract flies which had to be shooed away. It was an impressive feast, particularly considering they didn't have many of the modern conveniences that most cooks would think of as essential. The family didn't eat with us, but hovered around the whole time, serving the full table and happily answering questions. I was surprised by how German the husband sounded and was interested to learn that he worked as a builder both within the Amish community and on local jobs in the surrounding counties.

After dinner, the children came into sing some songs for us. It was very sweet and they seemed to enjoy the singing. Afterwards we had another little walk around the grounds and it seemed that they were leading a pretty charmed life. The countryside looked beautiful in the evening light and the children had gone outside to play in the fields again. Maybe all those rules were the key to this seemingly very happy life! It's hard to say really, because in some ways the Amish way of life is incredibly restrictive, education finishes at about age 13 and girls only have two options in life, being a teacher or being a housewife. Apparently though, despite all youngsters being given the option to join modern society, more than 90% of Amish stay within the faith and the number of Amish is actually growing. As we looked across the fields into the setting sun and saw the outline of a horse-drawn buggy, it struck me how much variety there is in the US. Despite the voluntary restrictions the Amish choose to impose upon themselves they were actually exercising that particularly American concept of freedom and living exactly as they wanted.

* * *

Jack and I parked up in the centre of Philadelphia on a side street (careful to park facing the right way) and figured we'd see a bit of the city before we headed to the hostel. We decided to walk to the Liberty Bell.

"What's this Liberty Bell all about then?" said Jack, who expected me, his resident tour guide, to give him the usual explanation.

"Well it's a Bell that they rang to announce the revolution," I said, struggling. I hadn't really read that section in the guidebook but I figured I probably knew enough to maintain my reputation as being *a generally knowledgeable sort.* Jack would get bored soon enough.

"And?" he asked.

"and... it's got a big crack in it," I said, running out of information. I looked at him. He could smell blood.

"You don't know anything about it, do you, you big bell," he said triumphantly.

The Liberty Bell is one of the attractions in Philadelphia's historic quarter, which featured a cluster of interesting sites. The best was probably Independence Hall, where both the Declaration of Independence and the US Constitution were signed in the late 1700s. It was an impressive place and the National Parks tour really brought the courtroom to life. They were clearly very proud of the history of the building and the importance it holds in the birth of the nation. Anyone who says that Americans don't know about or care about history is just plain wrong, and has probably never been to Philadelphia.

The US has a great reverence for history, albeit with a massive skew to its own. In the UK if you try to find any of our Civil War battlefields, you'll be lucky to even pinpoint their exact location. If you actually attempt to visit you'll probably find a massive supermarket has been plonked on it. In the US their major Civil War battlefields (Gettysburg, Antietam etc) invariably have a great visitor reception centre, multiple tours throughout the day and passionate National Park Rangers willing to answer any question you might have.

It's a little bit odd going to these revolutionary and independence sights as a British person, because sooner or later the history of how the plucky American colonials threw off the shackles of their "tyrannical British overlords" will come up. This time the guide asked if anyone was from overseas, and we sheepishly put our hands up and prepared to atone for the oppression of the despotic King George III or some other long dead British monarch.

There was some light-hearted banter about independence, with the guide ribbing us, for the benefit of the group, along the lines of *"I hope you boys aren't still too sore about it."* A quick retort about the burning of the White House, while claiming that we were on our way to Washington DC next, seemed to do the trick. The 1812 burning of the White House by the British (over 30 years after the revolutionary wars), is something that Americans seemed to bring up quite often. This is a bit odd, since the 1812 war is barely remembered in the UK these days.

Americans often seem to think that British people will have a really good grasp of history, because we are seen as coming from a historical place. Americans tend to have a good grasp on American history and their history is inextricably linked with the British, from the founding of the American colonies to the War of Independence, but even more than that many of their ideas and institutions have links to ours.

One American asked me about the Magna Carta and whether it was a really revered document in the UK in the way that the US constitution is in the US (the Magna Carta is generally recognised as the first ever bill of rights for people to protect themselves from a tyrannical king and was signed in England in 1215). Ideologically it is one of the founding principles for having a constitution such as the one the US has. He was shocked when I said I doubted many people in England knew anything about the Magna Carta, and it was almost never referred to (unlike in the US where the constitution is referred to everywhere, from the speeches of politicians to normal people's ranting facebook updates). He almost fell off his chair after the following exchange:

"I don't really remember learning about the Magna Carta in school," I said.

"They don't teach it in school, seriously?"

"No, I don't think I knew what it was until university. Although I do remember when I was growing up there was a place near us called *Magna Karta*, so I guess I had heard of it, but that place was actually a go-karting track."

We finished up at the National Constitution Center, an impressive museum, even if it is solely dedicated to a four page document. It bills itself as, "The world's only museum dedicated to the U.S. Constitution". *You're kidding me!? They don't even have one in Canada?* Americans may know a lot about American history but they can sometimes be confused of conflating the US with the World. Don't even get me started on The World Series of baseball.

We returned to the Van after enjoying the historical sites (although we never really learned exactly why the Liberty Bell was famous – apparently it may or may not have been rung to mark the reading of the Declaration of Independence, no one knows for sure). It was old though, had something to do with the revolution and did indeed have a big crack in it, so I felt vindicated. We approached the Ram and experienced some déjà vu.

"What the hell? Is that another bloody ticket?" I said.

"What now? Have they changed the direction of traffic? Are we somehow facing the wrong way again?" said Jack, only half-joking.

I picked up the ticket and read it out. "This vehicle does not have a current registration, it is out of date and should not be driven on public roads. Fine of $80."

"What the f***?" said Jack, not putting too fine a point on it.

I peered down and read the little sticker on the windscreen of the Ram, "apparently it hasn't been registered for about....18 months, nope, wait, 2 years."

We paused and then laughed at the stupidity of the situation.

"Sounds like we need to call Don," I suggested.

"I'm sure he will be dee-lighted to hear from us."

I dug his number out and called him again. The conversation began pretty much exactly as it had done last time, "Don! It's Rich here, with the Ram minivan."

"Who?" he asked. *Seriously?*

"Rich and Jack, we've rented the Ram from Florida and are bringing it to you in New York."

"Ok."

"Right well, we've had some more issues with the Ram."

"There is no breakdown cover," he said, as if his responsibility ended there.

"Yep – found out about that one the hard way," then I chuckled, hoping for a friendly laugh.

There was a stone cold German silence from Don. I continued, "Anyway, this time we've got a fine because apparently the Ram is not even registered."

"Hmm," I could almost hear the cogs in his mind whirring while he tried to figure out how he was going to be able to wriggle out of this one. He relented, "Just bring me the Van back, we pay for the fine. Ok?" he sounded like he was about to hang up.

"Thing is Don, it hasn't been registered for 2 years!"

"Ok." It didn't really seem to me a situation where *"Ok"* would suffice, but he went with it anyway.

"Right, but my point is that it says we shouldn't even drive it. To be blunt about it: is it even a legal roadworthy vehicle?"

"It's a good van. Where are you?"

"Philadelphia."

"That's fine then, not far, just bring it back," with that he hung up.

I turned to Jack, "He hung up."

"Good old Don."

Jack and I proceeded to the hostel, which again was on the outskirts of town because of our parking situation. We took in our surroundings, which this time was an old mansion in a park with a nice view down to the city. It's funny with hostels, it's the cheapest of accommodation, yet they are often situated in really nice buildings. Then you get into the rooms and find that you are sleeping in bunk beds with a load of random strangers and you remember why it's cheap. We introduced ourselves to our dormmates and tried to work out which one was the weirdo.

It didn't seem to be the first guy, who was a fairly normal guy, early 20's, American, from the West Coast. Next up it was Jurgen, Swiss, tall, about 6"4, utterly humourless but, nevertheless professing himself to be a "big time party guy." Ok yes, it was Jurgen, he was the weirdo. Nevertheless we agreed to accompany our dorm mates out to a bar in the city. Jurgen claimed to know a place where the beers were a dollar and promised us it would be a good time.

We entered the bar, which was cavernous and empty. It had two levels with a balcony wrap-around forming the top floor and a couple of pool tables at the side on the ground level. Jack fancied himself as a pool player and never tired of beating me, no matter how often we played. He saw the pool tables and his eyes lit up, "Pool?"

"I don't know if I can be bothered."

"C'mon you love a bit of pool."

"No, you love pool."

"Well that's convenient because there's a pool table right there. I'll rack them up."

After my usual run of three or four losses, I managed to score a victory by my usual method (Jack fouling by potting the black). Sooner or later, one of the very few other customers in the deserted bar approached us and wanted to use the pool table. We agreed to let him join in our games, which by now we are also playing with Jurgen and the other guy from the hostel. The conversation started in the usual way. The new guy was dressed all in black, with greasy unwashed hair and tatty bracelets on. He was young, early 20's and nervy.

"So you guys are really from England!"

"Yep," I decided to take this one on.

"I love England!"

"Really?"

"Oh yeah, I love it, the music, the people, the culture all of it."

"Oh ok, that's interesting, which music?"

"Well, like all my favourite bands are English, *The Smiths, The Stone Roses, Oasis, Doves.* They're practically all from the North West, from Manchester, which is freaking awesome."

"Oh ok, you've been to England?" I was vaguely intrigued, since most Americans haven't been to the UK and even if they have, it's normally London and Stonehenge.

"Yeah. Manchester's amazing, it's so atmospheric, like grey and gloomy, but really beautiful at the same time. It's really inspiring. You can see why all that great music comes from there."

I was reasonably impressed, I liked that same type of music and he seemed pretty knowledgeable.

We played more pool, and the one dollar beers were starting to affect Jurgen, the Swiss hosteller. He started singing, at first we laughed, but unfortunately the laughter encouraged him and he sang louder. His song choices on the jukebox also became more esoteric. They also changed to his native German and he sung louder.

"Ich kann nicht sagen und will nicht vergessen!!!"

Oh dear. He wasn't a good singer, his only quality was loudness, if that could be considered a quality. He reached the song's climax, "Oh nein, nein, nein."

"Jurgen. What are you singing?"

"It is a German love song! One of ze best!"

I turned to Jack, "That was a love song? It sounded more like he was promising he would have his vengeance against someone that had deeply, deeply wronged him."

Jurgen started singing drunkenly again.

The night had started poorly and was heading downhill fast. The place seemed even more deserted and we were surrounded by weirdoes. I turned to our new friend and decided to ask him more about his trip to England, "So where else did you go in England?"

"Umm, well I spent a lot of time in Manchester."

"You just went to Manchester?" I was surprised as that was a long way to go to see one place.

"Umm," he cleared his throat. "I didn't really go to Manchester, I just said it."

In a way I was used to this nonsense by now, but it was still inexplicable, "Why did you say it?" I sighed, "and why do you know so much about Manchester?" I looked at him and he shifted uncomfortably.

"I just read it in a magazine," he winced, as though he was disappointing a parent, "I just wanted to impress you guys."

I looked around the abandoned bar and said to Jack, "we've really got to stop going out on weeknights."

11. New Jersey: Mischief

North New Jersey is the car theft capital of the US, with more cars stolen in Newark than any other American city. This is still true even when compared to the 2 largest US cities, New York and LA, put together. That's one of things the guidebook told me, but I just wasn't sure what I was meant to do with that information, apart from worrying about the car, every time we left it anywhere. By the time we'd finished in New Jersey it struck me that the worst part of having your car stolen there would not be the fact you'd just lost the car itself, but that the lack of car would prevent you from actually leaving New Jersey. Maybe we were unlucky but a succession of things happened which tainted the whole experience.

Before we went to New Jersey, we tried to think about what foods New Jersey was famous for. Nothing it turns out, nothing at all! A lot of states have an official state food, so what's New Jersey's? It doesn't have one. It has a state fruit, which obviously technically is a food. I wasn't sure though what we could do with the highbush blueberry (even though it is the most common commercially-grown type of blueberry in the US).

Thirty-four states do have an official state food, some have multiple. Texas has eight state foods! South Carolina has an official state snack food! (boiled peanuts) Virginia even has a state muffin! (blueberry). If you think for a moment, that is actually quite staggering – the legislators in Virginia must have taken the time to file and approve a piece of legislation to make the blueberry muffin, the official state muffin. They must have a lot of time on their hands over there.

So what else could we do for New Jersey if not the state food? One thing that occurred was to track down famous foods that were manufactured in that particular state. So this could be a generic food type e.g. Florida orange juice or a brand e.g. Jack Daniel's (Tennessee). Well what does New Jersey have? It has Campbell's soup. That's about it.

Lacking anything better we decided to pursue the Campbell's soup option. This was not a wise move. I visited the Campbell's soup website. These types of companies always have quite good, flashy websites and I wonder why? Who the heck is eating their tinned tomato soup and thinking *I really need to get some more info on the soup. Better log on to campbells.com.* Even in that unlikely scenario, are they expected to do that while eating the soup? Having just finished the soup? Or at some other point in the day when they are surfing the internet but suddenly struck by the need for more info on soup? Unfortunately, even the Campbell's website doesn't provide any surfing suggestions....*Robyn wasn't impressed with that terrible joke either.*

Obviously *I had* to go to the website because I was tied to doing something food related in New Jersey. I had no other option. It was just my bad luck that the people of New Jersey have apparently lived through over 200 years of independence happily eating other states' food. So that had reduced us to tracking down a soup factory, whether they wanted us there or not. The first mistake made by Mr Campbell's Soup was the part of the website in the "about us" section: "Directions to the world headquarters - Find out how easy it us to find us." *Ok! Maybe this wouldn't be so hard after all then.*

We planned in a couple of days at the beach to start off with. We went to the South Jersey shore – where the motto is "Shore to please". Unfortunately it did not. Not on any level. Thinking about it, it didn't technically say "sure to please", so they maybe weren't actually promising anything. Perhaps they knew what they were doing all along with their nonsensical slogan.

It was pouring down as we got to the shore, not exactly what we wanted from a beach resort. The first meal we had was one of the worst Italian meals I've ever eaten. It was particularly heinous since New Jersey, rather like Philadelphia and New York, has a huge Italian heritage. Nevertheless this particular restaurant would have any self-respecting Italian Chef turning in his grave. The salad was appalling, it looked like it had been sitting in the fridge all day and was covered in some repulsive vinaigrette. I'm sure the Chef must've confused vinaigrette with vinegar since I couldn't taste the difference. The pasta and carbonara sauce was no better. It tasted like nothing at all. The white sauce was gloopy and horridly bland.

I wondered if the sauce was made from Cheez Whiz, but then realised I was doing a massive disservice to Cheez Whiz.

Perhaps it was our own fault, we were at the shore a week or so after Labor Day (which is the first Monday in September). Americans have a pretty rigid approach to the seasons, much more so than in the UK. In the US summer begins on Memorial Day, which is the last Monday in May and it finishes on Labor Day. That is your lot, it doesn't matter if it's 35 degrees (95F) in mid-May, it's not summer, because it's not Memorial Day yet. The outdoor pools will remain closed and not one of those ice cream parlours will open up. We hadn't realised the same was true post-Labor Day. We were at the seaside for what we figured was the shoulder season, it would be winding down, quieter than usual but still open for business. Not true, after Labor Day 90% of businesses on the seashore and boardwalk close down for about 9 months, pretty much overnight.

We endured a miserable couple of days, walking up and down the lonely boardwalk in front of the closed up shops. I don't know how the weather had also got the message that summer was over. Whereas the previous week was glorious sunny weather, the three days we were there were constant rain, grey, windy and gloomy. On the third day of rain we headed up to Camden, where Campbell's soup is located.

Camden looked rough, seriously rough. It brought to mind the zombie wasteland of Miami from

10 years earlier (I later found out Camden is one of the poorest, most crime-ridden cities in the US). We weren't in the best of moods, after the disappointment of the beach. Since alighting on the idea of going to Campbell's soup, I'd found out a couple of things that had made me begin to question the wisdom of this idea.

Firstly, the soup is not even made there! While Campbell's world HQ is in Camden, the majority of their soup is made in a factory in Ohio. Even worse, despite their welcoming website, it turned out they were not in fact very friendly at all. We rang up (hoping at best to blag some free soup and at worst to be given permission to take some photos of the building), and were told "you shouldn't come here" and "there is nothing to take any pictures of." Charming. Why put "directions to the HQ" and "find out how easy it is to find us" on the website and then act like *I'm the lunatic* when we want to come and say hello? I will admit that calling up a soup manufacturer and asking to come and visit doesn't sound like the actions of a sane person, but hey, everything makes sense in context.

Robyn was questioning whether this was really a good idea at all, but I was determined. We drove past the surprisingly high gates and looked for a place to pull over.

"I'm not sure about this," said Robyn.

"Why ever not!? We're here now!" I said, insistent, despite all available evidence that this was not a good plan.

"Well we've seen it now, can we go?"

"I'm starting to question your commitment here," I said, leaving my accusation hanging.

"Fine, trust me, I'm committed to you taking a stupid picture of a can of soup in front of the building."

It was a moral victory.

I was determined to at least get a picture. We were there, plus there were no other food things to do. We had stopped at a convenience store and begrudgingly bought one can of their soup for the photo opportunity in front of the HQ. We circled back around and pulled over just to the side of the gates. We could see a security guard pacing and pacing in the distance, clearly fuelled by a diet of endless soup. We were pretty quick about it, but I did manage to get various pictures of the can of soup in front of the gates. I imagined the receptionist inside who I'd spoken to some weeks earlier, staring out at us with binoculars. *"Oh dear, he's come. I told him not to come! For the love of God what does he want from us?"* Peering closer she would see me positioning the can of soup in front of the gates, *"Oh no! He's got one of our cans! No, don't hurt the soup!"*

We finished up in New Jersey with a visit to Atlantic City, which competed with everything else we'd done in New Jersey for the title of worst thing we'd done in New Jersey. Atlantic City is New Jersey's answer to Las Vegas, however, it contains none of the outlandish, gaudy charm of Las Vegas and all of its seedy, grittiness. Originally Atlantic City was a famous seaside resort, but as the years rolled round, it fell on hard times. The city decided to salvage itself by legalising gambling and casinos (gambling is generally banned in the US, so people will travel quite a long way for a casino in the few places they do exist).

It was depressing. The weather was still bad and the city was confusing to drive around. We needed fuel and pulled up at the gas station. I tried to get out to fill it up and a man raced round to prevent me. I was confused but it was clear he would be filling the car up. He did and we had the usual awkward moment about tipping.

Tipping culture is confusing for a lot of people visiting the US because it is so widespread and there are a lot of rules that are easy to fall foul of. People can get very touchy if you don't tip within the normal range. We'd got to the point where we knew what to do in restaurants (average of 15%, more if it was better), bars (a dollar for a single drink a few dollars for a big round), but gas stations? I had no frame of reference but it was clear it was a tipping situation. I gave him $2 and wound the window up as quickly as I could. I later found out that it is illegal to pump your own gas in New Jersey and a member of staff must do it for you. Crazy. It makes the law declaring the blueberry muffin as the official state muffin of Virginia look like a well-considered and sensible piece of legislation.

The casinos were very functional, with very little of the opulence I expected. They were full of grey people playing slots. There were no windows or sense of light and space. One of the casinos faced out to sea but had no views whatsoever, instead keeping all those inside in gloomy darkness. There was one highlight to the visit, on our way out of Atlantic City we stopped at The White House Sub shop and had the best Sub sandwiched we had ever had. The White House Sub shop is an institution. It has been serving subs since 1946 and is still owned by the same people.

Two theories exist about the etymology of "sub sandwich", one is that the bread was originally sold to sailors in Boston and was intended to resemble the hull of the submarines it was named after. The second (and the one subscribed to at the White House sub shop) is that the word sub just refers to the fact that the roll is sub-sized (i.e. smaller than a normal loaf or baguette). Either way they really serve up some fine examples there. We split a regular Italian (with delicious cold sliced meats) and one of their Meatball subs. It was a rare bright spot during the trip. I'm not saying I don't like anything about New Jersey, I like plenty of things from there. For example Bruce Springsteen and *The Sopranos* - although the beauty of those two things is you don't have to be in New Jersey to enjoy them.

* * *

Jack and I drove into New Jersey on our way to our rendezvous with the Crone. Jack was keen to stop off somewhere on the way. "Let's break the journey up a bit," he said.

"Why? Are you just trying to delay the inevitable?"

"No," he said defensively, "I just figured there might be some interesting stuff to see." He was worried about the Crone, I could see it, but I figured I wouldn't rub it in.

"Well we could have a quick stop off to look round Princeton University."

"Yeah let's do that," he said immediately.

We had a pleasant couple of hours wandering around some of the campus buildings and the town of Princeton. We returned to the Van with two takeaway coffees. We saw a traffic warden just finishing walking down the line of cars. He'd ticketed a few, but fortunately we had put enough money in the meter to cover our time.

"Ah it's a shame we weren't here 5 minutes earlier, we could've run down the line, putting in extra quarters on the meters just as the warden started writing out each ticket," I said.

"Yeah that's a shame. That would have been good," said Jack, "but you know what we could do instead?"

"What?"

"Well we could go down to the ones that have been ticketed and put a bit of extra money in those ones."

"Why would we do that?"

"Just because then, when they come back, they'll see a couple of minutes left on the meter, see they've got a ticket anyway and go mental."

"Alright." We were young and mischievous. Why not?

We put some money in the meters, waited 15 minutes with our coffees and none of them came back. It was frustrating. We deserved to see someone going mental. The meters ran out again. We looked at each other, realising how pathetic our plan to make mischief was.

"Shall we go and see the Crone then?" I said, realising that my opportunity for mischief was just beginning.

We approached her house; she lived in a shared flat which was part of the campus accommodation. Jack spoke up suddenly, "Oh God, she's awful isn't she?"

"She's *awfully* into you," I said, enjoying the thought of what was to come, "just relax and enjoy yourself."

Jack shot me a look, he wasn't happy about this at all.

We arrived and knocked on her door. She appeared, suddenly looming in the doorway, the hair looked bigger, the braces more prominent, she'd grown three inches and lost thirty pounds, she was skinnier and taller than ever before.

"Hello ya douchebags! Ya made it!" she grabbed Jack in a bear hug and then did the same to me.

We headed straight out for a tour of the campus, which was impressive, as most American universities tend to be. We walked through the courtyards, past the library and through the canteen. The range and scale in there was like nothing I'd ever seen, it was like a massive food court, except you could serve yourself on any of the dozens of stations.

"This is unbelievable, I don't think I've seen anything like this in England."

"No? Bet there's not much food in England anyway, or it's all terrible!" she cackled. I shuddered.

That evening, she told us that we would be heading out to a chain restaurant with her friend Jeff, then we'd come back and hang out with some of her friends in the evening. Jeff picked us up in his car. He turned out to be a significantly older guy (around 30), overweight, slicked back hair and obviously thought he was quite flash. We got in and he slammed the accelerator down.

"What's that Jeff?" I asked pointing at a little device on his dash.

"That is my little speed gun detector friend," he said proudly. The Crone cackled again.

We ate and drank a few beers. I noticed that Jeff was drinking a fair amount of beer. Jack and I had seen a lot of people drinking in bars who then walked immediately out to the car park and got into their cars. We weren't used to it since any level of drink-driving tends to be frowned upon in the UK. Jeff was on his third or fourth bottle.

"So, you're driving us back as well are you Jeff?" I asked.

"Course, how else are we going to get back? Why?"

"We just didn't know, cos we didn't know how many beers we were having here," I said gesturing at the beer in his hand.

"What, this?" he said "nothing wrong with a few brewskies," and took a big swig of his beer. "I don't mind having a few beers and driving. Ain't nothing wrong with that."

"Well I guess it depends how many, doesn't it?" I said tentatively.

"Nah, I got a system, I don't drink too many, just enough to get my buzz on."

I whispered to Jack *"so just enough to know he's definitely under the influence."*

The Crone left to go to the bathroom and left us alone with Jeff. He started explaining his friendship with the Crone, "You know her and I go way back. I mean it's fine, I do have to pay for her meals and drinks and stuff when we're out like this. But she knows loads of people and how else am I going to meet college chicks? So it's worth it, right?" he said conspiratorially.

It was odd because he was essentially telling us that he didn't like hanging around with the Crone, but that it was ok because she was using him and vice versa. Ah true friendship.

We went back to the Crone's house and her plan kicked into action. She had invited a few friends over and broke out some horrible, really light beer. We were introduced to the friends.

"So you're the gorgeous English guy she's been talking about?" one of them said, pointing at Jack.

"Guilty," he said uncomfortably.

The Crone positioned herself on the sofa next to Jack while Jeff did the same with some poor unfortunate girl on the other sofa. So the evening went and the Crone crept closer and closer to Jack. Suddenly he jumped up off the sofa.

"I've got to get some air," he said, "I'm feeling a bit light-headed is all," and before anyone could say anything he walked out the front door. The Crone looked a little shocked.

People started breaking off into smaller groups, chatting amongst themselves. I found myself alone with the Crone. *Not great*, I thought. Quickly the subject came around to Jack.

"I don't think he likes me, does he?" she said mournfully.

"Of course he likes you," I said, upbeat, "he couldn't wait to come and see you."

"But he doesn't like me like that, does he?"

"Well...not like that, no," I said tentatively.

We continued to chat and I began to empathise with the Crone. She'd had high hopes for Jack and clearly hadn't had a boyfriend for a while.

"Do you think I'll ever find my own Jack?"

"Definitely, of course you will."

She smiled and it was quite a touching moment. We continued to talk and she opened up about where she was in her life. She thanked me for some good advice and for cheering her up. After a while I noticed that Jack had still not come back and I told the Crone I was going to go out and look for him.

"Shall I come to?" she asked, concerned.

"Probably best if I go alone," I said, thinking Jack might not appreciate the Crone roaming the streets for him, hunting him down.

I went outside on to the street, it was pretty late, but I didn't think he could have gone far. I walked down the street, pleased to have a bit of space and fresh air anyway. I saw the Ram parked a little further along. Inside I saw a shape sitting in the darkness in the driver's seat.

I walked up and opened the passenger door and got in.

"Are you alright?"

"Yeah, I just needed a bit of space. It was all getting a bit intense in there. I thought I'd just have a bit of Ramtime."

"Fair enough. I think she's got the message though."

"Yeah?"

"Yeah, I just had a bit of a chat with her."

"Oh thank God. She'd told me earlier that there's a spare bed in her room and a sofa. She said that I could sleep in her room and you can have the couch."

"Charming. Why do I have to have the couch!?" I said, annoyed.

"Well that's it, I want the couch. You can sleep in the bed in her room. Can we just say you won a coin toss or something?"

"Sure, I'll take the hit," I said, not taking any hit whatsoever.

"Thanks Boss," he said, relieved.

The next morning we got up and prepared to leave. It was a bit awkward, like someone was escaping from a one-night stand. Even though the opposite had happened. We had breakfast and made small talk. It was time to leave. She showed us to the door, us with bags in hand, side-by-side, turned back to face her. The Crone loomed large in the doorway and was clearly getting a bit emotional.

"It's been so great to see you guys again," she said.

"Yep. Likewise. Thanks for having us," said Jack stiffly.

"Well don't be a stranger and just, you know, keep safe." She was looking intently at Jack and leaned in for the big bear hug. She pulled him in, squeezing him as tight as she could. Jack's arms were pinned by his sides. She held the hug a moment too long. She released him and I waited for my hug, but it didn't come. She stepped back in to the doorway, stared at Jack and whispered "Bye," and shut the door softly.

I looked at Jack and we walked away down the corridor.

"Where the hell was my hug?" I said, aggrieved, "I listened to her blather on about you for an hour last night! An hour! Ridiculous."

Jack laughed and we walked down the stairs to the street.

12. New York: The melting pot

New York is a city which impresses from every angle. If you approach by road you come round the gently curving I-95 and you are rewarded with the sight of the cluster of high-rise buildings of downtown Manhattan and that first sight of the Statue of Liberty, tiny in the distance but still instantly recognisable, visibly holding aloft her torch. If you fly in, then you have the view of Manhattan Island, densely packed but neat and ordered, with its familiar long shape, like a finger, bound by the Hudson and East River. It is a sight which will excite any traveller. Once you're on the ground, in the midst of the city, it is as iconic and uniquely identifiable as any in the world. The yellow taxis fly by as the traffic lights cascade in the "green wave". The buildings, so famous from the movies, each more impressive than the last: the Empire State, the Chrysler, the Flatiron to name but three. But it is the scale of the city which will impress any first time visitor the most. Take a walk from Midtown to downtown and you just have to look up, the skyscrapers tower above you on every side.

New York is rightly famous for a great deal of things, but surely one of the most important must be its food. There are few cities in the Western world that have given us so many iconic foods, but if one trumps them all it is pizza. You might argue that pizza is Italian and that New York is a mere imposter, that it has as little a claim to pizza as some of the more ridiculous types of pizza that have sprung up recently:

Greek Pizza? Egyptian Pizza? Seriously? No. New York pizza is something different, it is glorious and is sufficiently different from the Italian original to stand alone. For many people New York pizza *is* pizza.

New York pizza tends to have a smokier, thicker tomato sauce, a slightly thicker crust, a more even covering of cheese and a lot more meat than its Italian cousin, but is nevertheless deeply rooted in the Italian version. Gennaro Lombardi, an Italian immigrant from Naples, is credited with opening America's first pizzeria. He originally opened a grocery store in 1897 in New York and an employee of his began making pizzas and selling them. They were popular and if a customer could not afford a whole pizza (5¢) then they would pay what they could and receive a corresponding-size slice of the pie. So began the New York tradition of selling pizza by the slice. Lombardi recognised how popular the pizza was and opened the US's first pizzeria (Lombardi's) in 1905 in New York's Little Italy neighbourhood.

We got to Lombardi's (the oldest Pizzeria in NYC's Little Italy) and there was an hour-long queue, despite it being -10C (15F) with the wind chill. I like pizza, but I don't like it with a side of frostbite, so we opted out. The other pizzeria we wanted to go to, Grimaldi's, was in Brooklyn, just over the bridge. As the temperature had by then fallen to -14C in the wind chill, we didn't fancy walking on the bridge. Despite not being able to get in to Lombardi's we learnt they played host to pizza tour groups who got special access. I was delighted and we signed up for the walking tour the next day.

We battled our way to Midtown. The wind was ferocious. However, New York's grid system was creating a curious effect. Since the wind was blowing consistently in one direction it meant that as we walked west to east (on the "streets") we were pretty sheltered from the wind by the tall buildings, this was until we turned north to walk up one of the "avenues" (all the north-south roads are called avenues, it's very logical). On the avenues it was like trying to walk in a wind tunnel. It was almost impossible.

"This is ridiculous!" Robyn said.

"Yeah, I can barely move forwards," I said as the wind buffeted us.

"Do you want to go back?"

"No way! We're not going back. Just imagine you're a fisherman working on an Atlantic trawler or something!"

She pulled her hood fully over her head and closed the drawstring so I could barely see her face. She strained to move forwards, "Yes, I don't think that's helping."

We spent the rest of the day making the most of some of New York's excellent museums and art galleries. Once the wind had died down we took a walk through Central Park which looked particularly beautiful as the all the leaves were covered in frost and the lake was icing up.

The following day we took the pizza tour, which I thought was a great concept. The Little Italy area of New York is just a few blocks in size so you can see all the historic pizza places within a relatively short distance of each other. The pizza tour also busted us past any queues, and the guide was very passionate and informative. I couldn't decide if being a guide on a pizza tour would be an excellent job or one that would make you feel like you were living through *Groundhog Day*. Surely being force fed pizza day after day would eventually turn you against it? Our guide still seemed enthusiastic though and was more than happy to have a big slice in each of the three places we visited.

The tour started at Lombardi's, and we got in half an hour before opening, which was great as we had the place to ourselves. The guide took pizza seriously and she talked about the difference in styles and regions, and also the history of it (both in Italy and in the USA). Unfortunately the original Lombardi's (which was the first pizzeria and opened in 1905), closed in the 1980s and relocated a couple of blocks away. However, when the location was moved the original coal oven was moved over, and is still in use today, so they maintain their claim to be the nation's oldest pizzeria. Interestingly the huge oven's coal-fire is kept burning all the time, all year-round, apart from the week when it's closed down for a thorough cleaning. That week comes directly after the busiest day for pizza consumption in the US (have a guess which that might be……the day of the Superbowl).

The pizza they make at Lombardi's is still very traditional, a full covering of tomato, and huge individual slices of Mozzarella cheese, much closer to the original Italian style of pizza, rather than covering the pizza evenly by grating the cheese. Most of New York's notable early pizzerias can be traced back to Lombardi's, either people who worked there (e.g. Totonno's) or relatives of Lombardi (e.g. Patsy's and John's). At Lombardi's they proudly display a family tree of New York pizza, you can see Lombardi right at the bottom starting everything else off and see how the different pizzerias branched out from there.

We were also taken to John's of Bleecker Street – "No slices! Whole pies only!" and to Pizza Box a mid-50's establishment that specialised in the type of pizza we're perhaps more familiar with as being New York pizza (i.e. heavy on the cheese – huge floppy slices you can fold up and whole pizzas the size of dustbin lids). All three places were great in their own way.

New York City is undoubtedly one of the world's biggest melting pots and it wasn't just Italian immigrants who had an effect on New York's food culture. The Jewish were one of the most prominent groups to migrate to the US, many of them from Central and Eastern Europe. While it is nowhere as easy to find Jewish cuisine as Italian, there are a few choice spots.

We went to Cafe Edison, a Jewish restaurant in Midtown, where I'd read they did the best Matzo ball soup. It was a tasty soup, chicken, noodles and a huge dumpling ball in the middle. We scooped bits of dumpling off with every spoonful, and it was a warming treat on a cold day. It reminded me of food in Hungary, hearty and slightly stodgy, and it was interesting to think of the mixture of cultures, Jewish, via Eastern Europe and then a New York twist that combined in this single dish.

We also tried a Pastrami sandwich, which was the type of thing I'd heard of, but never seen or eaten. Pastrami is a sliced deli meat, made from beef, brined then smoked. We knew to order them "Pastrami on rye" since that's what they do in *Seinfeld* and *Friends* and so on. It was very tasty; although it did seem like a competition to get the most slices of meat between two pieces of bread without it falling apart. The pastrami sandwich's origins can be traced back to a Lithuanian immigrant to New York, who had learnt the recipe from a Romanian Jew. He began selling the sandwiches from his butcher's shop in the city, but rather like the story of Lombardi and his pizza, the sandwiches were the most popular thing in the butchers and he converted it to a restaurant and the trend for Pastrami sandwiches grew from there.

When you drill down into the food culture of the US it's interesting to see that the local specialities tend to emerge from one of two things. If a region is blessed with a particularly bountiful supply of something (e.g. crabs in Maryland or oranges in

Florida) then those dishes or drinks are likely to be prevalent there. The second determining factor is often the immigrants that came to that particular area and the foods and traditions they brought with them from their homelands. Italians are one of the most obvious examples, but elsewhere in the country where German, Polish, Swedish, Mexican or Cuban immigrants are concentrated you will find their food traditions influencing the local cuisine or even becoming the speciality of that region. What's even more interesting is that these foods that they brought with them were often modified either because of what was available in the US (or what wasn't) or for local tastes. Lombardi, apparently unable to construct a wood-fired oven like those found in Naples, went with a coal-fired one. At the time he was also unable to reliably source buffalo mozzarella (which is what they used in Southern Italy) and started using fior di latte (cow's milk mozzarella). This is still by far the most common type of mozzarella found on American pizzas today.

* * *

It was nearly time. Soon we would be parted with our beloved Ram. She had done us proud by getting us from Miami to the outskirts of New York. We'd done nearly 3,000 miles and with the exception of the flat tyre and her ridiculous consumption of fuel, she'd not put a foot wrong. It was true that we were no nearer San Francisco than when we had landed in the US over a month before, since we had chosen to go drive north all the way up the coast, rather than start our journey westwards, but this leg of the journey was drawing to an end. We had arrived at the car rental and we were looking forward to our showdown with Don.

We pulled into the non-descript rental place. It had the desperate end-of-the-world look of a lot of out of town car rental places. There was one low slung building at the front of the lot for processing customers and a few lines of shabby cars, parked in such a way that they were all trapping each other in. We pulled up and went inside. A young man, with long hair, was at the desk.

"Hello we're returning the Dodge Ram - we've brought it to you from Florida," I said. I felt like he might congratulate us on our epic drive or perhaps thank us for bringing the precious Ram back or maybe even just compliment us on the fact we had driven an unregistered, clearly unserviced deathtrap safely back to him. Unfortunately he said none of those things.

"Ok we go outside and check it out," he said. He had a German accent. *Was this Don?*

He looked round the car, checking a few of the scratches. She was in pretty good shape, although it did occur to me that since it must have been at least two years since this guy could have possibly last seen the Ram, how would he even know what damage had occurred in the last 30 days?

The long-haired German seemed pretty happy with the Ram.

"Can I just ask," I said tentatively, "are you Don?"

He laughed, "Me? No, I am not Don," he continued, "I am happy with the van. So since you pay already, you owe only $100 for the spare tyre you used."

"Whoa, whoa mister!" We did not want to pay $100, we were the ones who had been wronged by Don, with the lack of breakdown cover, the absence of a jack and the fact the van was unregistered.

I thought quickly and continued, "Yes we used the spare tyre, but if you had included the jack then we could have changed the spare tyre. Instead we had to go to a mechanic, which cost us...you know, loads."

He paused for a moment. I pressed my advantage. He wanted $100, *ok, let's double it*.

"That mechanic cost us $200! So you owe us $200!"

Jack chipped in, "we'll take the $100 we owe you off that and settle for the $100 you owe us."

Perhaps it was the language barrier, perhaps it was the fast maths, but he relented, "Ok no problem, no one owes money to anyone."

"Ok fine," we said, gleefully.

We went back inside to sign the final papers.

"So if you're not Don then, where is he?" I enquired.

"He's in the back," he said and gestured down the corridor behind him. I glimpsed down and saw a couple of office doors.

"Can we say hello?" I strained my head and could see a pair of feet, crossed over and resting on the desk, as if the owner was leaning back in a chair making some important business call.

"No, he is busy."

And that was that, no chance to meet him. No showdown. We would not be able to unmask the puppetmaster, the man behind the curtain, the Wizard in our very own Oz. Instead the long-haired German agreed to drive us to the station so we could take a train into the city. Before long, that view of downtown Manhattan opened up and all thoughts of the Ram and Don began to disappear.

Jack and I had a week in New York and it was the first time that I had ever visited the city. It was an assault on the senses, busy beyond words and just a bit crazy. Not just in the sense of the pace of the city life, but also in terms of how many crazy people there were about. At every turn (or at least at every subway station exit) there was a crazy person just waiting to jump out and show off and/or scare us in equal measure. I was unused to the subway train "etiquette" of these people, it was something I'd never seen on the London underground. In New York it was common for a crazy person or busker (or someone who was both) to walk down the carriage doing something (like a song or just ranting about our sins) and then ask for money. Most New Yorkers seemed to be adroit at avoiding their gaze as though they didn't exist. I wasn't sure whether it was the insane busy nature of the city that had turned these people crazy or whether they had gone crazy somewhere else and thought, *"Right, better get myself to New York City then."* Whatever it was, there were a lot of them.

For the first few days we stayed in Midtown Manhattan in an anonymous hostel. We met some of the other hostellers and in contrast to some of the chilled-out people we had met in earlier hostels, they seemed vacuous and shallow. Many of them were doing round the world trips. They were "doing the US" but typically that included flying into New York, flying across the country to Los Angeles and then a side-trip to Las Vegas or San Francisco. They weren't doing the hard yards. Hundreds of miles of interstates, forgotten towns in unfashionable states – *that* was a cross-country trip. Since many of them were doing round the world trip, apparently we were the ones who weren't doing it properly, since we hadn't been to the full moon party in Thailand or picked fruit in Australia for months on end.

Unfortunately there is a lot of competitive travelling within the backpacking community. Often when backpackers meet each other, they will size each other up, judging each other on length of trip, number of places they've packed in and hardship endured (with the more unnecessary hardship the better.)

"How long you been on the road?"

"Oh, about three months, I got three more to go though. You?"

"Well only two months, but I haven't had a shower in four weeks, you?"

"Three weeks, but it doesn't matter because I've found a way to really get in touch with the locals because I've been drinking yak's milk for the last two weeks, you?"

"Yak's milk? I've been drinking rat's milk, that's what the locals drink. And I've been drinking it for three weeks. Warm."

And so it goes on, because a lot of these conversations are just a competition to prove who is the most authentic, who is the *real* traveller. It can be quite tiring. When I first went to Thailand, I told some other hostellers I'd just been for a fantastic meal at a restaurant. I couldn't believe how cheap it was or how fantastic it was.

One of the other travellers replied, "Oh you went to a restaurant? We only eat street food."

It was so dismissive and just rude. It didn't matter to her how good the food was, she wasn't interested. It didn't fit her model of what *travelling* was, so she dismissed it out of hand. At the end of the day though, unless you can speak the language fluently and are living with the local people then you are still a tourist. As a backpacker you can travel more sensitively and go a bit deeper, both of which I actually endorse wholeheartedly, but whether it's tourism, travelling or backpacking, or whatever you want to call it, you are a visitor in a foreign land and you should leave the judgmental and competitive attitude at home.

By this point Jack and I had decided to spend the days separately, meeting up in the evenings to hang out. This wasn't because we'd fallen out, but there is a limit to how much time you can spend in someone else's company. The drives were long and the cities were a chance for us to explore individually. Of course we were getting on each other's nerves occasionally; at one point we were waiting on the subway station and Jack had his iPod on, with one ear in and the other earphone dangling out.

"Are you listening to me?" I asked.

"What, yeah sure, of course I am," he replied.

"What did I just say then hmmm?"

"Something about...doing stuff," he said tentatively.

"Oh, something about doing stuff? So you *were* listening! *I apologise*. Take that bloody earphone out when I'm talking to you."

"Why? I can hear you."

"Yeah but you're also listening to music."

"Yeah and listening to you."

"The music is distracting you. You can't listen to me while listening to the music."

"What, like if we're in a bar and there's music on then it's not possible to have a conversation?"

I looked at him, with his stupid, well-made point, "Shut up."

"Great, I'll listen to my music," and he popped his other earphone in.

I went for long walks, I visited the Statue of Liberty and Ellis Island, where immigrants to the US were processed by the boatload between 1892 and 1954. The Ellis Island museum told the story of all the many thousands who passed through. They came mainly from Europe and sailed across the Atlantic and arrived tired but hopeful into New York harbour. They would have sailed past the Statue of Liberty, that symbol of America and docked in at Ellis Island, anxious to be let in to this new country, all hopeful of starting a new and better life. They say over 40% of Americans have at least one ancestor who came through Ellis Island, which is staggering when you think there are around 300 million Americans. The tour gave a great insight into the diversity of people who came and the melting pot that America is today.

Mostly though I enjoyed walking in Central Park, it was always a refreshing change to the madness of the city. Central Park is one of the great city parks. It's an oasis, with its relaxing trails, the fields where ordinary New Yorkers play Frisbee and softball. It's got a huge lake in the middle fringed by wooded areas. There are little bridges and boathouses and places for peace and quiet. I sat on the rocks watching the last tinges of frost recede in the early April sunlight.

The ice-skating rink was still open and I watched the skaters laughing and enjoying themselves, I walked on past the kids and stopped at the Strawberry Fields memorial. It commemorates John Lennon, who was shot and killed nearby in 1980. Lennon's ashes were scattered in Central Park and it seemed like an appropriate place for the singer and peace activist. Central Park is undoubtedly the peaceful heart of this thriving, chaotic and always fascinating city.

13. Connecticut: Half and half

Beyond New York, in that far North Eastern corner of the US, is New England, a cluster of six states bound together with a shared identity, but enough little differences to make them distinct. The best time to go to New England is the autumn (or fall), when the leaves turn colour in a riot of golds, reds and burnished yellows. Driving around the region to look at the foliage at this time of year is affectionately called leaf-peeping. It sounds a little seedy, but tell that to the legions of pensioners careering around in their oversized Winnebago camper vans.

The first New England state we came to when leaving New York City was Connecticut. A small state but one which divides neatly in two, the western half, the side closest to New York City, comprises a belt of commuter towns which are effectively the outer-lying suburbs of the city. New York has such a big pull, such a big sphere of influence, that it dominates both the northern half of New Jersey on one side and it does the same with Connecticut on its other side. You can take a train from these commuter towns into the city in less than an hour. Therefore many people commute into the city, but choose to live out in the suburbs (in another state).

I once saw an interesting map of the US which showed where the support for each baseball team lay. The support was represented by bubbles spreading out of the city where the team was located. Some teams had massive bubbles and some were confined to a small bubble not much bigger than the city itself. In some ways that graphic told you something about regional identity (as well as the fact that the more successful you are as a baseball team, the more popular you are.) Connecticut (which doesn't have its own major league baseball team) neatly followed that theory. Those in the New York side of the state tended to support the main New York team, the Yankees, while those in the other half, by-and-large rooted for the main team of New England, the Boston Red Sox, in the neighbouring state of Massachusetts. I think the character and people of the state in the western half of Connecticut definitely look towards New York and those in the east are characterised more by a distinctly New England identity.

So what is Connecticut famous for food-wise? Well according to our bible of food, the ominously titled "500 things to eat before it's too late" – it's also pizza. Of the book's top 24 places to get a pizza in the US, six of them are in Connecticut, including their number 1 and 2. Many think New York is the king of American pizza and as we've seen the very first pizzeria was indeed founded there. Others think Chicago, with its distinctive deep dish pizza, is the only place to rival New York. However, those in the know think the real battle is between New York and Connecticut. Strange, you might think, but perhaps not when you consider the amount of Italian immigration into Connecticut. The wave of Italian immigration in the late 19th and early 20th century began in New York City but it spread throughout the North Eastern US, down through New Jersey, on to Philadelphia and as far as Baltimore. On the northern side of New York the Italian influence can also be found in Connecticut, which brings us neatly back to the food. For our purposes we can imagine it not so much as a wave of people, as a wave of pizza.

The top two places for pizza in the country according to the book are in New Haven, Connecticut, which is also famous for being the home of Yale University. We duly went to the top dog, "Franke Pepe Pizzeria Napoletana", founded in 1925 and renowned for its white clam pizzas. Seafood is prevalent in New England so it makes sense that seafood features so heavily on Connecticut pizzas.

I'm not sure I can create a better description of the white clam pizza than the book, so I'll quote; the clams "are spread across the pie with just enough of their clear nectar to give the wafer thin creation a salubrious ocean savor. This is not a cheesy pizza, in fact there is no mozzarella at all, just scatterings of grated sharp pecorino. The bite of the cheese and sweetness of the clams, along with a salvo of minced garlic and spices and a drizzle of oil, make up a topping that does not cover the crust as much as meld with it…" It goes on like that, and my verdict was, if not quite as evangelical, that it was a damn good pizza. It was also unique, given the seafood topping, and lack of mozzarella (and tomato). It tasted authentic, and I loved the brick oven that we watched them cooking the pizzas in.

There is though another pizza connection in Connecticut. The following day, we moved further east into the state. The scenery changed, it became more rural, the suburbs gave way to little villages. We stopped at a historical town, Mystic, famous for its old seaport where all manner of wooden boats including whaling ships and trading ships used to dock in the 18th and 19th centuries. Mystic has the biggest maritime museum in the US, with plenty of preserved buildings and restored wooden ships. The museum comprised the whole of the dock area so we wandered round outside to our heart's content. Breathing in the salty sea air while looking around the ships definitely added to the experience.

We had been drawn to Mystic though for its (somewhat) famous pizzeria, called "Mystic Pizza". Does that ring any bells? It was the real-life inspiration for a 1988 film starring Julia Roberts. So the story goes: a screenwriter was spending the summer in Mystic and decided to set her coming-of-age story in the Mystic Pizza restaurant. Julia Roberts played one of three waitresses and they learned that true love was where they least expected, right on their doorstep, probably. Who knows, who cares? I watched the movie about a year and a half ago and I can't remember. This is my point, it's a pretty forgettable film. I bet you can't even remember if you've seen it or not.

I think that if Julia Roberts hadn't become a superstar then the film would've sunk into the annals of Hollywood like so many other 80's movies. If not for the stardom of Miss Brockovich, I doubt it would be remembered at all; who, for instance, knows what happened to the other two stars of the film, Annabeth Gish and Lili Taylor? If you must know, Gish starred in "Shag" (1989) and "Desperation" (2006) (TV movie), while Taylor took a leading role in the curious sounding "Penguins Behind Bars" (2003) (TV movie).

A trip to Mystic Pizza on Main Street will transport you back in to the scenes of your 68th favourite movie of all time; complete with special T-shirts, never-ending 80's music, and the movie playing silently on a loop on a widescreen TV on the wall. To be fair, it wasn't bad, the pizzeria had a more general movies theme and they had loads of black and white stills from other movies on the walls. Besides, how many "themed" bars and restaurants have you been to that have no real connection to anything famous, let alone being the subject of a bona fide Hollywood movie? Even if this particular movie is as forgettable as say, any Jennifer Anniston movie. Oh and the pizza? Robyn, who is the real pizza connoisseur, gave it her approval, although her rule seems to be that all pizza is good pizza.

The trip did give me the following thought though. Apparently when the movie was first released the queues to get into Mystic Pizza were down the block. When we were there, it was about 2/3 full. So over 25 years on from quite a forgettable film, at what point will it no longer make economic sense to hold on to the movie tie-in? There can't be that many Mystic Pizza movie devotees yet to make the trip.

* * *

Jack and I were ready to leave New York. We had moved from the Manhattan hostel to a Brooklyn hostel, for a change of scenery and because it was cheaper. It wasn't a particularly great move as, even though the neighbourhood was decent, almost all the sights were back over the river in Manhattan. We'd also ended up at a YMCA, which is a hostel more in the sense of the "long-stayers/soup kitchen" style. Grizzled-looking middle-aged men with straggly beards were omnipresent in the communal showers and the place had a functional, utilitarian air.

We decided to head to Boston next and given the difficulties with parking in cities we figured we'd take a bus or train then pick up a car after that. We weren't overly keen on the Greyhound and the train seemed expensive, but we had heard of an altogether cheaper option. At the first New York hostel we were talking to a backpacker who had come from Boston.

"I'll tell you the best way to get to Boston," he said conspiratorially.

"Oh yeah?" I asked, intrigued.

He leaned in, "The Fung Wah," he said with a smile on his face.

"The what?" I wasn't sure if I'd heard him correctly, as they weren't words I recognised.

"The Fung Wah Express man! It runs from Chinatown in New York to the Chinatown in Boston. Direct! And it's only $15!"

"$15? That's half the price of Greyhound."

"I know, crazy right."

"No catches?"

"Nope!"

The matter was settled and Jack and I found ourselves waiting on one of the busiest streets in Manhattan's Chinatown. I was impressed by Chinatown, it seemed pretty authentic to me, not just a token few restaurants, but grocery stores, banks and clothes shops all covered in Chinese writing. Obviously a block or two in either direction it all dissipated and it was like any other part of Manhattan, but right here it felt like a proper community, like we were in Hong Kong.

In fact some of the rules of the rest of New York didn't even seem to apply here, people sold belts and handbags right on the pavement, many of them were counterfeit high-end designer labels. I was just telling one of these hawkers for the third time that I definitely wasn't interested in a belt, or a watch or even a handbag, when the Fung Wah Express pulled up. Despite the Chinese characters along the side, it looked like a normal enough coach. It even had a little sign for Boston in the window. Jack and I, along with about 50 Chinese people, crowded around the door and then clambered aboard.

14. Rhode Island: The small-time

After Connecticut we drove the mere hour and a half to get into Rhode Island. If you know anything at all about Rhode Island, it is probably that it is the smallest state in the US. In fact it's about half the size of the next smallest (Delaware). In American terms it's tiny, being only around 40 miles by 50 miles, and it's actually smaller than the largest cattle ranch in the US. That's right, it's a state that's essentially smaller than a farm (the largest being King Ranch in Texas). So there you go, Rhode Island – it's small (and not even an island).

When we visited a state one of the things I liked to do was have a look at the state flag. Unlike state foods, they all have a flag, just as they all have an official seal, a nickname and a motto. The mottos are also intriguing. They range from the poetic, Kansas: *"To the stars through adversity",* the feisty, New Hampshire: *"Live free or die",* to the frankly bizarre and possibly sexist, Maryland: *"Manly deeds, womanly words".* I think you can tell a lot about the state from its flag and motto. Rhode Island's motto is endearingly simple, being just one word: *"Hope".*

The flags are even better. They all have flags, but they don't all look like they've spent much time on them. National flags tend to conform to a system. They tend to be made of two to three bold colours, making liberal use of stripes, crosses and other simple shapes. National flags don't, for example, tend to have a man standing on another man, having just beaten him up, like Virginia does. Nor do they tend to feature a giant cartoon pelican, considerably bigger than its own nest, like Louisiana does. Rhode Island's flag though is a good one; it's a picture of an anchor, ringed by 13 gold stars (which represent the original 13 American colonies – which coincidentally is also why there are 13 stripes on the American national flag). The anchor is a nod to Rhode Island's ocean links (and its nickname *The Ocean State*). To top the flag off the word *Hope* is inscribed beneath. Certainly one of the better flags.

We visited the city of Newport, tucked into Rhode Island's craggy Atlantic coast. The city made its fame as the summer retreat for millionaires from New York in the late 19th and early 20th century. Each millionaire (who I suppose were the equivalent of billionaires in today's money) seemingly tried to outdo each other by building ever more spectacular mansions on the cliff top at the edge of the city. Each one faces out to sea to make the most of the spectacular view and benefits from the refreshing ocean breeze that relieves the heat of the steamy and oppressive summers.

We couldn't really see any of these mansions from the road, since they were set back with big gardens and high hedges. However, we did a wonderful cliff top walk, which skirted right past the amazing buildings. Their long gardens ended with small fences (so they had the view) then there was the path, and the cliff fell away to the dramatic coastline beneath, with little coves and jagged rocks at each turn. Even better, the millionaires of Newport were kind enough to line their mansions up one after the other as if in some kind of beauty pageant. We were treated to spectacular coastal views on one side of us, with the marvellous sight of some of the most beautiful and ornate examples of late 19th and early 20th century architecture on the other.

Of course, as interesting as it was to see the outside of these mansions, it was only natural to want to have a peek inside as well. Fortunately a lot of them have been turned over to the public and are available to go round. This is because these massive mansions, complete with ballrooms and music rooms and all manner of extravagances, were hideously expensive to maintain. Therefore many were sold off when the families died and their heirs squandered their wealth or fell on bad times.

The owners of these fabulous buildings were the *Who's Who* of rich and famous people in the US at the turn of the 20th Century. The Vanderbilts, who made millions from the shipping and railroad industries, the Astors, whose wealth originated in that peculiarly American industry, the fur trade (and later real estate) and the Wideners, rich from steel and tobacco. They each constructed some of the most impressive mansions in Newport, which they oddly called 'summer cottages'. It made me wonder what their main homes must have been like.

We decided to take a tour of the 70 room *Breakers*, which was Cornelius Vanderbilt's "cottage" and one of the grandest in Newport. The mansion, built in 1895, was really something to behold. We got audioguides which were great for giving the background on rooms such as the Grand Hall, laden with marble and measuring fifty feet (15 metres) by fifty feet. All the rooms were constructed in Europe and then shipped over to be reconstructed in Newport. The little details were also fascinating, the small early electric bells to call the maids, the internal fountains constructed behind the staircases and the platinum leaf on the walls of the room designed by Tiffany's, the jewellers.

For the food, we went to rather less salubrious surroundings. On the other side of Newport, we visited Bishop's 4th St Diner, which is an old style dining car on the outskirts of town. Despite its diminutive size Rhode Island has a few particular state delicacies, so we didn't have a problem finding something to eat. In the end we went with jonnycakes, which are a type of pancake, and typically eaten at breakfast. A jonnycake is a cornmeal flatbread, served with butter and syrup. Although not an official state dish, Rhode Island did go to the trouble of producing legislation about the jonnycake – for instance jonnycake cannot be spelt with the letter H, i.e. johnnycake, the cakes must not contain sugar or flour, and the only type of corn that can be used is white cap flint corn. Too much time on your hands there chaps! Seriously, legislation for spelling and corn type? Come on, you haven't even got an official state muffin yet! I seriously question the priorities of some of these state governments.

The diner was renowned as a particularly good place for the jonnycakes. One reason we chose the jonnycake over such other Rhode Island food specialties as Hot Weiners (a type of hot dog) or the snail salad (exactly what it sounds like), was that apparently the jonnycake is made differently depending on where you are in Rhode Island (and bear in mind how tiny this state is). So we figured Rhode Islanders took jonnycakes pretty seriously.

The jonnycakes were undoubtedly tasty, although seemed to cry out for a lot of syrup, being a little heavier, darker and drier than regular pancakes. I'm not sure they were as good as a regular American pancake (which itself is heavier and doughier than its cousin, the British pancake). Perhaps the fact that jonnycakes are made with cornmeal makes them that bit heavier. That said, despite their heaviness, they weren't too thick, which would have really made them hard work. Since they were served up pretty thin, covered in syrup with butter on top, they were delicious.

Sometimes regional specialities break out and become popular nationally, e.g. the Frappe drink was originally a New England specialty and has since been co-opted by those mega-corporations, Starbucks and McDonalds. Other times you have to say that while you can see why people might like a particular dish you still can't see it catching on in a big way. Given the existence of the (superior) pancake, I'm afraid I don't think jonnycakes are ever going to hit the big time, but then again that's probably appropriate for the dish from the smallest state.

* * *

The Fung Wah in Fung Wah Express is actually Cantonese for *Magnificent Wind*. I can't understand why they didn't have that translated. I mean, if you were in the bus station and you had a choice between the Greyhound, the Megabus or the Magnificent Wind, which one would you take? Unfortunately the Fug Wah had a rather un-Magnificent history of serious safety violations and has stopped running in the intervening years since Jack and I rode it. According to the Department of Transportation Fung Wah drivers rated in the worst 2 percent of drivers nationwide based on regulatory violations, and nearly a dozen Fung Wah drivers were suspended after inspection between 2004 and 2006. In 2013 multiple buses were found to have cracked frames. The Fung Wah Express was declared an "imminent hazard to public safety" and ordered to stop all operations immediately. 10 years earlier though Jack and I were happy as the bus rattled along, wrapped up in the comforting blanket of blissful ignorance.

Unaware that our driver was probably half-blind and driving a bus with the structural integrity of an egg, I gazed out of the window thinking about the journey ahead. We were eating up the miles between New York and Boston, but we were barely halfway through the trip. We were still on the East Coast and had about 6 or 7 weeks to get to San Francisco in California. Surrounded by our fellow passengers happily chatting away in Chinese, Jack had his headphones in, but I gestured for him to take them out.

"So where do you want to go next?" I asked simply.

"We're going to Boston," he replied quizzically.

"Well yes, obviously we're going to Boston next, but after that where shall we go?"

He looked back at me, "Don't know, what do you think?"

Acting as travel agent (as well as tourguide), I gave him the options, "Well I figure with a couple of weeks to cross the country and a couple of weeks for California, we've got a couple of weeks to spare."

"Ok," he waited for me to continue.

"So I reckon we can either continue north to Canada, or we can try and get a car and start driving West. If we do that now we might have a chance to go to Mexico."

"Well how far are we from Canada?"

"I mean relatively speaking, we're really close. It's not that far north of here."

"Well why don't we just pop to Canada then?" He started to put his earphones back in.

"Wait! Wait! I don't think we can just *pop to Canada*."

"Why not?" He continued to hold his earphones close to his ears, as if this debate was very close to being over.

"Well because we're only close, relatively speaking. I bet it's still 6 hours or more on a bus."

"But relatively speaking or otherwise, we're close right? Let's do it Boss," and with that he put his earphones back in and the matter was settled. I had to admire his decisiveness.

The rest of the journey was uneventful, apart from when we made a stop at a service station. It appeared to be solely selling Chinese products, which was strange. To be honest the bus driver had garbled something so unintelligible that we dared not leave the bus for more than a few minutes, so we didn't get much of a chance to look around. The bus driver had used that language peculiar to all people who make announcements on public transport, I couldn't honestly say whether it was in Chinese or not. It was short and abrupt and something about the tone indicated that the Fung Wah Express would wait for no man. We got back on the bus as we quickly as we could and a couple of hours later pulled into Boston.

15. Massachusetts: The ballgame

In the case of Massachusetts it is worth quickly considering both the flag and the motto. The flag comprises a plain white background with a blue shield in the centre. A Native American with a long bow stands in the middle of the shield. However, unbeknownst to him, there is a sword rising above the surface of his shield-home and pointing directly down at his head. It is almost like a shark fin, breaking the wave and bearing down on the poor man underneath. Confusing, but without doubt there is an undertone of violence.

Underneath the picture, the Latin inscription (and state motto) means; "By the sword we seek peace, but peace only under liberty", eh? So, that's saying: "By this implicit threat of force and violence, i.e. the sword, we want peace. However, it better be the type of peace we like, with liberty and stuff, otherwise we'll get that sword back out." So yet more threats of violence; but is that surprising? Well Massachusetts holds a very special place in the history of America. As its flag, motto and everything else suggest, if they don't like stuff, they violently attack it. I am of course referring to the tyrannical colonial British, because it was here in Massachusetts that the American Revolution began.

Boston, the largest city in New England and state capital of Massachusetts, is extremely proud of its revolutionary history and Boston is well set up for tourists interested in this type of thing. The first

American revolt against the British was the "Destruction of the Tea in Boston" in 1773, later called "The Boston Tea Party" (which sounded a lot more fun than it actually was). The colonialists, angry with a new tax on tea imposed by their British rulers, refused to accept a consignment of tea and tipped it in the harbour. They were furious and demanded; "No taxation without representation" (they hated tax even back then!) They were resisting this new tax from their colonial overlords since they had no representatives in the British parliament. This is despite the fact that the average American colonist was considerably richer than the average British resident at the time. The British government responded harshly, withdrawing powers of local self-government from the colonies. This prompted the all-out revolutionary war that began (also in Boston) in 1775 and the Declaration of Independence the following year.

There is a museum to the Boston Tea Party and the city centre has plenty more Revolutionary sights, and even numpties dressed in period costume. There is also a red line running through the city which is called "The Freedom Trail" and if you follow it, then it takes you to various historic places, including the site of the Boston Massacre, Quincy Market, Boston Common, a revolution era gravesite etc. Tip - if you ever go to London, it also has some of these red painted line trails, called "red routes", follow these and you can see such sites as "The North Circular" and "Chiswick Roundabout"- very authentic London.

I'd been to Boston a couple of times and thought it was ok, but nothing special compared to New York City or even Philly, but this time I really liked it. We had three days exploring the city, and just over the river on the Cambridge side. We barely went into the centre, instead exploring some of the outer central part and some of the neighbourhoods which in some ways gave a much better sense of the city.

We wandered through Harvard, which is over the water in Cambridge. It's always pleasant to investigate these universities; as usual there was some enterprising student hanging around willing to give tours. They generally do them with enthusiasm and gusto (although this is obviously the upside of working for tips). Harvard was impressive, with an inescapable sense of money and grandeur. It clearly benefits from that virtuous circle between high-achieving students who then earn lots of money and then give it back to the university. Splendid buildings, ornate statues and wonderful landscaping give the campus a very pleasant feel. I thought about my own time at university and wondered how strange it would be to see tourists traipsing around the campus, while you were trying to make your way to a lecture (inevitably five minutes late).

Massachusetts has a variety of food traditions and we were keen to try as many as possible. One of the most famous is clam chowder. There's just something about chowder that is so New England that it begs to be pronounced in that very strong Boston accent (chowder becomes Chowdah!). Boston has a peculiar accent, think of someone like President John F Kennedy. If you can't conjure up his accent then if you've ever seen Mayor Quimby in *The Simpsons* you will know what I am talking about. He is forever shouting about *Chowdah!*

Clam chowder is sometimes called "New England Clam Chowder" or "Boston Clam Chowder" and the perfect place to try it is Boston's Quincy Market, a historical building in the city centre with a huge food court. Chowder is a stew or soup typically made with milk or cream, so is normally white. Clam chowder obviously features clams, which are molluscs (similar to mussels). They are found in abundance on the coastline of New England.

The recipe for chowder is fairly rigid. Apparently adding tomatoes to clam chowder is controversial in New England. In 1939, the neighbouring state of Maine had to take action and legislated: making tomatoes in clam chowder *illegal*. Clearly when you believe in something strongly you have to stand up and say something. I couldn't find out whether anyone was prosecuted under that law, but if they were, then that would probably be the one jail on earth I could cope with. *What was your crime? Tomato in chowder? You ghastly beast! I can't believe you would do something like that, on the other hand I'm a serious criminal. I spelt jonnycakes with an "h" and now I'm doing 10 to life.* No wonder the US has a problem with prison overcrowding.

But let's be honest chowder is just a fishy white soup, tasty, but not a huge amount to write home about. There are two vaguely interesting things about the chowder. First is that it is served in a bread bowl, as in the bowl itself is a big bread bun. The top is sliced off and the middle is hollowed out and the soup is poured right into the bread. This is quite fun (as far as soup goes). You can tear off little parts of the bread roll and dip it in the soup. The second intriguing element is the saltine crackers you get with it. To be clear the crackers themselves are boring. They are little salty crackers to dip in the soup, even though you already have a massive lump of bread to dip in it. However, you still get millions of the crackers. No one knows why. I think Americans liken the crackers to paper napkins, whereby if one napkin is good then eighteen must surely be better. In summary there are too many napkins and far too many saltine crackers in a lot of the dining experiences in the US. For instance if you go to a McDonald's Drive-Thru and get some coffees they'll give you about 6 paper napkins. No one has explained to me why or what I should be doing with them.

We also visited the Sam Adams brewery which is a few miles from the centre of Boston, and it is a journey well worth making. They did skip us through the tour part pretty quickly (since it was so popular) and the site is quite small (as most brewing is now done in Pennsylvania and Ohio). The tasting session was nevertheless excellent. They went through a good few different styles of beer, and seated us at German-beerhall style tables. The guide was funny and imparted some interesting information, including the fact that because of the strict German beer purity laws, no American beer could be imported into or served in Germany until the 1980s with the introduction of Sam Adams. The tour was worthwhile, although the sheer number of people coming through did compromise it somewhat. The tour was free and Sam Adams is one of the best known beer brands in the US so perhaps we shouldn't have been surprised (who would have thought free beer would be such a big pull?)

The real food highlight of Boston was tied up with the highlight of the trip, which was a visit to see the Boston Red Sox at the oldest stadium in Major League Baseball, Fenway Park. It was noticeable just how mad about the team and the sport the whole city seemed to be. In most American cities, you see an equal split between people wearing baseball caps and clothes of both the local team and the generic biggest teams in the sport (typified by the New York Yankees – you can go to Los Angeles and see people in Yankees gear). Not so in Boston, it was like a rule, if you had a baseball cap on, it was a Red Sox cap. That's the type of passion and unity you rarely see. What's more, the Red Sox have had about ten years of consecutive sellouts at their ground. That's for every game, and when you consider that baseball teams play *at least* 162 games a year(!) so more than 80 home games, that's a real achievement. It helps that

Boston have been pretty successful in recent years, and that the ground is fairly small, but it's still impressive.

Fenway Park is 100 years old, and was a really good place to see a game. As well as having a full crowd, the place had a great history about it. We walked through the back concourse and tunnel and went past all the old logos and various bits of memorabilia. There was a great feel to the place. Whereas a lot of baseball stadia are often half full (partly because of the amount of games they play), Fenway Park crackled with anticipation and excitement and made us feel like the game really mattered.

Baseball also has its own food culture. From the multitude of food stands around the stadium to the vendors walking up and down the aisle constantly, you're surrounded by food. The archetypal snack of the baseball stadium is definitely the hot dog. In fact, some say the term "hot dog" was coined at baseball stadia, where they would sell German sausages, originally called "dachshund sausages" because they were so long and thin.

We dutifully had some hot dogs, and while I won't pretend it was the most amazing hot dog I ever had, it certainly was the right place to be having it, and it did the trick. The Red Sox won the game which kept them on track for an appearance in the playoffs and possibly "World Series" that October. Unfortunately, since the American Football season would have started by then, the nation may not care much, but Boston sure would.

Baseball is often referred to as America's pastime. For a long time it was the most popular sport in America (although since the 70's that has probably not been the case). Baseball is deeply rooted in the American culture and psyche. It was popular as both a participation sport and a spectator sport. Baseball used to draw huge crowds around the country (especially in the interwar years) but has lost ground since then. It's still a big tradition though, from little league (the baseball children play), minor league (renowned as a great family day out) to major league baseball (where the biggest stars can still earn tens of millions of dollars).

The deep impact of baseball can also be seen by the number of phrases that the sport has given the English language (and many are so universal, that they are common in British English as well, even if your average Brit won't have the foggiest about baseball). For instance; heavy hitter, ballpark figure, play hardball, cover your bases, step up to the plate, out of left field, touch base etc. The list goes on and it's interesting to see how many are used in corporate business speak. It's like business decided that instead of inventing their own language they would just co-opt just about every baseball phrase going.

Baseball is still a popular sport and it remains an accessible, cheap and fun way to see professional sport. Going to the baseball is also full of its own traditions. The most popular thing is probably stuffing your face with all manner of hot dogs, nachos, funnel cake and beer, but there other endearing traits, like the 7th inning stretch (where the crowd get up to stretch) the listless shouting of *Charge!* at regular intervals at the prompting of the stadium announcer, and the kiss cam, where the jumbo screen zooms in on a couple in the crowd and they have to kiss, otherwise everyone else in the stadium boos them (it's less creepy than it sounds).

It's easy to see why (American) Football has become the nation's most popular sport, by almost every measure, from television audiences, to revenue even to the fervour it inspires in the fans. The problem for baseball is just that it's not that exciting. Yes it has exciting moments, a home run, 3 outs in one play or that crunch situation in the 9th inning where the last batter needs to win the game - they can all generate excitement. But those moments are few and far between, and baseball is so slow. The games last around 3 hours (and studies show they're getting longer and slower). Often you'll watch a game with fewer than 10 hits, which given that's what all the players are trying to do over and over for three hours, is not very many at all. It's easy to see why football (both college and professional league) with its excitement and big plays is now the top sport in America.

* * *

Jack and I arrived in Boston and walked to the hostel. Walking with backpacks is one of the worst parts of backpacking. Contrary to what you might think, it's not an especially big part of it. Obviously it's where the term backpacking is derived from, but it sucks all the same. The only time you really need to walk around with all of your stuff on you (i.e. your full backpack rather than a daypack) is when you are arriving in, or leaving, a place. Clearly arriving in a place is the worst of the two since you don't know where you're going or anything about your surroundings. That fact is obvious to everyone around you (and that you've got all your stuff on you). Therefore the best thing to do is pretend that you are just leaving the place and actually do know where you're going. Admittedly, that pretence is hard to keep up when you're walking away from the bus station and holding a map.

Before long though, we did arrive at our hostel, a rather anodyne place, with rules aplenty and a strictly rationed breakfast. Staying at places like these gave me a good insight into what living through wartime on the home front must have been like. The rules were printed and pinned up around the hostel by some unseen committee, designed to guide every aspect of life in the hostel and carefully regulate any sense of fun. *Home by 12! Lights out at 1! Silence in the rooms! Two pieces of toast per hosteller, with a ration of 20 grams of butter OR 15 grams of jam! Please do your washing up, remember we're all in this together!*

The hostel though did do a bar crawl every night. What the poster didn't say was that they ran these regardless of how empty the bars were or how few people signed up. So it went that Jack and I traipsed around some desolate bars on a midweek night with a group of other unfortunates from the hostel. It was the type of bar crawl that was so bland that by the end of it you seemed to know fewer people then when you set out. It did at least serve to establish whom in the hostel you should avoid; Alan, the trainee accountant, Lisa, whose best conversation was asking who my favourite character in *Friends* was; and Darren, who'd been drinking rat's milk for the last week. They all made the list.

There was one person who seemed reasonable. An Aussie guy, similar age to me, he seemed laid back. Given Jack and I were still exploring the cities separately I arranged to hang out with him the following day. He was a backpacker, so unsurprisingly he didn't want to spend any money. Money was for beer and the daytimes were an exercise in doing the most you could for the least amount of money. We decided to go for a walk around the city and agreed to walk the Freedom Trail, the painted red line that ran past all the historical sites.

We walked up the slope of Boston Common and past the capitol building with its golden dome. We walked past Paul Revere's house, he who launched the famous ride to warn the colonists that, "The British are coming." This apparently saved the day, as the colonists mustered themselves and fought off the dastardly British. In American history Paul Revere gets treated as a hero, while Benedict Arnold, a colonist who passed information to the British, is regarded as a traitor. However, you could say that Revere was actually just a loud-mouthed tattle-tale, while Arnold was a loyal and dedicated sort. *I* wouldn't say that, but you could. History is written by the victors, as they say.

The Freedom Trail was interesting though, the 2.5 mile walk took us past 17 revolutionary-era sites. It showed just how much Boston was the epicentre of the revolution. My Aussie friend and I continued to talk. It was ok, but it was quite an effort. I really had to *make* conversation. Of course the problem is that once you've committed to doing something like a 2.5 mile historical walk with someone you've only met once before then you're in it for the duration. We both knew silence wasn't really an option. You really have to be at a certain level of comfort with a person to be able to spend time in their company in silence. Clearly we weren't at that level. As time wore on it was a bit of a strain to maintain a constant conversation.

The historical sites did at least give us something to talk about and we reached the end of the Freedom Trail at Bunker Hill. The grassy hill is over the river from the centre of Boston and features a large stone tower monument. It commemorates the Battle of Bunker Hill, one of the first significant battles of the Revolutionary War. We decided to climb the tower, which was pretty tall. There was a sign at the bottom saying that there were 300 steps and the climb should not be attempted if you were infirm or lazy.

My Aussie friend and I dutifully made the climb and were rewarded with some impressive views back over the river towards Boston. We climbed all the way back down the steps and arrived at the bottom of the monument. I thought to myself how unpleasant it would be if you had forgotten something at the top and had to go back. Seized by this thought, I saw that my friend had his sunglasses resting on the top of his head.

Without thinking I said, "Hey didn't you have some sunglasses? You didn't leave them at the top did you?" He instinctively reached for his face as if they would in fact be in front of his eyes. They obviously weren't and I assumed that his hand would then naturally reach to the top of his head and find the sunglasses and we'd both laugh at my witty comment. Instead his hand dropped.

"Oh crap. Crap! I've lost them. What if they're not even up there? I need to go back up there," he started to walk back to the tower before I could even think.

He started to jog and was already inside the door when I shouted out, "Wait! Wait!" Fortunately he came back out, "What?" He was agitated and clearly wanted to climb the stairs.

"Umm it's just that your sunglasses are on your head," I said awkwardly. His hand reached up slowly to his head, felt the sunglasses and brought them back down. "Yeah, sorry about that," I said sheepishly.

"Not cool man," he said quietly, although his eyes silently added *"you halfwit."*

"Yeah sorry about that," I repeated. It was clear the joke hadn't gone as well as I hoped.

"I think I might walk back on my own," he said and turned on his heel and started walking. I watched him go. Where was Jack when I needed him?

16. Maine: The forest

Maine is a big state. It could easily fit the other five New England states in it, yet very few people live there, apart from Steven King. As we entered it felt like we'd reached the wilderness, as though we'd crossed a frontier. We'd come from densely populated Massachusetts and all of a sudden the landscape just seemed to open up. There was forest everywhere we looked, and it had an untouched appearance.

The interstate hugged the coast as we drove north, but soon it became two-lanes and then just a single-lane in each direction. We skirted very close to the water, over little bridges and then through forests. On pretty much any drive in Maine you can't help but notice the sheer number of trees. In fact, over 90% of the state is forest (the most heavily forested in the US). Interestingly the public (via the state government) own about one million acres of this – about 5% of Maine's total area. However, paper mills and logging companies own more than 5 million acres, which is over 25% of the total area of Maine! That's a lot of paper.

We stopped at the flagship LL Bean store. LL Bean is an outdoors adventure and outfitter shop. It's pretty popular throughout the US and was founded in Maine in 1912 (which makes sense since it is a pretty outdoorsy kind of place). The original Mr. LL Bean sold just a single product - waterproof shoes - to hunters. Not that you would know it now, if you were to visit the flagship store. In the hundred years since Mr. LL Bean first started selling shoes in Freeport, Maine, the shrewd folks now at LL Bean had transformed things beyond recognition. They had created a megastore complex for "destination" shopping. It was an impressive place, just for its sheer scale. And it was busy, with hundreds of people milling around.

Clearly seeing the inside of an outdoors shop was the thing to do in Maine. The irony was that we saw many more tourists there than anywhere else in the state. It was not just individual shoppers that had turned up, they had tourbuses there! This store is actually in the book, *1,000 Places to see in the USA and Canada Before You Die*. All I can say is that I guess 1,000 is a pretty big number to get to. I honestly don't think anyone will be any the poorer for not having seen an LL Bean store that can only be described as bigger, but nevertheless similar, to all the other LL Beans in the US. Certainly not worth getting off your deathbed for.

We continued north up the coast and the towns became more spread out and the scenery even more stunning. My mind turned to the food. One of the culinary experiences I was looking forward to most was Maine. I'd heard of a place serving lobster rolls that everyone raved about. To be honest it's hard not to hear of this place, it was in our 500 things to eat book, the Lonely Planet, and 1000 places to go before you die, so it's pretty famous. But the place in question, *Red's Eats* in Wiscasset, is not a particularly impressive place to look at; it's just a shack with some picnic tables out the back. Yet it's so popular the town have considered asking for a bypass because of the traffic jams that it creates in the summer. *The New York Times* even wrote an article about it. I'm going to guess that probably didn't help matters.

So why is it so popular that people will queue up to an hour to eat there? Because it's universally acknowledged to serve the best lobster rolls in the state, and therefore the country. Maine is the lobster capital, they thrive in cold waters, and Maine has got an awful lot of coastline, so they're abundant up there. The popular consensus seems to be that *Red's Eats* serves the best lobster roll partly because they put the most lobster in the roll: they promise more than the meat of a whole one pound lobster in each roll. That and the lobster is always freshly caught.

The concept of a lobster roll is actually pretty simple, take a long bun, toast it, stuff lobster meat into it until it is overflowing and then pour drawn butter over it. They have an old fashioned metal kettle on the hob and they just pour melted butter into a little cup for you to pour it on the way you like it.

I'll have to be honest, it was delicious – so simple yet so decadent! Huge knuckle-chunks of lobster meat, as fresh as can be, melding with the warm butter. Whenever I'd had lobster before it was always in very modest portions, delicate pieces sprinkled throughout some dish. Clearly that was wrong way to do it. What you need is just great big chunks of juicy, succulent lumps of lobster meat. Why shouldn't it be served in that way? It was so indulgent, so damn tasty. I suppose the reason is that even served from a shack, in the land of lobster, in a roll, each one still cost $16. But it was worth every penny.

But Maine's charms extend further beyond the lobster. It's full of wilderness, great craggy coastline with lighthouses galore. Robyn and I spent a fantastic couple of days at Boothbay Harbor, a coastal town about halfway up the state. The hotel was the type of place that offered canoes for free. They were tied up on the river at the end of its extensive gardens. The little river led out into some bigger lakes and within 10 minutes of paddling we were in wilderness in the middle of nowhere. Maine is one of those states that is just so massive and devoid of people that it reminded me of the sheer scale of the US.

Robyn and I were paddling the canoe, we rounded a bend to see yet more steeply forested hillsides. Around another bend we saw a seaplane. A seaplane! Imagine living somewhere where that would be a logical purchase. It was all so peaceful, quiet and majestic. We agreed it was hard (and unfair) to believe that anyone got to enjoy on this on a daily basis. It's amazing the different environments people live in, having been in the bustling centre of Boston not long before. If I lived there I didn't think I would ever get sick of the views, the tranquillity, or those lobster rolls.

* * *

Jack and I had a plan, we had decided to head directly north out of Boston and go to Montreal in Quebec, the French speaking part of Canada. Since we'd be arriving in another city, we figured we'd continue with the bus and get a car when we'd finished with the cities. Unfortunately the French, unlike the helpful people of the Chinatowns, were not the types to run a low-cost direct coach service. Instead we had to get back on the Greyhound for a bus through to Montreal.

There weren't many passengers on the bus; it didn't have the down-at-heel feel of the other Greyhound we had taken back in Florida, before we picked up the Ram. No, this was international travel (of a sort) and the other passengers were of a (slightly) higher class than usual; this Greyhound clearly wasn't being used purely to ferry convicts and former guests of the *Jerry Springer show*. We were still a little apprehensive though, as we weren't sure what to expect from an overland border crossing, whether there would be inspections or customs barriers of any sort.

Most of the other passengers were on their own, which always seemed to be the case on Greyhound (presumably travelling on it cements your status as a social outcast). One of the other passengers was particularly nervous about the border (I wondered exactly what he was carrying). He kept repeating that he had heard the border was a lot tighter these days, since the terrorist attacks in 2001, a few years before.

One man, who appointed himself as the *Captain of the Passengers*, had made the journey to Montreal before. He was the type of man who clearly got off on being "special", if having travelled on Greyhound before qualified him as special. He told us what would happen at the border: that we would get off the bus, walk through customs and the bus would go through separately. It was good information and well worth the 5 minutes it took for him to explain that part. The next hour and a half of him continuing to repeat that bit of information and seemingly everything else he knew was less interesting. In the end I had to resort to putting my earphones on (while he was still talking) and then pointing to the earphones apologetically, in a manner that suggested; *Yes, I would love to hear where the third hour of this conversation will lead, but somehow my earphones are in now and the music is loud, so I'm afraid you really are going to have to turn round in your seat now. Sorry about that.*

In the end the journey went smoothly enough and we arrived in Montreal, which was a breath of fresh air. After more than 6 weeks in the US, it was nice to be somewhere different, and city-wise Montreal is about as different as it gets in North America. It's the second biggest city in Canada and also one of the five biggest French-speaking cities in the world.

The French influence is obvious everywhere and it certainly looked more like France than the US to us. Across from our hostel was not the typical Dunkin' Donuts, but a *boulangerie* with fancy coffee and artisan pastries. Jack in particular was over the moon. He was a man whose tastes ran to the finer things in life; he was beginning a transition, his late night cravings for snacks could no longer be satisfied with a Budweiser and a Pepperami. Like some kind of drug user searching for a purer high he had transitioned to Genoa salami, ripe brie and high end red wines. He tended to treat himself almost continuously with products that were altogether more decadent these days. I had lost count of the number of times on the trip that, late at night, he had rustled up from who knows where, a deli pack of very thinly sliced salami and munched his way through it slice by slice.

The next morning we were in the boulangerie and he was in heaven. His face alighted upon pain au chocolats, homemade croissants and Colombian coffee.

"Now this is more like it," he said, happily gazing at the menu.

"We're backpackers, this place is a bit fancy," I said hesitantly.

"Calm down Boss, we deserve to treat ourselves don't we? Don't we? It's pretty cheap anyway, I think."

"Says you," I looked at him sceptically. "You're the one who used to throw away money... literally!" It was true; he had a famously carefree attitude to money, one which did not match my own. I once found out he had literally no clue how much a pint of milk cost. It was the type of silly question that would flummox out-of-touch celebrities and millionaires, yet Jack (even though he was a student at the time) was similarly clueless. His guesses weren't a little bit out, in a kind of *'oh I guess you don't buy milk often'* kind of a way, but in a way that suggested he had no grasp of the fundamental costs of basic staples. His estimate for the price of milk was approximately 400% out. It was remarkable. Around the same time I found out that he used to actually throw away small denomination coins. I was shocked then and only mildly less shocked three years later. Occasionally, like then in the boulangerie, I brought it up to prove he had a careless attitude to money.

"Yeah, but it's an encumbrance isn't it? All those little coins," he smiled, because he knew it annoyed me.

"Only you would describe money as an encumbrance."

"It's not like they're really worth anything is it?"

"Well that's exactly the point! It's money, so of course it's worth something, you imbecile."

He was smiling again.

Just being somewhere different had livened both of us up. We had fun exploring the Olympic park, where Montreal had hosted the 1976 Olympics. The project had been so expensive that the citizens of Montreal were still paying off the cost of the stadium

30 years later. Out at the Olympic Park they had since built a planetarium (fair enough) a biodome (cool) and an insectarium (my least favourite kind of –ium). Nevertheless we visited both the biodome and the insectarium. I was reminded of the film *Biodome* where two moronic young men get trapped inside an experimental biodome and for reasons unknown are forced to stay in there for years. I looked at Jack and wondered if the same thing happened to us how long it would be before our *Biodome* turned into *Lord of the Flies*.

The best thing about Montreal was probably the Vieux Montreal area, which was the old town. It was full of olde-worlde restaurants and shops, it even had some cobblestones, which made a nice change. There was an embrace of the old in Montreal which was different from a lot of the American cities we had been in.

We ate well and saw some of the interesting underground city. Montreal is one of the coldest cities in North America. It snows on average more than 60 days a year and experiences a dozen days a year where the windchill factor is more than -30C. That is seriously cold. That type of temperature might be acceptable if you were conducting research at an Antarctic scientific base, but it's rather inconvenient in a place where people have got to get to their job as an accountant or estate agent. Montreal has developed an underground city to deal with the ferocious winters. It's a complex system of tunnels and walkways stretching over 20 miles. There are shops, restaurants and offices down there and it connects to a lot of the metro. Clearly some of it had been built at different points, as some of it looked like a little old-fashioned, made of beige tiles, while other parts looked more futuristic and gleaming. Nevertheless it was a novel idea.

By this point in our journey it was mid-late April, but it was still surprisingly cold in Montreal. We had arrived at the end of winter in Florida and tracked up the coast as winter rolled back and spring emerged. However, by the time we got to Montreal it felt like we had caught up with winter again and ice still fringed the lakes in the parks. Undaunted, we figured we would pick our way west across a little bit of Canada before dipping back into the US for the long journey across the middle. We decided to go to the Canadian capital, Ottawa, and hopped on another bus for the 3 hour journey.

17. New Hampshire: The leaves

Robyn and I were still driving around New England. We continued from Maine inland into New Hampshire. This was where we really hit the fall colours that the region was so famous for. Amidst the mountains and the abundant signs for "Moose Crossing", we got a sense of a very different New England than coastal Maine and the more populated (almost suburban) feel of Connecticut and Rhode Island.

We decided to stop for a couple of nights in the White Mountain National Forest. The White Mountains cover more than a quarter of New Hampshire and are at the northern end of the Appalachian range of mountains. The Appalachians run for 1,500 miles down as far as Georgia and continue even north of New Hampshire, all the way up to Newfoundland in Canada. They are the most significant mountain range in the east of North America and it was incredible to think that they stretched south through practically all the states we had visited on the Eastern seaboard.

We were particularly keen to visit the National Forest since we were, after all, there as leaf-peepers. The whole fall foliage spotting is a difficult thing to time correctly. Since it is a natural phenomenon it always takes place at a similar-ish time of year (late September and throughout October), but the peak of it, when you get the most vivid colours, is in a very small window. This window, which is about a week or so, always shifts from year to year. This means it's tricky to plan when exactly to visit.

There are websites which track the foliage colour change which rolls down from the north, as the most northerly places have their leaves change first (since winter arrives a little sooner). These websites do their best to try and predict when and where the best colours will be, but predicting more than a few days ahead seems to be largely guesswork. The actual colour change of the leaves results from summer suddenly departing and the winter arriving. The trees start to lose the chlorophyll in the leaves, the green disappears and it is replaced by bright yellows, oranges and reds for a few weeks before the leaves eventually turn brown and fall off the branches.

They say the fall colours are best in New England because it's a pretty cold place and the change from summer to winter is more sudden than elsewhere. The abruptness of the change makes the leaves turn colour quickly. They light up in a riot of colours and that is what everyone wants to see. Unfortunately unless you live in New England or you have the type of boss that is ok with you saying *"Look I'd love to do the big client meeting tomorrow but I've just heard that the fiery reds and golden yellows in New England are out of this world right now so I'll see you next week,"* then you just have to book your trip and hope.

We were pretty lucky. The colours had been fabulous in Maine and when the sun shone on the leaves the colour spectrum was glorious. The drives were magical, particularly because, despite what we'd heard, it really wasn't busy and the winding roads were peaceful and quiet. In the White Mountains the colours were still there, but perhaps a little past peak.

We went for some lovely walks in the mountains, strolling on quiet paths, past little rivers and to a waterfall. Despite the *Moose Crossing* signs that we saw everywhere around New Hampshire, unfortunately we didn't see any, but the scenery was great anyway. Occasionally we'd come to viewpoints which offered sweeping vistas and we could see thousands upon thousands of trees. They swirled together in a pleasing palette of autumnal colours.

There wasn't any one particular food thing we wanted to do in New Hampshire, so we were open to ideas. One thing we wanted to do was have some authentic maple syrup, which in the US tends to be associated with New England (it's also very strongly associated with Canada). Maple syrup is made by "tapping" Maple trees. The trees are generally found in cold northern areas and the syrup is derived from the tree sap. The sugary sap is a by-product of the tree storing starch and come spring time, they bore a tap into the tree and sap comes out. After that, it's a case of heating the sap to evaporate a lot of the excess which leaves the concentrated "syrup".

The Canadian province of Quebec, just to the north of New Hampshire, produces the majority of the world's maple syrup, with the New England states the next biggest producers. The production of the syrup was first carried out by the Native Americans and it has been culturally significant in the US and Canada ever since. Tapping the sap of the maple tree and producing maple syrup was one of the only agricultural practices used by Native Americans in this part of the continent prior to European colonisation.

Maple syrup became popular with abolitionists and during the Civil War since most regular sugar was being grown, processed and transported with the use of the slave labour in the South. When the Civil War broke out, the North obviously lost a lot of its sugar supply and so they substituted maple syrup in a lot of products since the syrup was something the Northerners could still get their hands on.

Since then the maple leaf has only risen in power and significance, and as well as working its way on to the Canadian flag it has even taken over its own professional ice hockey team. Well it had an ice hockey team named after it at any rate (the not very fearsome sounding *Toronto Maple Leafs)*.

Unfortunately since the maple sap actually gets tapped from the trees in the spring, it seemed like we wouldn't be able to watch it get made, and instead would have to settle for just eating a lot of it. We had heard of a place called "Polly's Pancake Parlor" in the excellently named Sugar Hill which is on the western side of New Hampshire, near the border with Vermont.

The logo for the restaurant was a maple leaf which was a good start, and the place had an excellent reputation. It had started serving pancakes back in 1938, and they made a variety of maple products including maple sugar and maple spread on the premises. The setting of Polly's Pancake Parlor was great. It had amazing views of the White Mountains straight out of the big plate glass windows in the annex to the restaurant. We were also very impressed by all the maple products on the table, there was maple spread, maple sugar, maple pepper and of course maple syrup. They were obviously purists.

Despite the fact they had a rather large menu, with all sorts of country sausage, home fries and smoked ham, we both just wanted the homemade pancakes. We ordered a sampler of all the different pancakes which included plain, buckwheat, wholewheat, cornmeal, oatmeal and then we chose add-ins from the huge list: blueberries, choc chip, walnuts and coconut.

What I liked was that rather than serve all the pancakes at once and have them get cold, they served them in two batches of three so that they were warm, which was smart thinking. The blueberry ones were absolutely delicious and probably the best pancakes I'd ever had. I particularly liked the maple spread which was like a maple syrup version of Nutella.

They made a perfect lunch and perhaps unsurprisingly the Pancake Parlor was only open for breakfast and lunch. A pancake parlor clearly isn't the place to go for date night (although Robyn didn't seem to mind). It was great trying the pancakes with all the variations of the maple products on the table, like some kind of rotating buffet where the only condition was the inclusion of some kind of maple product. They also had a shop for all their delicious maple goodies. One such delicacy is maple hurricane sauce, a specialty of the Parlor since the 30's when one autumn they were left with a huge bounty of apples. Unsurprisingly they decided to boil the apples in, what else but maple syrup, and created a new apple-maple sauce. Delectable.

* * *

Jack and I stepped off the bus in Ottawa, Canada's diminutive capital. Some people recommend skipping straight through between Montreal and Toronto, but we were keen to see Ottawa. We were rewarded with a handsome little city, situated next to the river. Since it was a capital city there were plenty of things to see and yet there were practically no tourists at all. Ottawa is on the border of French-speaking Quebec and English-speaking Ontario, a site deliberately chosen in the 1850s to ensure fairness between the two key groups of Canadians at the time. That said, apart from their love of poutine (a French-Canadian snack of fries, gravy and cheese) Ottawa seemed much more English than French to us.

Despite Canada's vastness (it's actually the second biggest country in the world and bigger than the US, which is fourth, Russia is first), Canada remains a fairly small country in its outlook. It doesn't think it is one of the great powers of the world and Canadians are often pretty self-deprecating, which for all their great qualities is not one you tend to find much amongst Americans. One of the more unusual benefits of this small country mindset is that Canadian politicians are not nearly as removed from the people as in the UK and the US. For instance if you fancy observing the Canadian parliament and you're in Ottawa with an hour or two to spare, you can simply enter the gallery and see what they're up to. This is exactly what I chose to do. Unlike in the UK where you have to write to your MP and wait patiently to see if you can get an invite in 6 months time, in Canada you just wander in. Of course the downside in Canada is that they're generally just legislating about ice hockey or maple syrup, but nevertheless it was a novel experience.

In the hostel we met a guy called Sammy who was attempting to set up an adventure and ecotourism camp out in the woods. He had been visiting the hostel and offering to have people to stay with him for a few days in his log cabin in the forest. The volunteers would help him for a few days doing some work to get the camp up and running, while he would let them do some of the activities for free. He had just brought some people back and they recommended it. Sammy made the same offer to Jack and me. Jack, being a lazy man, agreed to the offer with just one proviso: that instead of us doing any of the chores or jobs we would just pay him some money. Sammy was happy, he had his first paying customers, while Jack and I would go to the ecotourism camp for what was a very cheap price, particularly since it also included a couple of nights at his log cabin. Sammy had convinced two Korean girls to come along as well, although they were on the "do some jobs" package, unlike our own "executive" package.

Sammy drove the four of us out of Ottawa in his battered Ford for about an hour or so back into Quebec. We stopped at a village for "supplies", which mostly consisted of Doritos and beer. He asked for the money that we had agreed on and we noted he immediately spent the majority on the supplies. We got back in the car and ploughed on down some country roads before entering a large pine and spruce forest. After a little while the road ran out and the last part was on an unsurfaced track. It was remote.

As we pulled up in front of the log cabin Sammy turned to us, "Now guys, I've actually got a roommate at the moment, a guy called Lens."

"Ok," we said, we hadn't heard this before but it didn't seem like it would be a problem.

"Oh and also, you two," pointing at us, "will be staying in his room." Well that definitely was news to us, "and you two," pointing at the girls, "will be staying in my room." One of them giggled. I was beginning to doubt they actually spoke any English at all.

We entered the log cabin, it wasn't that big. There was a central area with two rooms leading off from it and some wooden stairs on one side which led to an upper level. A guy was sitting at the small table in the corner, wearing glasses, looking at a laptop. He looked up and a flash of anxiety crossed his eyes.

Sammy bellowed "Lens! How many f***ing times have I told you about my laptop!?" Sammy leaped at him and slammed the laptop lid shut, it looked like it caught Lens on the finger. Lens jumped up. With one hand Sammy scooped up the laptop and with the other he gave the bookish-looking Lens a hard shove. Lens stumbled backwards and caught himself on the wall, "this is my laptop," Sammy shouted, rather obviously.

Lens started to slink away, "you're such an assclown," he said and the two stared at each other for a moment with mutual hatred. Lens went through one of the two doors to another room and slammed the door hard.

Sammy turned around and gave a wide smile as if nothing had happened and he hadn't just blown up in an explosion of violence, "so I reckon half an hour to unpack and then we'll go out and climb a tree."

I gestured at the closed door, "And we were in Lens' room were we?" I said tentatively. Perhaps heading out into the wilderness with this guy wasn't such a great idea after all.

Sammy disappeared upstairs with his two Korean hostages and we knocked on the door of the room that Lens had disappeared into.

"What? What do you want?" came the voice from inside.

We opened the door and hesitantly stepped inside. "It's just us," I said, fearing he would slam the door in our faces, thinking it was Sammy coming in for round two of their argument.

"You're staying in my room are you?" he asked in a wearied and resigned fashion.

"Yeah, I'm afraid so," I said.

It turned out that Lens had been staying in the hostel in Ottawa at the beginning of winter (it was now mid-April) and had agreed to stay in Sammy's log cabin for six months. He'd been promised a bargain rate and had been attracted to the romantic idea of overwintering in a remote log cabin. It sounded like it had turned into a hell for both of them. They didn't get on at all and at one point had been snowed in, with just each other for company for days on end. Things had gotten worse in the spring as Sammy had brought in a succession of guests to help him build his camp, many of whom he placed in Lens' room.

"That guy is mad, totally freaking insane. Oh and don't ever touch his stupid laptop," he warned gravely.

"Yeah, I really wasn't planning on touching his laptop," I replied.

The next couple of days passed in a bizarre fashion. For a man who claimed he was building an ecotourism camp, he seemed to possess almost nothing that you would need to run one. His camp seemed to consist of one log cabin (complete with bitter cabinmate), some tree climbing equipment and an old rowing boat with no life jackets. Nevertheless we proceeded to do some of the activities and mooch around while Sammy and the girls set to work doing activities that seemed only marginally related to the building of an ecotourism camp (chopping wood, building fires). I began to wonder if Sammy really just brought people to his log cabin for the company. I didn't observe him say another word to Lens after their original altercation.

As well as climbing a 60 foot tall tree which was something Sammy seemed to take seriously (since he did actually have some safety equipment), we also went for a night walk. There was still frost on the ground and the residual snow of what must have been some serious drifts during the winter. As we walked by the moonlight out into the forest Sammy announced the real purpose of the night walk, "In a few minutes we will reach our own tree, our special tree and we will know it when we see it."

Jack and I muttered to each other, unclear exactly where this was heading. I asked Sammy, "and what will we do, when we find our special tree?"

"We will commune with nature. You will hug the tree and you will feel the connection."

Before long, Sammy had found his tree, he literally hugged it, embracing it for a minute or so as we stood bemused, unsure what to do but watch him hug it. After this long minute, he turned to us, "See? It's about being in nature." There didn't seem any obvious response to that. He turned to me, "now which one is your tree?" he looked around and pointed seemingly at random, "That one is your tree." We approached a huge pine tree and he nodded his head from me towards the tree in encouragement.

"Look Sammy, I'm not sure about this, isn't treehugging just something people say? I'm not really sure it's an actual thing."

"Dude, of course it's a thing," he said slightly affronted. "Look if you've never tried, you don't know, so hug that tree man. Hug it!" I was afraid he was going to start chanting at me so I stepped against the tree and gave it a hug. It wasn't unpleasant, but it was exactly as I imagined, cold and solid, with the bark against my face.

I turned my head back to the group, "What now?" I asked, while still holding on to it.

"Hold it, feel it. Be one with it," he said in a wise manner.

The tree was massive so I wasn't anywhere near getting my arms all the way round it. I wasn't sure if that mattered, but it felt like hugging a giant whale of a person that I couldn't really get enough of a purchase on. Before long I was allowed to release the tree. Sammy turned to me, "See?" he said again. I was fearful of a good shoving, so I decided to let it go and we walked back to the cabin.

18. Vermont: Liveability

The final stop in New England was Vermont. When we met Americans and told them about the food quest, one thing that often came up (totally unprompted) was Vermont. Why? Because of Ben and Jerry's, the famous ice cream makers. A lot of people know that you can visit the factory in Vermont, and since everybody likes ice cream, pretty much everyone wants to go. The only problem is that it's located in the north of Vermont, nowhere near anywhere really, and only about an hour south of the Canadian border. The Ben and Jerry's factory seemed to represent the holy grail of American food for a lot of Americans so we couldn't pass up the opportunity to go.

To our surprise despite the fact that it's about five hours from the nearest major city, there sure were a lot of people there for the tour. It was so popular that the tour was running every 10 minutes, on a weekday, in October. The facility is pretty much what you expect, a huge gift shop at the front, with all sorts of ice cream paraphernalia like pint tub cosies which were little neoprene covers designed to fit snugly around a tub of ice cream, presumably so you can hold it and eat the whole tub on the sofa without your fingers getting cold, which is about how 99% of Ben and Jerry's is consumed. They also had special spoons shaped like little shovels, and even some kind of lid lock to stop light fingers making short work of your ice cream in a communal freezer (could be aimed at students, or those with an untrustworthy partner, who knows?)

As we waited for our tour to start we looked at the various displays, including a list of their top 10 selling flavours (in US supermarkets) – 2nd is Chocolate Chip Cookie Dough and 1st is......Cherry Garcia. We also saw a display of all the flavours currently on sale – apparently there are over 40 at any one time in the US, while the poor Brits have to make do with only 10!

Then we went on the tour, watched a "moo-vie" about Ben and Jerry, about how they bought an ice cream machine because it was cheaper than a bagel machine, how they doubled the amount of flavouring in their mix because one of them had such a poor sense of taste and so on. We also learnt that Ben and Jerry now have nothing to do with the company since it was bought out by Unilever. I can't think why they didn't change the name; surely "Unilever's all new Chunky Monkey Flavor" would be just as popular. After all that we went through into the factory and saw it being made and then finished up with a tasting of one of the newer flavours.

We also took a walk to the "Flavor Graveyard" which is located back behind the factory, and is a rather humorous resting place for dearly departed flavours. Apparently over the years, there have been around 400 flavours in production at one point or another. The more fondly remembered ones get their own headstone with a witty little eulogy e.g. "In memory of *Urban Jumble*: The chaos and cacophony of busy city life lies peaceful now under a maple tree, the flavour lost its strife. 2000-2001."

It was a good tour, and a fun place to be, but it didn't take too long. Fortunately there were plenty of other food-related things to do in the area. Just down the road is a cider mill (the American non-alcoholic version of cider), where they also make cider doughnuts.

Vermont is a small state both size-wise and population-wise. Its capital, Montpelier, is tiny; the state capitol building is smaller than a lot of town halls. We went in for a look around and within a few minutes accidentally wandered out the back and straight into the woods. We then visited the extremely pleasant city of Burlington – the largest in Vermont, with barely 40,000 residents. It is situated in the north of Vermont (near the Ben and Jerry's factory) on the shores of Lake Champlain. The lake is long and thin and you can get a ferry to Canada, which lies not too far away.

Burlington was a great little city, full of healthy-looking active people strolling around and cycling on the lakefront. It's got a decent-sized university and it definitely has that college town feel to it, which means is lots of great places to get coffee and characterful cafes. It also tends to mean that there is a nice centre to actually walk around and Burlington had all these things in abundance. It also had lots of nice touches like swing-seats on the lakefront area, so we had a sit down, swung back and forth and watched the world go by.

We visited the Magic Hat brewery which is just outside Burlington. Magic Hat is a large craft brewery, with an emphasis on real beer. Their tour is a lot more informal than the more corporate Ben and Jerry's. The guide was great, very informal and told us funny tales including the story of the most disgusting beer they ever invented – garlic beer, with a clove in each bottle. Apparently 90% of it was returned by the bars and shops the day after it launched. They also hold a Mardi Gras party on the streets of Burlington every March, in defiance of how freezing it is in Vermont at that time of year. After the tour we were allowed to hang out in their bar area and have as many free samples as we wanted, for as long as we wanted. It was very cool and all the staff were really friendly. It was definitely the best brewery tour we'd been on.

We really liked Vermont. Robyn and I agreed that it was one of our favourite places in the US. The scenery was lovely, with its rolling countryside and charming villages. In contrast to next door neighbour New Hampshire with their right-wing libertarian attitude *(Live Free or Die)* Vermont has a very green and liberal attitude *(Freedom and unity)*. We really got the sense of a community of open-minded and independent people. The food was also uniformly great.

"Robyn, I really think I could live here," I remarked, while we were staring out on the lake in Burlington.

"Yeah I agree, it's so beautiful."

"There's only one drawback," I said after a moment or too.

"What's that?"

"It gets seriously cold here in the winter. The average temperature in winter is about -15C."

"Hmmm" she considered it. "Could we just hibernate in the winter? There seems to be a lot of good ice cream and beer here that we could stock up with."

"Sounds like a plan," I said and we continued swinging on the seat, looking out across the lake.

* * *

Back in Ottawa, we prepared to leave the hostel and go to Toronto, where we would finally get a car to drive back into the US and then to the west coast. Right there and then though we still needed to get to Toronto. We had seen a flyer advertising transport on the hostel notice board. It was handwritten and it said, *"Need to get somewhere? Take a ride with me. I'll drive you anywhere in Canada!"* That seemed unlikely since Canada was massive, but we thought we may as well try the number. A guy picked up the phone and rather surprisingly told us that he just happened to be outside. He came in; he was about thirty, Chinese, with long-dark greasy hair and a plain white t-shirt. He didn't look especially clean, like he'd been working all day in some manual job in that same outfit. We discussed that we needed to get to

Toronto the next day and he quoted us a price that was similar to the cost of bus tickets for the both of us. Since it included door-to-door service we were pretty happy with it and we agreed to meet him at 8am the next day.

We woke up and packed our stuff and left the hostel and went outside to the driveway. Immediately we saw a fairly new looking Toyota Corolla parked on the driveway. On closer inspection it looked like our driver was inside. We went a little bit closer and we could see he was asleep in the driver's seat.

"Should we knock on?" I asked Jack.

"Well it is 8.02am, so technically he is sleeping on the job."

We knocked on the window and he woke up with a start. He jumped out of the car and I noticed that he was in the same clothes as the night before.

"I'm sorry, if we woke you," I said.

"You didn't wake me, I was just resting, waiting for you guys," he said a little abruptly. I wondered if he'd slept the night there.

We packed our bags in to the boot and got in the car. Jack took the backseat and I went to get in the back as well. Our driver looked at me, "Hey man, come ride in the front." It was not an offer to be refused and I came round to the passenger seat. I didn't really mind as I was sure he would be an interesting character. As we set out for the four and a half hour journey to Toronto, he told me about his "business." Basically he rented cars from the airport for 30 days at a time, which was the longest they gave cars for at good rates. He then exploited the fact that the car rental companies allowed unlimited miles and gave lifts to backpackers huge distances around Canada. Given the money we were paying him and the cost of fuel and the fact he had to get back to Ottawa, it didn't seem like a particularly clever idea or a business that was likely to make him a millionaire any time soon.

"What's the furthest you've ever driven someone?" I enquired.

"Oh, I've driven someone all the way to Winnipeg before."

"And how far is that. To Winnipeg?" I liked saying Winnipeg, it was a funny-sounding word and I hoped to have the opportunity to say it a few more times before the conversation was out.

"Oh I'd say 1,400 miles, there or thereabouts."

"To Winnipeg?"

"Yeah."

"But if you drive to Winnipeg and back – that's nearly 3,000 miles. Don't the car companies get annoyed when you bring the car back with all those miles on?"

"Oh no, they plan for it," he gabbled. "I'm like an outlier, but it all averages out so it's like it's all planned for." He continued to stare straight ahead with his eyes on the road. It seemed extremely unlikely to me that any car rental company would plan for a man to use their cars to drive backpackers thousands of miles around the country and in all likelihood to also use that same car as a mobile home.

"But don't the people in the airport recognise you if you're constantly going in there to rent cars?" I was puzzled.

"Oh yeah they recognise me. But it doesn't matter, it's all factored in." I didn't agree with him, but I had to admire the fact that he was playing the system against the faceless multinational corporations. The workers at the desk probably knew what he was up to, but it wasn't against the terms and conditions (it would be a strange and very specific condition if it was). So the workers on the desks weren't going to stop him.

He dropped us off in Toronto and we had a couple of days to explore the city. Toronto is the largest city in Canada and in appearance is not too dissimilar to a lot of American cities, in that it is fairly modern and big and full of large concrete and glass buildings. It's not an unpleasant city, but it didn't strike me as a particularly unique one either.

One thing that was interesting was just how multicultural it was. Over 180 languages and dialects are spoken in Toronto and 30% of Toronto's residents speak something other than English or French as a first language. One consequence of all this diversity was an absolutely mind-boggling choice of restaurants. We ate a different ethnic cuisine for every single meal including Lebanese, Chinese, Kurdish/Turkish and Ethiopian.

It was the first time I had ever tried Ethiopian food and it was an unusual cuisine. It was a very communal experience. We shared a big central plate, which had a big flat spongy bread known as injera spread across it. The bread was covered with several different piles of stewed and curried vegetables and meat in big dollops. We then tore off pieces of the bread to eat with the different fillings. They were tasty but to me the spongy bread tasted like a washcloth – not ideal. In the intervening years I've only had Ethiopian food one more time. The pick of the cuisine was probably the Lebanese since the falafel was amazing. That was one of the first times I'd had Lebanese food and it showed me how good it could be.

    We knew that our time in Canada was coming to a close and our thoughts turned to the long journey across the US. We still needed to find a car and a way to get to California.

19. Illinois: The middle

Chicago is one of America's greatest cities: the third largest in the country and the gateway to the Midwest. Although you could define and categorise the US in any number of ways, I'd say the simplest and easiest is to divide it in three parts. The first part is the East Coast, characterised by the big cities of the North East, New York, Boston and Philadelphia. The East Coast tends to be rich, fast-paced, urban and with a sense of history.

Then there's the middle, often used interchangeably with the term Midwest. I think of the middle as something broader. The Midwest tends to refer specifically to the farming states (Missouri, Iowa, Kansas, Wisconsin, Nebraska etc) which tend to be sparsely populated, full of conservative values, religion, small communities, high school football and with a predominantly white, Christian homogeneity.

I think though that "the middle" is something bigger than the Midwest, I would also lump into it: the Deep South (the most conservative, religious and "backwoodsy" part of the country), the mountainous West (more ranching than farming and even more sparsely populated), the desert South West (still pretty conservative, fans of guns, lots of pensioners and some liberal city enclaves). All of those places in the middle though, along with the Midwest, have something in common, which is a less urban character and a more insular, community-centric outlook.

Finally the third part of the US is the West Coast (of which more later).

Chicago is the entrance to this vague area of the middle. Historically its development was reasonably similar to New York and it started to boom in the early 19th century. This was a little while after the 'Big Apple', but still about the time when the modern US was being born and the West was being opened up. In that sense the inner city looks and feels a little like New York. As we walked around the downtown, we were consistently struck by the size and number of skyscrapers.

Chicago's buildings are probably even more interesting than New York's. While New York has a uniformity to its skyscrapers and buildings, Chicago's are a bit more playful and inventive. Chicago experienced a huge fire in 1871 which razed most buildings to the ground, so they practically had to start again and this started a great building boom, which coincidentally was around the time that skyscrapers were first coming into being. In fact the world's very first skyscraper was built in the city in 1885 (the boringly named Home Insurance building). Chicago even gave rise to two models of architecture, "the Chicago school" and "the Prairie school".

Prominent architects like Frank Lloyd Wright lived in Chicago and left their indelible mark on the city with some fantastic buildings. Wright believed in organic architecture where the building would be in harmony with the environment. There are also lots of other interesting architectural features in the centre of the city including Grant Park and Millennium Park. We walked over the remarkable, snakelike, shimmering, curving footbridge which took us from the centre of the city, over the highway and into the park. In Millennium Park we saw *The Bean* (officially called Cloud Gate), which is a huge shiny sculpture in the shape of a bean (obviously). It cast crazy and distorted reflections of the cityscape behind it while tourists wandered around it trying to capture weird and wonderful photographs.

It was a nice day and we decided to take an architecture cruise, it seemed like a very Chicago thing to do. It was a very pleasant way to see the city skyline and hear a little bit more about the background to the fantastic buildings. Chicago is intersected by the Chicago River and fronts on to the massive Lake Michigan (one of the Great Lakes) so we got great views of the cityscape from the water. It was a wonderful cruise, made even better by the bright sun and blue skies, the city looked fantastic.

Rather like New York City, Chicago has some food traditions of its own, it has hot dogs and it has pizza and….wait a minute, exactly like New York City has. Let's just say that when trying to uncover the food traditions of the US, you do become old friends with pizza, hot dogs and burgers, but then again the variety and tradition almost always surprises.

First on the list for Chicago was the hot dog; the Chicago area has more hot dog restaurants than

McDonald's, Wendy's and Burger King restaurants put together. This is interesting because a lot of American cities seem to contain more McDonalds than every other business put together.

What makes a Chicago Dog unique? Well due to the incredible number of toppings that are often put on a Chicago hot dog, it is said to be "dragged through the garden." We went to "America's Dog" on Navy Pier, which is a pier that juts out into Lake Michigan. America's Dog offered a staggering variety and we tried a few. One that stuck out was the "Mac and Cheese". It was a hot dog covered with Macaroni Cheese and bacon bits as though it was a sauce. It sounds like an odd combination, but what's not to like? The softness of the pasta went pretty well with the softness of the dog and the cheese and bacon is obviously a winning combination.

In the US fast food adverts and adverts for chain restaurants (places like TGI Friday, Red Lobster etc) are on TV constantly. They are always advertising new meals and dishes, often in quite dramatic style. An enormous burger will suddenly fill the screen and then massive rashers of bacon will fall out of the sky and crash land perfectly on the burger while huge flames rear up around the whole mega meal and a very serious voiceover tells us that *The new Chipotle Cheese Chargrilled Bacon Burger HAS ARRIVED!*

I always wonder who is coming up with these new burgers and new pizzas, because all these chains seem to constantly need new products to throw around the TV studio for the next 10,000 adverts they've already booked. No problem you might think - because restaurants are always creating new meals and they are always changing their menus. True. But what if you were serving pretty much just burgers? And what if you needed to come up with a new burger four times a year? And what if your customers *only liked* cheese and bacon?

The amount of "new" burgers from these chain fast food places that are basically just a bacon cheeseburger is unbelievable. Yes, sometimes a curveball gets in there like guacamole or mushrooms but basically it's a new bacon cheeseburger every time. I feel even sorrier for the people trying to come up with a new pizza, since cheese is already a given there. I kid you not, but one "new" pizza being offered by Papa John's was the "six cheese" pizza. That's six kinds of cheese. I can just imagine the guy charged with coming up with a new pizza screwing up endless pieces of paper as the deadline approached and then his boss walks in, "Well, what did you come up with?"

"Errrmmmm you know the four cheese pizza?"
"Yes, what's your angle?"
"I was thinking……six cheeses?"
"You are…..A FREAKIN' GENIUS. I LOVE IT."

The other food we wanted to try in Chicago was Chicago Mix popcorn from the popcorn specialists Garrett's – also on Navy Pier. Chicago Mix popcorn, like the Mac and Cheese hot dog is another rather strange combination. They take a big bag and add a mix of salty cheese popcorn with sweet caramel popcorn, half and half. It really sounds kind of revolting, but hey sometimes these things work. I'm not saying it was quite the revelation of other unusual combinations like salted caramel chocolate, but it was surprisingly more-ish and soon enough the whole bag had disappeared.

Obviously we also had to take the chance to sample one of Chicago's best known foods, the deep dish pizza. Unlike the New York pizza with its 19th century roots and its strong links to the Italian original, Chicago pizza is a more recent invention and can be traced back to the 1940s. The pizza is cooked in a pan, with a much thicker crust and base than other types of pizza. Interestingly because the cooking time needs to be longer (since it's thicker), they tend to invert the toppings i.e. they put on the cheese first, then the tomato sauce and other toppings, otherwise the cheese would burn, since it is in the oven for close to an hour.

No one knows exactly who created the deep dish style, but it is often said it was invented at Pizzeria Uno in downtown Chicago in 1943. So that's where we went; Uno has been a pretty big success story and now has over 150 restaurants across the US, so while it was good, it did look more like a chain place than something with that truly authentic, old-fashioned appearance. Nevertheless, we couldn't complain about the pizza. I was surprised by just how deep it was, but then again, this was a genuine

Chicago style pizza, rather than just a generic deep pan pizza. The crust rose up a good few inches so it was more like a fruit pie and the base was seriously doughy. In addition because of the inversion of the toppings, the top appeared very red in comparison with a normal pizza. Robyn and I spent a good half an hour discussing the relative merits of the different styles of pizza. We agreed that the thick, buttery crust and the chewy base was indeed tasty and that we welcomed pizza in all its many forms. However, when the votes came in, New York pizza won it unanimously.

* * *

10 years earlier, Jack and I didn't know it but we were about to take a trip to Chicago. We were in Toronto and we needed to get to California. No more buses for us, we wanted a car, but we faced the same problem we had in Florida. Not many people wanted to rent cars to under-25 year olds and the fees for one-way rentals were exorbitant. Fortunately we had a plan. We wanted to get a "driveaway" – a service where you drive someone else's car from one place to another. Due to the size of the US, often when people move to the other side of the country they don't actually want to drive their own car all that way themselves (since it can be thousands of miles). Driveaway companies charge the person who needs the car moving and then match the car up with a person who wants to make that journey anyway (e.g.

New York to Los Angeles) – the driver gets the car for free (although typically has to pay the fuel). The only restriction is that the driver has to get the car to the destination in a certain time limit and within a certain mileage limit.

We called the two driveaway places in Toronto to seek a car to the West Coast. Unfortunately (and to our surprise) there were no cars going to California. They did however, have a couple of cars that needed delivering to Vancouver on the West Coast of Canada.

"What do you think Jack? Should we go to Vancouver?"

"Well then we'll still need to get to California," he said reasonably.

"That's true and isn't the whole point of this to drive across the US?"

"Yeah, we don't want to drive across Canada, I don't think it would be the same." We were in agreement: it had to be the US. We phoned around a few more places and eventually looked further afield. We found a place in Chicago that had a car that needed delivering to San Diego in California. We were back on and our dreams of cruising across the American West in a Mustang or Chevy convertible were alive. Even better than that, we were going to follow pretty much the entire original Route 66 which runs 2,200 miles from Chicago to Southern California.

The only issue for us now was to get to Chicago which was 10 hours away from Toronto by road. The driveaway company were keen for us to get going and said they could only hold the car for three days. We had a final night in Toronto and then quickly hopped to Niagara to see the famous waterfall and then took a singularly unpleasant overnight Greyhound from Niagara to Chicago. If there's something more disagreeable than being woken at 2am during a Greyhound coach journey to be told that you need to get off and wait in a bus station for an hour only to get on a second Greyhound for another 6 hour journey, then I don't know what that thing is.

We arrived in Chicago knackered and with only one night there before picking up the car the next morning. We were excited to get going on our cross-country journey the next day. We'd been told that we could have a maximum of 11 days to do the journey – the guy said he was being generous since it could be done in 5. The distance was about 2,200 miles and after a bit of arguing they said we could have up to 2,900 miles. That was still a bit tight for the route we wanted to take, but there was a lot of nothingness in the middle that we knew we wanted to just drive straight through. Also, with the exception of a few detours, we'd be following Route 66, which given our desire to do the ultimate road trip, suited us just fine.

20. Alabama: Division

After the chills of early autumn in New England and a stop in Chicago, Robyn and I decided to head to the Deep South and arrived in Birmingham, Alabama - a city as synonymous as any with the civil rights struggle of the 1950s and 1960s. Back then segregation was the norm throughout the American South. This meant segregated schools, hotels and shops for whites only, separate public bathrooms and divided public transport (i.e. black people had to sit at the back and stand if there were only enough seats for whites). It was a shameful system, not much different to apartheid in South Africa. The public justification by the authorities at the time was that segregation just meant "equal but separate" i.e. that schools for blacks would be the same as the schools for whites. Clearly this was not the case though, since many services and places were out of bounds for black Americans. Effectively they were second class citizens.

In 1963, as Martin Luther King Jr. was leading his campaign across the South for equal rights, he was invited to Birmingham. The leader of the local civil rights movement, a preacher named Fred Shuttleworth, wanted King to help fight segregation in his city. Birmingham was one of the most segregated cities in the US and King was keen to confront discrimination and segregation wherever he found it. King and Shuttleworth began a series of nonviolent protests including a boycott of businesses, demonstrations and sit-ins. However, Birmingham had a particularly nasty chief of police, Bull Connor, whose response was to confront the protestors with every means at his disposal.

In one particularly disgraceful episode in early May 1963 when the protestors had run out of adult volunteers (many of whom had been locked up – including King himself), they recruited schoolchildren to protest instead. The police arrested them in droves and the following day when the children came to protest again the police realised the jails were full. Bull Connor ordered the police and fire department to turn the water cannon on the protestors (set at such a fierce pressure that the water would separate bricks from mortar). Finally they set the police dogs on them. One journalist, who had been in war zones, said he was left sickened by what they were doing to children. The pictures shocked the country and President John F. Kennedy called the episode "shameful". The action backfired hugely for Connor and the city of Birmingham. The next day senators from states that did not have segregation started pressing for immediate national civil rights legislation.

Unfortunately, the struggle for civil rights was not won and Birmingham was the scene of several violent episodes over the next few years, it even gained the nickname "Bombingham". One Sunday morning in September 1963 the Ku Klux Klan, fighting the end of desegregation, planted dynamite under the steps of the 16th Street Baptist Church. The victims of the explosion were four girls aged 11-14 attending Sunday school. Once more the events shocked the nation. However, it took until 1977 before anyone was convicted of the bombing and not until 2002 when the last of the bombers was sent to jail.

    Birmingham is an altogether more peaceful place now and it is hard to see any visible lasting effects of segregation and the struggles for civil rights (at least as a visitor). Birmingham elected its first black mayor in 1979 and to commemorate the fight for civil rights opened the Civil Rights Institute in 1992. This is where we found ourselves on a hot sunny day. The museum was fascinating, with interesting recreations of lunch counters, train carriages and waiting rooms which were commonly segregated in the South. It was amazing to think that this was all in the lifetimes of a lot of Americans, being only 50 years ago.

    I was particularly impressed by the story of the Freedom Riders, a group of both black and white Americans who set off on buses in 1961 to ride through the Southern states in order to challenge the segregation of buses. The passengers were attacked by mobs in Anniston and Birmingham, Alabama. One of the mobs (mostly of Ku Klux Klan members) was organised by non-other than Bull Connor. Even though a lot of the passengers were hospitalised after the attacks, most were refused treatment at local hospitals. The Freedom Ride was called off after the passengers were attacked again (this time with baseball bats and iron pipes) in Montgomery, Alabama. By this point though, they had again drawn national attention to the situation and won more supporters to their cause.

The Civil Rights Institute is situated across from the (rebuilt) 16th Street Baptist church, scene of the bombing, and is also opposite the public square where the police dogs where turned on the schoolchildren during the protests. Both the church and the square feature memorials to what happened and despite being a rather melancholic visit, they really bring home how important and difficult the struggle for civil rights was.

After this we had a much more relaxing visit to the Botanical Gardens, which were a pleasant surprise. Alabama is so far south that it is in the humid subtropical zone. This is why cotton was traditionally grown across the Deep South and it was the cash crop of choice for a lot of slave-owners. Cotton is still grown today in the South, although it's not as common. The upside of the subtropical climate is that the Botanical Gardens were absolutely fantastic. The gardens (which were free) contained over 12,000 different types of plants in 25 distinct garden areas. The rose garden in particular was an absolute joy. I'm not the biggest fan of flowers, but there were so many different types, in such vivid colours, that it was a real pleasure walking around in the sultry Southern heat, exploring all the different areas of the gardens.

Our thoughts eventually turned to food. Alabama is known for its barbecue and fast food, and unfortunately all this unhealthy food is having an effect on its citizens' waistlines. Alabama has the unwanted accolade of being the third fattest state in the Union. Over 30% of adults are classified as obese and if you include the overweight that jumps to over 65%. Sadly this is not a problem particular to Alabama. America has been gaining weight everywhere. In 1990 every state had an obesity rate lower than 15%. By 2010 every single one of the 50 states had an obesity rate *higher than* 20%, with Mississippi topping the fatties list, with an incredible 35% of its adults classified as obese.

You could say the Deep South in particular is weighing the rest of the US down as the obesity problem is especially bad across the region. In fact, 8 of the 10 fattest states are in the South East of the country. Still though, as they say: *When in Rome, do as the Romans do.* So off we went looking for fast food. At the time I had heard of one of those new fast food products that are constantly being invented, but instead of being just another new Bacon Cheeseburger, this time it sounded genuinely revolutionary. I am talking of the KFC Doubledown. Oh yes! It sounded like a new fast food sensation.

The Doubledown is touted as a sandwich. But what's missing? That's right, the bun. Instead of a bun, it has two fried chicken pieces which act as the "bread". The filling is bacon, melted cheese and the Colonel's "special sauce". That's it, just batter, fried meat, cheese and sauce. It was a revelation! Despite the stomach cramps later that evening, I have to say it was one tasty sandw...whatever it was, it was tasty. Only in America! Even though I knew eating it was wrong, and that it was like just eating the topping off a pizza or the icing off a cake, it was still damn tasty, and that I think is the essential problem of fast food. A lot of the time it is delicious and if your will power is low (or it's the only thing you can afford) it can be genuinely hard to resist.

The other thing I was keen to try which is more a snack food than fast food was the "Twinkie", a product I'd heard a lot about on American TV programmes when I was growing up. I'd always been curious about the oddly-named snack. I remember being particularly interested since characters would often talk about Twinkies without ever actually eating them e.g. *"there's no food left in this whole house except four freaking Twinkies!!"* I noticed that the Twinkie was often talked about in a disparaging manner or in situations bordering on despair (like the above), so beyond the name I had no real concept of what one was, except that it was probably pretty bad.

You may also be familiar with the product if you've seen the Woody Harrelson film "Zombieland", since Harrelson's character is on a post-apocalyptic quest for Twinkies. He was one of the few people I'd seen who genuinely seemed to want a Twinkie. To be honest, I'm not really sure why. The Twinkie wasn't exactly bad, but it was one of the most fake-tasting foods I've ever had. It's basically a really dry sponge cake with a synthetic-tasting cream inside. It genuinely tasted like *a bathroom sponge* instead of sponge cake. Perhaps it would be good on the bottom of a trifle, but as a straight-up snack, it was strangely displeasing. Suffice to say, should I survive a zombie-led Armageddon, it won't be the snack I'll be breaking into a 7-11 for.

* * *

10 years previously Jack and I were on our way to pick up a car to take us across America. It was an exciting prospect, although our surroundings didn't really match up to the expectation. We'd taken a local train out of Chicago and arrived in an outer-lying suburb: a suburb that was so outer-lying that it was in a different state (Indiana to be precise). We were waiting outside the train station, looking at more abandoned buildings and empty car parks, surrounded by chain link fences, many of which were locked.

Our thoughts turned to what car we were likely to be driving. Jack and I had had our initial conversation with the company and then exchanged a couple of emails with them. In one of the emails (when we were hammering out our mileage and time limit) we had asked what type of car we would be driving.

"It was weird how they didn't reply when we asked what type of car we'd be getting," Jack said.

"Yeah that was weird, I wonder why?"

"Maybe it was just an oversight, like you know the guy was just getting straight to the point about the other details."

"Or maybe he was hiding something," I pointed out.

"I don't know, I mean if you're someone using a driveaway service, you must be pretty wealthy, so you'd think the car must be pretty good," he reasoned.

"Look around Jack, it doesn't look like we are in Beverley Hills exactly, does it?"

"Hmmm good point."

After what seemed like an eternity, the driveaway guy came to pick us up and took us to the company headquarters (essentially a car park). We arrived and went inside a hut, where a man was behind the desk.

"So which one is ours?" I asked the man excitedly.

"C'mon I'll show you." We walked outside and there it was, an old beaten-up white Honda Accord. Boxy and low to the ground, it looked like it was about to be junked.

"Someone is paying for this to be driven across the country?" I asked incredulously.

"Yeah, some people just love these old cars," he said, without acknowledging my concern.

"How old is it?"

"1989 I think, only done about 180,000 miles," he said.

Now to me, I don't think the word "only" goes with the phrase "180,000 miles". Not unless someone was issuing me with a warning of an incoming asteroid, then it might be appropriate, but not for a car.

"Do you think it will even get there?" Jack asked.

"Of course it will get there! So long as you Brits can drive on the right," he said half-seriously, as if that was a real impediment to our ability to drive a car.

So there it was, we had 11 days, a little under 3,000 miles and a beaten up 16 year-old car that probably looked old-fashioned the day it rolled off the production line. On the upside we had some wheels and we had a destination; we were ready to hit the road.

21. Tennessee: The beat

Tennessee's state motto "Agriculture and Commerce" leaves a little to be desired. Agriculture and Commerce? That's about the least descriptive thing you could say about a state, it distinguishes it from no other states, or even any semi-modern society. In fact it doesn't even signify a semi-modern society; even an agricultural land of peasants and serfs that had developed a rudimentary bartering system could be said to have "Agriculture and Commerce". So it doesn't really tell you a lot. Maybe Tennessee just wants to keep your expectations low.

But it needn't, because Tennessee has a lot going for it, lots of great food, amazing music, and some decent scenery.

Tennessee actually has three very distinct regions, which is pretty good going for one state. On the east side the Appalachian Mountains run down the state, and Tennessee has preserved a large part of them as the Great Smoky Mountains National Park (with the other half of that park in North Carolina). The middle section of Tennessee is flatter, plains-esque terrain and is dominated by the city of Nashville, and then on the western side there is the Mississippi River, and the lowlands of the Mississippi Delta, with the main centre being Memphis.

The one food that dominates across the South is "barbecue"; this comes in lots of varieties, but is generally centred around slow-cooked/smoked meats. Within the South the barbecue varies substantially, for example in Texas it means beef, in the Carolinas it means pork. The sauces and rubs also vary by region. In North Carolina the speciality we had was pulled pork in a vinegary sauce; elsewhere the sauces tend to be sweeter, or stickier or smokier. In Tennessee the first place we stopped was in the east of the state, near the border of North Carolina, in the foothills of the Smoky Mountains. We stopped in at an old shack-style restaurant, the Original Ridgewood Barbecue, which has a huge separate smoker off to the side of the restaurant where they smoke all their meats (typically for hours at a time).

This restaurant is famed for its barbecue beans, which have little shreds of pulled pork mixed in with the beans. They were absolutely delicious, and I was quite amused to see on the menu that they were just called barbecue beans with no mention of the meat. This new-fangled vegetarianism mustn't have reached the foothills of Eastern Tennessee yet. The beans were a perfect complement to the pulled pork sandwiches. There was a lot of pulled pork on the menu, which was similar to the barbecue restaurant we'd been to in North Carolina: it was interesting to see the similarity between the two neighbouring states. The whole restaurant had a very local feel to it, being a long way from the highway, practically in the middle of the woods. There were an array of pickup trucks parked out the front and the waitresses looked like they had been there for the past forty years. It was a very authentic restaurant and one that had probably not changed since it opened.

Tennessee is just as well known for music as it is for food and its three distinct regions, each with their distinct food culture, have even more distinctive and well-renowned music cultures. Eastern Tennessee and the Smokies have bluegrass. Unfortunately a lot of people think of banjos when they think of bluegrass, and when they think of banjos they think of THAT SONG from *Deliverance*, which is fine, as it's a great song and a great scene, but then they think of everything else that happens in *Deliverance* (spoiler: basically hillbillies killing a bunch of city slickers). Certainly not a great advert for the Deep South.

When we were in the Smokies area of Tennessee we went to a bluegrass evening at the Rocky Branch Bluegrass club. It's just an evening held by the local people in the community hall, where they jam and play old time bluegrass music. You don't pay anything more than a nominal amount which helps cover the cost of the hall. It's basically just a get together for the local community on a Friday night. The musicians wander from room to room, joining in with different groups and just start jamming. We were free to wander between the rooms and see what was going on with each different group. The standard was exceptional, and every room had a different style going on, from a kind of concert led by a charismatic, evangelical Vietnam vet, telling jokes in between songs, to a group of young guys playing in a circle, all instrumental. It was great to see that community spirit, keeping up traditions that had been going on for centuries, ever since Scots, Irish and English settlers brought their fiddlin' to the Appalachians.

Next up we went to Memphis, which is a different proposition altogether. Memphis is poor, really poor, there's even a section in the Lonely Planet entitled "Abandoned Memphis", which lists the best abandoned buildings to go and have a look at. Take that Detroit! Detroit is pretty much the poster-child for American cities in decline, but you could make a case that a dozen other cities – including Memphis – are just as bad. A lot of the abandoned buildings in Memphis are actually pretty central, and they are too expensive to tear down. They wouldn't be profitable to refurbish so they just stand there derelict. I got the sense that Memphis was one of those cities that probably was just about growing during the good times, but post-crash it had suffered. Regardless, you can't take away Memphis's fine food and music culture. For me, outside of the obvious food capital cities like New York, Memphis is right up there.

Robyn and I have eaten in some pretty dodgy-looking places over the years and we ate in two barbecue places in Memphis which would both stand a chance for winning the title of dodgiest of all. Certainly that would be the case when looking at them from the outside, although both were much more welcoming on the inside. They were both outside the city centre and the neighbourhoods did look a little down on their luck. One of them actually looked closed, but that was just shabby-chic, and besides it really didn't matter, because Memphis barbecue was the best barbecue we had ever eaten, hands down.

The two places that we ate at, Cozy Corner and A+R barbecue, were absolutely leagues ahead of anything I've had anywhere else. We went to Cozy Corner first, an institution in Memphis, founded in 1977, a couple of miles out of the centre. The founder, Raymond Robinson, said, "My desire is to serve a few people the best they ever had." That's something I really admire, I think the corporate philosophy these days is to make a product or service that captures the biggest possible market share and satisfies the most number of people as possible. My feeling has always been in line with Raymond; it is better to really connect or mean something to a few people, than have a horde of people think – *yeah that's ok*. Talk about being damned with faint praise.

This idea about seeking out the unique and the niche is definitely a part of this food quest. If we were visiting a lot of chains and eating homogenised dishes, what would be the point of that? Sometimes you have to go the extra distance and put the extra effort in, but it's worth it when you find something unique. The point is that you have to go to Memphis to eat Memphis barbecue, it can't just be packaged up or reproduced. Raymond can be happy, because without a doubt the barbecue was absolutely the best we'd ever had.

We had read about these two barbecue places and they had sounded so good that Robyn and I couldn't just order one thing each; it was obvious that we had to order as many things as possible and share them out. We had pork sandwiches where the meat was so tender and so flavourful, that it almost melted in the mouth. We ordered plates of ribs that were delicious beyond words. We indulged in the Memphis tradition of barbecue spaghetti, similar to the barbecue beans from before. They were just the icing on the whole barbecue experience. Delicious. We were so enamoured with the barbecue that we also made the trip out to A+R barbecue, which some people believe is the best in Memphis. This time it was lunch time so we settled for pulled pork sandwiches, which once again were out of this world good.

As well as the food, Memphis is a fantastic town for music. Although most of the tourists are there because of Elvis, the real soul of Memphis is the blues. Elvis helped popularise that style, fusing it with pop and rock and roll (and general crooning), and a trip to Graceland is a must, even if it is so expensive that you feel like you are taking part in an organised pickpocketing event, where you are the main attraction. Nevertheless we enjoyed it.

I was dragged around a lot of country homes and manors during my youth, houses from hundreds of years ago, perfectly recreated or preserved. However, I'd never seen a house preserved in homage to the excess of 70's luxury, shag pile carpets on the ceiling, lurid yellows and vinyl everywhere. In one room there were three TVs installed next to each other since Elvis liked to watch all the main news programmes at once. He would have loved NFL red zone (where you can watch about 7 American Football games going on at once).

The Graceland site also contains several museums, some frivolous (Elvis's cars, Elvis's two planes and Elvis's costumes) but it also has a more serious exhibit on Elvis's rise to fame and the rise of rock 'n' roll in the 1950s. I found it really gave me an appreciation of the cultural impact of Elvis, who I think in some ways was the most important cultural American icon of the 20th century. I could certainly see the rise of the "teenager" linked to the rise of rock 'n' roll and that was personified most by Elvis. For the first time kids didn't just want to grow into being their parents, they wanted to be distinctly different.

It was interesting how conservative Elvis actually was in his interviews. Despite the scandalous hip-shaking of his performances, when he spoke he really set himself *against* any kind of rebellion. In 1956 as all sorts of commentators were complaining about his "outrageous" antics he said, "I don't feel like I'm doing anything wrong. ... I don't see how any type of music would have any bad influence on people when it's only music. ... I mean, how would rock 'n' roll music make anyone rebel against their parents?" Well indeed, but that's a pretty different message to say punk music just twenty years later. Nevertheless, in the 1950s the trend for teenagers to follow their own heroes and establish their own identity was set.

From one musically influential city to another; we stopped finally in Nashville, which is a fun place, and is again very distinct. Country music is the order of the day, which is a different beast entirely from bluegrass or the blues. Nashville is a bit of a strange city as the centre feels like it's in festival mode all the time. There are dozens of bars in the centre; they completely dominate (along with shops selling cowboy boots). Every single bar has live music, some of which even have two bands playing at different ends of the bar (or on different levels). This is true from the time they open at about 11am, all the way through to closing. It's incredible, I don't know how there are so many bands and musicians in Nashville to fill them all.

For the most part these bands are pretty good, although they are generally fronted by a Billy Ray Cyrus lookalike (mullet, lots of denim, cowboy boots). They seemed quite talented and I guess they were all trying to get discovered since Nashville is the centre of the Country Music industry (which is phenomenally successful in the US). It did make me wonder what would happen if you lived in Nashville and you just wanted to go for a quiet drink though. I don't think it would be possible, every time you tried to talk you'd be interrupted by a bemulleted singer smashing out a cover of Bryan Adams' "Summer of '69".

While Nashville doesn't quite have the food traditions of Memphis, it has nevertheless carved out a niche for itself as being *the place* in the country for spicy fried chicken. The two leaders are generally acknowledged to be Princes' Hot Chicken Shack and 400 degrees Hot Fried Chicken. We chose 400 degrees because it was walkable from the centre. They do their fried chicken in various degrees of spiciness: 0, 100, 200 and 400, which was the spiciest of all. We chose some fried chicken pieces in the 100 and 200 varieties. But we learnt that when they said hot fried chicken, they really meant it. Even the 200 degree chicken was fry your lips off hot.

Fortunately we'd ordered some 100 degree chicken and sides, but I valiantly kept going back to the 200 degree chicken. After a few bites I would have to stop and drink a load of coke as my mouth was burning so much. It was tasty but it was incredibly spicy, which was strange, because truly spicy food is not that common in the US. A lot of restaurants will put warnings all over their spicy dishes on their menus and yet when they are served they tend to be only very vaguely spiced. In this case though, they were so spicy as to be almost nuclear. I couldn't even imagine what the 400 degree chicken would be like. Regardless, it was still good - there is something about fried chicken that makes you want to devour it. What's the phrase - *finger-lickin' good*? It was a fitting end, Tennessee is a great state with its three distinct music and food cultures and is a wonderful example of the diversity you can find under the surface in the US.

* * *

Jack and I were heading deep into the middle of the country now and as usual he was driving. We had a lot of miles to cover and by our calculation we wanted to drive around 400-500 miles a day. We'd set off and had escaped the outer sprawl of Chicago. We had nearly 3,000 miles of road ahead of us. An hour or so into the journey and already bored with each other's conversation, our thoughts turned to the car.

"I can't believe it doesn't even have a CD player" I said, half-despairing at the thought of the journey in front of us.

"I'm not even sure they'd invented CD players in cars in 1989," Jack said, "she does have a top of the line cassette player though," he said, tapping the crappy looking tape/radio.

"Lucky us! We don't actually have any cassettes though."

"Well why don't you have a rootle around and see if there's some in the glove box."

I began rummaging around and came across two cassettes. One was by 80's band INXS and one was a self-made mixtape.

"Jackpot! Two cassettes. This one's a mixtape," I said.

"Ok, what are we working with?"

I began reading the handwritten track list, "We've got Pet Shop Boys, Go West, Lou Bega. Frankie Goes to Hollywood. All the big boys really. Basically every awful 80's group you can imagine, plus some 90's one hit wonders."

"Sounds ghastly. Like what?"

"Jimmy Ray's *Are You Jimmy Ray?*" That song, unbeknownst to us then, would actually grow to become one of our favourites.

"I don't know that one. What is it?"

"Well if I remember rightly I think he was some kind of Fonz look-a-like, you know big quiff, leather jacket etc. Pretty sure he was a one-hit wonder, he was called Jimmy Ray, and his song was about whether other people were also called Jimmy Ray."

Jack looked sceptical, "Go on sing it."

I cleared my throat, *"Are you Johnny Ray? / Are you Jimmy Ray? / Are you Sting Ray? / Who wants to know? / Who wants to know?"*

He paused and looked at me, "Honestly? Is that how it goes? ...Sounds good, stick it on."

An hour later, after doing the full circuit of the tape (both sides) fast forwarding only when strictly necessary (Queen, Erasure) we had reached Jimmy Ray again. We listened to it for the second time and by the end even Jack was joining in the chorus, singing along with Jimmy's enquiries about who else was also Jimmy Ray and who was a Sting Ray. With that finished I pressed stop.

Jack spoke, "How many tapes have we got again?"

"Two."

"Hmmm...There's going to have to be some good chat then. What chat have you got?" he asked.

"I've seen you every day for the last two months and most of the things I've been doing, you've been there as well."

"Right," he paused, "Shall we have Jimmy Ray on again?"

We went round the tape again and when it finished Jack encouraged me to have another look around the side pockets of the doors and the glove box. This time I found a letter.

"Ok now we're talking – a letter!"

"What does it say?"

"It's from the owner," I read the letter and it wished us well on our journey across the country. It asked us to take care of the car, noting that while it was old, it was well-loved. The owner hoped that we would have an enjoyable and safe journey across the country and it finished up, with the words, "All the best, Laura Glinski."

"I know a Sklansky," Jack said in a self-satisfied manner.

"This is a Glinski."

"Glinski, Sklansky," he paused, "Now you mention it, where is my Sklansky?" Taking one hand off the wheel, out of nowhere he slowly drew up a battered bright yellow book until it was in my eye line and then once he knew I'd seen it, he smiled at me. It was a book that always seemed to be about his person, even in the most unlikely of scenarios. He would take great pleasure in producing it at curious moments or when it was least expected, such as in a random gas station. Occasionally I would even find it hiding under the covers in my bed or ensconced in my suitcase. I wasn't surprised to see that he somehow had it on him even now, while he was driving. It was *David Sklansky's Theory of Poker*, a highly mathematical book which advised how to win at poker.

"Enough!" I said. "What chat have you got then?"

"I'm driving, you're responsible for chat, or you can read me some Sklansky, or if you prefer, some more Glinski."

California seemed like a long way away. I put the tape back on.

22. Louisiana: Influences

New Orleans is probably the most unique place in the Deep South. This grand old city has a fascinating history and while it is definitely Southern in nature, it's quite a different proposition from the backwoodsy, rural nature of a lot of the Deep South. The city was originally established in the early 18th century by the French, back when they still had an interest in the modern-day US. However, the French then sold their claim to a huge swathe of the US to the newly independent American government in 1803 in the "Louisiana purchase".

While the city was originally influenced by these early French colonists, a second very significant influence was the Cajuns, who are still present today across a lot of Southern Louisiana. The Cajuns are descended from the French-speaking "Acadians", who were kicked out of Nova Scotia in Canada by the British. Around 1760 the British asked the French Acadians to swear allegiance to the British crown (and convert from Catholicism to Protestantism), many refused and so began the "Great Expulsion". Searching for a place to live they eventually found their way from Canada to Louisiana, which already had a fair amount of French-speakers living there. Many Cajuns learnt the ways of the land, and lived in and around the swamps of Southern Louisiana. The word "Acadian" got mangled into the word "Cajun" and voilà, a new culture was born, which mingled with the Creoles (the descendants of slaves who had been brought to Louisiana) and other settlers in the area. Interesting stuff, but why the history lesson? Well, because Louisiana, and New Orleans' food culture is heavily influenced, and often interchangeable, with Cajun and Creole cuisine.

The most well-known area of New Orleans is its "French Quarter". This central district is the oldest quarter, with lots of streets having French names, "Bourbon", "Chartres", "Dauphine" etc. However, most of the distinctive colonial buildings that line the streets were built in the late 18th century during the period where New Orleans was ruled by the Spanish. Because of New Orleans' geographical position on the Gulf of Mexico, pointing out towards the Caribbean, a totally separate set of events was happening in that region to what was happening in the North East around New York, Boston and Philadelphia where the British were ruling. Because of the poor land links and vast distance, it was almost as if New Orleans was a different country altogether.

In a treaty in 1762 the French ceded New Orleans and Louisiana to the Spanish, intriguingly a year later the French agreed to let Britain have Canada in return for the Caribbean island of Guadeloupe. The French believed Guadeloupe was more valuable since Canada was just "some acres of snow." When the British took full control of Canada that was the point at which the French Acadians were expelled and came to Louisiana. Unbeknownst to the French Acadians though, at around the same time the

French had given away Louisiana to the Spanish, so when they arrived in New Orleans they found they were once again living under foreign rule.

The Acadians, who at this point became the Cajuns, settled all across Southern Louisiana. In many ways it was easier for them to preserve their own culture in smaller communities outside the city of New Orleans, which already had a ruling class, somewhat hostile to the newcomers. For that reason a lot of them settled in the swamplands that make up the coastline of Louisiana. The swamp here is called the bayou (which is a word that originated in Louisiana) and is derived from the original Native American word. The Mississippi River (the biggest in the US) flows all the way from the Great Lakes in the North and it empties into the Gulf of Mexico in Louisiana. There are lots of streams and tributaries which flow into the Mississippi River which make this area of Louisiana very swampy and marshy. The water moves very slowly in these swamplands, so much so that it's almost stagnant. Combined with the humidity it actually makes the bayou a good habitat for a lot of wildlife including catfish, crawfish (like shrimp) and alligators.

Robyn and I did a swamp tour from New Orleans. Within about forty minutes of the city we were in a different world entirely. The bayou was hot and humid, with low hanging cypress trees and other vegetation half growing in the water and half in the marshy shoreline. Most people were on the tour to see alligators, but there was plenty of other wildlife there as well. We saw lots of birds and some sizeable snakes (and an alligator). We also saw some homes within the bayou. The houses were either built up the banks of the shore or incorporated stilts so that they jutted out over the water.

The guide explained that most of them were owned by Cajuns who lived there permanently. Many of them still hunt, trap and fish right off the bayou (famously documented in the TV series *Swamp People*). Apparently other people, who live in the city, own second homes out in the bayou too. They go there to relax at the weekend, go hunting and even swim in the bayou. To me that seemed a remarkably unpleasant prospect, what with all the alligators dwelling there as well. Not the type of thing I'd want to go swimming with.

New Orleans has so many food traditions that it is difficult to cover them all. The most obvious influences are the French, Creole and Cajun traditions, and the key "gift" from the bayou is crawfish. Crawfish are quite like shrimp, they are crustaceans, except they live in the swamps and bayous rather than the sea. As you can imagine that makes them abundant and therefore very popular across Louisiana, where they are often called "mud bugs". They are typically boiled up and cooked in spices. They are served up in baskets in their bright red shells and are often eaten with the accompaniment of beers.

To eat crawfish, as the saying goes – "you pinch 'em and suck 'em." You crack them open and suck both halves out of the shell. This essentially means you are eating the meat, the interior and the brain. Doesn't sound great, but if you put that out of your mind, it's good eating! Crawfish are also often one of the main ingredients in that other Louisiana Creole speciality – gumbo (a soup/stew). Gumbo will often make use of Tabasco sauce, which also originates in Louisiana and is still made there today. It's like one virtuous circle!

One of the more obviously French delicacies in New Orleans is the beignet. One of the great pleasures of New Orleans is indulging in beignets in the cafes (there is a big rivalry between Cafe Du Monde and Cafe Beignet). Beignets are essentially donuts, but they're French donuts. They are served hot (i.e. freshly cooked) and they look more like small paninis rather than donuts. They add a mountain of powdered/icing sugar over the top and you scoff away.

The beignets are incredibly popular with tourists and pretty much everyone lines up outside Cafe Du Monde to get in on the act. But why are they so popular? Err, because they're like donuts. I actually thought they were better than donuts, I liked the fresh/hot aspect; it was like when you get freshly baked bread and it's still warm. We had about three lots of them.

The beignets were ideal for enjoying with a coffee, although annoyingly they tended to be served in threes. This was a very strange number. Three beignets was clearly too many for one person, yet it did not divide easily between two, so unless you happen to be dining in a group of three, it was a tricky number to work with. Robyn wasn't overly keen on my solution, "Two for me, one for you." But I thought it worked. For my money Cafe Du Monde, on the edge of Jackson Square had the better ambience, and Cafe Beignet had the better beignets.

Jackson Square commands an excellent position close to the middle of the French Quarter, a two minute walk from the banks of the Mississippi River, where you can still see paddleboat steamers out on the water. Robyn and I took a walk up there and watched the boats drift by. Unfortunately we were accosted pretty quickly by some local scammers. The two young hoodlums, early twenties, scruffy-looking, one man and one woman approached us. Having travelled a lot (and being British) I'm wary of anyone that strikes up a conversation with me in the street.

"Hey, hey guys, how's it going?" the girl asked.

"Yeah no thanks, we're fine."

Undaunted she continued, "Hey I bet I can tell you what city and what state you got yo' shoes."

"Yeah I'm fine thanks," I replied. Robyn chose to stay silent, allowing me to deal with our new friends.

"I bet you $5 that I can tell you, any city, any state, where you got dem sneakers."

"Well you can't, because I bought them in England." I thought it was highly unlikely that she could tell me which provincial English town I had bought my shoes in. She was somewhat flummoxed by my response and it had at least shut her up.

"Yo dude, let her guess," the man chipped in.

"Yeah, I really am going to have turn this opportunity down." I knew that somehow, even though she couldn't possibly know that she would nevertheless win. I didn't fancy paying $5 to find out how the trick worked. It must take a pretty stupid or bored person to imagine they were going to win a street challenge from two ruffians in a game that they had invented. Unfortunately they wouldn't relent, so we had to walk away and decided to head back into the French Quarter.

The French Quarter is generally a pleasure to walk around. There are not many cars and it's pretty friendly for pedestrians. It's compact and the architecture is uniformly stylish and pretty. New Orleans suffered a great fire in 1788 and the buildings were rebuilt in the Spanish style with stucco render being mandated in the new buildings to mitigate the fire risk. They are all painted in colourful pastel shades with plenty of ornate iron balconies and wooden shutters everywhere. The French Quarter is very strictly controlled and preserved these days with the seeming exception of Bourbon Street. Bourbon Street is the "party" street, full of drunken tourists, bars with rubbish live music, shops selling tat and trinkets and (unusually for the US) lots of strip bars.

Wander away from Bourbon Street though and the situation improves dramatically. I'm not sure there is a more European-looking city in the US, and it is generally a pleasure to walk around. Contrary to popular assumption the very centre of New Orleans (i.e. the French Quarter) was pretty much unaffected by Hurricane Katrina. That is not to diminish the effects of Katrina, which devastated the majority of the city. The average elevation of New Orleans is six feet *below* sea-level and it is surrounded by water.

On 29 August 2005 Katrina struck - the hurricane was 400 miles across and had a wind speed of around 120 miles per hour. Katrina left around 80% of the city under water; it was an economic and human tragedy. Although there were plenty of warnings about the incoming megastorm, about a quarter of the city's half million residents had no access to a car and chose to stay. The city actually issued its first ever mandatory evacuation order the day before, but over 100,000 were still there when it hit. Some of them took shelter at the Superdome (an indoor stadium) and some stayed in their homes. When the city flooded, many people, in districts like the Ninth ward, had to escape on to their roofs and await rescue. Robyn and I did a Katrina tour, which we feared would be a bit like disaster tourism, but wasn't at all. It was informative and sensitively done. This was a good few years after Katrina but the effects were still very noticeable outside the centre of the city.

New Orleans lost about half its population in the months after Katrina as displaced people found that their homes had been so badly damaged that they could not return. Even five years later in 2010, the population was still a quarter less than it had been pre-Katrina. As we toured around we saw where the levees broke and whole streets that were still abandoned. We visited the lower Ninth and you could see where whole houses had been removed and the plots remained empty. Other derelict houses still bore the markings painted on the outside by the fire department and federal emergency responders in the aftermath of Katrina. They indicated that the houses did not have people inside and that the gas supply had been shut off and made safe - it was eerie.

Huge mistakes were made by the George W. Bush government in dealing with Katrina. The response was slow and ineffective. Media reports of looting, which was a problem, were nevertheless exaggerated. This created a poisonous atmosphere, when what was needed was immediate help. Two days after the storm hit, with thousands of people stranded or waiting for help in the Superdome, the Louisiana Governor announced the military was heading into New Orleans to tackle the looters. She put it rather forcefully, "they have M-16s and are locked and loaded. These troops know how to shoot and kill and I expect they will."

The tour also showed us how the city was being rebuilt and everywhere we could still see people living life fully or rebuilding their homes. We were both impressed by how vibrant the city was and the pride the residents seemed to have. Immediately after

Katrina, some politicians and commentators were talking about whether New Orleans was still a viable city and whether it should just be abandoned (given its vulnerability to storms and the fact it is below sea level). It was pleasing to see just how proud the people were and how they weren't going to be beaten or allow their city to die. It felt resurgent.

One of the joyous things in New Orleans is the residents' love of music. I'm not talking about the Bon Jovi cover bands on Bourbon Street, but elsewhere in the bars outside the very centre and even amongst the buskers. At one point we were walking down the street and a full brass band was coming the other way. It was clear this wasn't a proper band, just a collection of friends. They were young black guys in their Timberland boots and white Tees: in any other city in the US they would be into rap music. Here they were playing some fantastic gospel blues, with trombones, trumpets, saxophones, big bass drums and even a tuba. Crowds of people stopped as they passed by and they were a joy to watch.

We also went to Preservation Hall, which is the home of the traditional New Orleans jazz style of music. Old guys, who looked like they probably knew New Orleans native Louis Armstrong, play jazz and blues to appreciative audiences. The old hall is one of the most unique venues in the US; it started hosting jazz in the 50's and there are performances every night of the year. They were great and seeing those guys belt out the song most associated with New

Orleans, "When The Saints Go Marching In" was absolutely fantastic.

To finish we had a couple more dishes we wanted to try (such is the diversity of New Orleans). One was the muffuletta which is essentially a manhole-cover sized bap. I'm not sure Americans use the word bap, but that's what it is (a round circular bread bun). It's huge, and is a Sicilian-New Orleans creation. We went to the home of the original muffuletta – the Central Grocery in the French Quarter. It's a pretty cool Italian deli and reminded me of the Italian market we had visited in Philadelphia's South Street.

The muffuletta is made on a focaccia loaf; it's cut four ways and there are no options to alter what comes in it. It comes as it comes, which is to say: with an olive tapenade which gives it a vinegary tang, and a very generous helping of Italian meats and cheeses. We took ours to the levee behind Jackson Square and ate it with some Barq's Root Beers (another New Orleans staple). It was absolutely huge though and I don't know what you would do if you didn't have someone to share it with.

Finally we wanted to try a Po' boy. The Po' boy is a type of sub. The only real ingredient that differentiates a Po' boy from other subs is that the bread must be cut from a proper French baguette. But really it's just a submarine sandwich. Since there's so much seafood in New Orleans (given its access to the coast and the Gulf of Mexico) Po' boys often have seafood in them. Given there are so many types (we went to Johnny's Po' boys in the centre of New Orleans and they offered at least 40 varieties) it's hard to say what the definitive type is. Anyhow, the one I got was big and tasty - enough said.

We didn't even get around to some of the other New Orleans' specialties such as gumbo, the hurricane cocktail, jambalaya, etouffee, bananas foster, red beans and rice etc. New Orleans is a tough place to match when it comes to food. Finally, just in case you were wondering about those scam artists: the answer to where you got your shoes is - *you got your shoes on your feet, in New Orleans, Louisiana*. Smart!

* * *

"Are you Johnny Ray? / Are you Jimmy Ray? / Are you Sting Ray? / Who wants to know? / Who wants to know?" We finished singing and I pressed stop on the tape.

A moment of silence passed, I spoke, "It's weird that Jimmy's asking if other people are also Jimmy Ray. What's the likelihood of anyone he's asking actually being another Jimmy Ray? Pretty bloody low, I would guess."

"Yeah, but even weirder is that he asks, *who wants to know?* Even though it's clearly him that wants to know, since he's the one that's doing the asking. He's even the one who has written a song about it. So it's him, isn't it?"

"Correct," I said confirming his analysis.
"Must have a split personality disorder."

We drove on and I looked at the landscape. We were following Route 66 west across the middle of the country but a lot of the original Route 66, so famous as the original highway for great American road trips, actually no longer exists. Disappointingly in many places it has fallen into disrepair or simply been built over by interstates. The US is absolutely massive and still takes a long time to drive across, but 50 years ago it took a lot longer. The roads meandered, the cars were slower and people had more time. They took roads like Route 66, nowadays people zoom by on Interstate-44. They want to drive fast and get to their destination quickly.

The scenery in these middle states, Illinois, Missouri, Oklahoma and Texas was boring. It was flat and featureless. Mile after mile rolled by. It was hard to distinguish one section of road from the next or the one before it. Jack had set the cruise control on and the road was straight. We didn't want to listen to the tape again and the radio was irritating.

One way to pass the time was to watch other people driving. I've witnessed some truly terrible driving in the US, lane drifting, pulling over on the central reservation, rather than side of the road, that type of thing, even people missing an exit and then reversing back down the highway to try and get back to it. Of course a lot of Americans can drive very well, although there are a great number that clearly can't. I think the main problem that afflicts a lot of American driving is inattentiveness, it's not that they can't drive, it's just that driving is a very low effort endeavour in the US. Cars are automatics as standard, cruise control is used all the time and indicating (using your blinkers) is strictly optional.

    I think this inattentiveness may be something to do with the fact that Americans spend so much time driving and that it is so central to American life, that driving is not really seen as a separate and distinct activity. Need to put your make-up on? Do it while driving. Need to make a call? Need to eat breakfast? Fancy finishing the crossword? I've seen all these things being done while people are driving. One time, I kid you not, one of the people eating breakfast was doing so with a cereal bowl and a spoon. That is an activity that requires two hands.

    Driving is just so integral and commonplace in the US, that people do everything in their cars. You have drive-in movie theaters, drive-thru coffee shops even drive-thru banks. For many Americans there is no alternative to driving on a daily basis, even when perhaps they shouldn't. While a lot of British people will say that they wouldn't even have a sip of alcohol if they were driving, if you asked a lot of Americans what their attitude would be, then they would reply, *"Of course I'm going to drive, how the hell else am I going to get home from the bar at the end of the night?"*

    I know any American readers won't take offence at my criticism of some people's driving, it seems to be pretty well-established. Incredibly I saw an advert for a Ford pick-up truck that used the average American driver's inattentiveness as the main selling point of their new truck. As the impressive and mean-looking pick-up truck was driving along, another car came into view. The serious voiceover started, "That guy over there's eating his sandwich, and talking on the phone when he's driving. If he crashes into you, don't you want to know that you're coming off best?" My question is this: What if the guy who's scoffing a burger and texting while he's driving, is the one who's driving a 3-ton pick-up truck? What then Ford?

23. Nebraska: The law

Robyn and I were driving west. We were pretty much smack bang in the middle of the country in Nebraska. Nebraska is part of the Midwest and also one of the Great Plains states. The Midwest is associated with farming and states like Iowa are covered in cornfields. Nebraska though is more like featureless prairie and they raise a lot of cattle there. There is not much to look at as you drive and it's perhaps not surprising that Nebraska is sometimes dismissed as a "fly-over" state – i.e. you fly-over it to get to somewhere more appealing, but we weren't doing that, we were driving.

Nebraska is one of those states that unless you live in the US you could spend a lifetime never hearing about. It has no major city to speak of, no professional major league sports teams, no massive festivals, it just carries on with an understated *"Nothing to see here"* kind of vibe. That's not to do it down, 90% of Nebraskans live in towns with 3,000 residents or fewer. That is a serious small-town culture. You get the sense that it is community-centric, rural-based and slow-paced.

Robyn was driving and we were ploughing on along the arrow-straight interstate. I was trying to find something of interest in the guidebook. Finding nothing, I decided to look up some facts about Nebraska on my phone.

"Do you want to hear some interesting facts about Nebraska?" I asked Robyn.

"Go on then," she said, a little warily.

"Did you know that Nebraska is the nation's largest producer of centre pivot irrigation?"

"No, I did not know that. But then again I don't know what centre pivot irrigation is. I thought you said that these facts were interesting?"

"Ok, ok, here's another one. Did you know that as well as being the largest producer of centre pivot irrigation, Nebraska is *also the nation's largest user* of centre pivot irrigation?"

She sighed, "Is that really the most interesting fact there is?"

I started scrolling, "Ok here's one. In Blue Hill, Nebraska, no female wearing a hat that would scare a timid person can be seen eating onions in public," we both laughed.

"What numpties!" she said. "That's the type of fact I like. I'd say more like that and less about spigots and pivots please." I sensed a richer vein of comic material and started looking up stupid laws.

We've all heard of these types of laws e.g. "In North Dakota, you may not wear your hat while dancing" or "In Vermont it is illegal to paint a horse." Humorous, and while these types of odd laws do exist in other countries, you generally tend to hear about them in association with states in the US. I wasn't really sure why that was. A lot of people dismissively would imagine that it's because the US is filled with crackpot legislators just waiting to crackdown on horse-painting or hat-dancing, but I imagined it was something more credible than that. It's true that because each US state has a state government as well as the national government there are therefore a lot more laws being passed. Clearly that provided scope for a lot more stupid ones, but that still didn't fully explain it.

The reality is that while there are indeed a lot of stupid laws out there in different states (even sometimes within different towns and cities), there is often a good reason for them, strange as it may sound. For one, many of these laws are often exaggerated or fabricated, becoming more and more ridiculous as they get repeated, like in a game of Chinese whispers. A lot more of them are just twisted from a single ruling in a local court of law. The idea is that if a judge in a city ruled on one thing once then they have established precedent in common law. For example someone successfully sues their neighbour for disrupting their sleep because they keep having night time barbecues. The noise and smells are disturbing their sleep and they successfully win damages from the offending neighbour. This is then interpreted as establishing a precedent and the stupid law gets presented as "it is illegal to have a barbecue after 9pm in wherevertown."

Other times the laws can make sense at the time and seem ridiculous now. For instance, in New Orleans if a woman wants to drive a car it is only legal if her husband walks ahead of the car waving a flag. Sounds ridiculous, but back in 1908 or whenever the law was passed it was quite common to have to warn pedestrians of an oncoming car and this was often done by waving a flag.

There are though still a load of ridiculous laws left on the books that cannot be explained by either of the two reasons above. For example: in Washington state, there is a law that "a motorist with criminal intentions must stop at the city limits and telephone the chief of police as he is entering the town." Great law! It must be easy being a policeman there. Or how about this one, "In Eureka, Nevada, it is illegal for men who have moustaches to kiss women." That just sounds like someone who had a chip on his shoulder about men with moustaches. I like the idea of a jilted city councillor whose wife had run off with a moustachioed scoundrel trying to put a stop to the affair. *Ok moustache-man how about I make it illegal for you to kiss my wife and, for good measure, any women at all in this whole gosh darn town?!*

Robyn and I arrived in Gering, Nebraska, one of these typical small town communities in the Plains. The reason we had come was to try one of the few specialities of Nebraska – the cabbage burger, also known as a bierock or runza. As you might be able to tell from those names, this is a food with its origins in Germany. Germans were one of the biggest groups to come over and settle in America, and the Great Plains states had a lot of German settlers. Nebraska (which is about 90% white) has the highest proportion of Czech Americans in the US and one of the highest proportions of Americans with German ancestry.

The Germans (like every other immigrant group) brought over their food and drink traditions and these are now firmly associated with particular states. For instance Wisconsin is known for its beers and bratwursts. Wisconsin (Milwaukee specifically) was the centre of American beer-brewing in the mid-19th century and one of the biggest brewers, Miller, is still based there. The biggest American beer brand (Budweiser) was also founded by a German, Adolphus Busch, and is based in St. Louis, Missouri, also in the middle of the country. Those other states got beers and sausages, but Nebraska got the cabbage burger.

One place that specialises in cabbage burgers is the Gering Bakery, so much so that it puts a neon sign for them in its window. That's why we had come to this town in the middle of nowhere. I feel that the name cabbage burger is a bit misleading though. The product in question is really more of a soft-doughy bread bun stuffed with minced (ground) beef, and cabbage shreds with loads of seasoning. Americans tend to use the word "sandwich" to mean just about anything that involves bread (including most things served at fast food restaurants) unlike the stricter British definition. I think the Nebraskans are doing the same thing with "burger" here. How can a doughy bread thing be a burger? They're playing pretty fast and loose with the definition by my standards.

The cabbage burger reminded me a lot of a Cornish pasty, which has a similar minced meaty filling but is encased in pastry instead of a doughy bun. I wouldn't be surprised if, like a pasty, it was designed back in Germany for workers to take one with them on a day in the fields, in the way that the Cornish pasty was taken down the mines by the miners.

Anyway – I thought it was a very tasty dish, and it really did remind me of the Cornish pasty, which was nice since they are impossible to find in the US. I think though it would have been better if they'd retained the name "Runza", rather than "cabbage burger" although asking for Runzas does sound a bit like asking for some strong medicine for a nasty disease.

* * *

We were still driving. Mile after mile with little to think about apart from how far we would drive that day. We'd passed through all of Illinois, stopped overnight at St. Louis, Missouri (and looked at the arch – it's just a big arch) and did a quick tour of the Budweiser factory (suitably commercial). We pressed on through Missouri, seeing little but what we could spy from the interstate.

I don't think any country is shown in its best light by viewing it from its highways and motorways. Back roads and quieter roads definitely do offer interesting insights, but the big highways tend to be functional and traffic heavy. The US does better than most, in certain parts of the country, the scenery (even on the interstates) is fantastic but there in the middle of America, it was dull and repetitive. For a long time we had noticed the profusion of fast food places, chain motels and chain gas stations that clustered around interstate exits. You can't miss them; they advertise themselves with giant neon logos shining and glaring from on top of huge poles. Around any interstate exit that led to a town of any size at all we would see the logos held aloft. They looked like the banners of some approaching army, huge golden arches for McDonalds, the yellow circle of Burger King, the looming creepy face of the KFC Colonel, the cowboy hat of Arby's, the tolling Taco Bell, the frightening pig-tailed Wendy's child, we came to know them all.

The effect was particularly stark at night. As we approached a town, we would see a cluster of neon lights. As they became larger and clearer, we could see the logos competing with each other for height and size. Some of them were ridiculously tall, 100 foot or more, topped often with huge golden arches. Yes it was convenient for the interstate traveller and often for us when we were looking for some motel as close to the interstate as possible, but I couldn't help feeling that it was just a blight on the landscape. I felt sorry for people that lived near the interstate in these towns. They often lived in small rural communities, yet if they came outside, perhaps to look at the stars, they would instead see the giant illuminated face of Colonel Sanders smiling back, imploring one and all to try his finger lickin' good chicken.

The other thing that was vaguely unsettling about the huge neon signs was that it made it evident just how many of these places existed. Seemingly small communities would have a dozen fast food restaurants and those were just the ones visible from the interstate. Jack and I found it difficult to comprehend. It's not that we didn't have fast food in the UK, just not in that frequency. They were literally everywhere. For a while we had a game where the first one to spot the Golden Arches would say "There's your Macca's." It wasn't a very fun game, but it was based on the premise that it didn't really matter how small the community was, there always would be a McDonalds to spot. This is not surprising considering there are over 14,000 McDonald's in the US. However, McDonald's is only the second most numerous fast food chain. The no. 1 chain Subway has over 25,000 stores. Staggering.

Pretty soon we were bored with the McDonald's spotting game since it was far too easy. Over time it evolved so that you could only win the game if you could spot two McDonald's in a single field of vision. This was actually reasonably easy as well (since the signs were so damn large). Eventually to win the game you had to find two (or more) of a lesser-spotted chain in the same field of view. These included the 70's looking Waffle House, with its sign that looked like a fully revealed phrase on the answer board of *Wheel of Fortune.* On one memorable occasion, we spotted two IHOPs (International House of Pancakes) and three McDonald's all in the same field of view. God we were bored.

I'm not really sure why fast food is *so* popular in the US. Americans do tend to eat out a lot more than Europeans. A lot of Americans will eat out every single day (not necessarily for their evening meal) but perhaps grabbing their breakfast or lunch on the go. All that time spent in the car necessitates a type of food that can be purchased (and consumed) in the car. It's no surprise that the US invented the Drive-Thru. Maybe our busy lives are another contributing factor. However, fast food may have finally reached saturation point in the US. The only sector in the US fast food market that is still growing is the breakfast sector, which is why fast food chains are putting so much effort into new Sausage Griddles, Chicken Biscuits and Breakfast Burritos.

There is one McDonald's for every 20,000 residents in the US, which doesn't sound too bad. That is until you realise that a community of 20,000 residents will on average also have two Subways, one Starbucks and a one in two chance of having a branch of each of the following: a Wendy's, a Burger King, a Taco Bell, a Dunkin' Donuts, a Pizza Hut, a KFC, a Domino's, a Dairy Queen and a smaller (but still significant) chance of having one of a hundred more fast food chains. They are totally inescapable.

US fast food chains are also priced very attractively. They often have a dollar menu (single items for one dollar) and meal deals, where your whole meal will be less than $5. It is practically impossible to cook up meals as cheap as that. They use the fact that their business is very high volume and they have immense purchasing power to keep costs very low. If you are on a low income, then fast food can often seem like the only choice. Furthermore the amount and frequency of advertising of fast food is incredible. Watch practically any commercial break in the US and you will see at least one advert for fast food, if not two or three.

I think the final aspect of their popularity is cultural. There is a lot of fast food in the UK, but not really on the same scale as the US – take McDonald's with its 14,500 branches in the US. The UK is a lot smaller, but if you take a *per person* measure then there are 2.5 times as many McDonald's in the US than in the UK and we don't even have a lot of the other chains that the US does: Taco Bell, Chick Fil A, Wendy's etc. I think the difference is a class and snobbery issue. In the UK the majority of people will have eaten fast food, some will eat it regularly, but if you are middle class then you will know there is something a little bit naughty, perhaps even shameful about eating fast food. Many will be proud about never eating it while others will eat it, but not tell anyone about it, like some vaguely mischievous secret. Or I've noticed that a lot of people will admit they eat fast food, but only in an ironic manner like; *"Yeah I did a bad thing, I had a dirty great big burger for lunch, and some chicken nugget chasers, but it had to be done."* Or they might admit it in an apologetic manner, *"I was just really tired last night, so I had to go to KFC, I just couldn't face cooking."*

In the US though there is no sense of shame, handwringing or snobbery about fast food, it's just a normal part of life. Why wouldn't you go to McDonald's or Subway? In fact often the opposite is true, many people are passionate about fast food, especially niche or more unusual chains, and that's people from all social sectors. Fast food is important to them. I've known people complain about living in a state just because it doesn't have In-N-Out Burger or Five Guys. I've known people be evangelical about certain chains and products, imploring me to try a particular burrito or burger. There is no snobbery at work whatsoever, the opposite, they're passionate about it.

The same is true of soda, most people in the US love fizzy drinks. Again they are a lot more popular than in Europe and the sheer variety of them is overwhelming. I knew one American guy who went to Italy to stay with a family and when he ordered a coke at dinner they were scornful of his choice, saying that it was not very classy and not really appropriate for dinner. He was suitably admonished, telling me that he'd never realised it could be seen in that way. He told me he rarely drank coke again after that. It's hard to say whether this snobby European attitude is preferable to the American attitude that can be so welcoming to fast food. Whatever the answer is, I wish they'd make those neon signs just a little bit smaller.

24. Colorado: The mountains

Robyn and I continued to drive west and we left the flat, treeless plains behind. We were in the foothills of the Rocky Mountains now. As we drove into Colorado, we started to gain elevation quickly. Denver, the main city, is known as "the mile high city" due to its altitude (about 6,000 feet). Some people even experience mild altitude sickness if they fly straight in from sea level. Colorado is very mountainous and interestingly 75% of the land area of the U.S. with an altitude over 10,000 feet is found in the state. Perhaps because of this it is a very outdoorsy kind of place. It certainly helps that much of Colorado gets an average of 300 sunny days a year (which I think is about 100 times the number England gets every year).

We visited the Rocky Mountain National Park, which was surprisingly varied. The road climbed as we approached the park and once inside we drove between several different peaks and valleys. The park contains the highest through-road in the US (its highest point is 12,183 feet / 3,713 metres) and is closed by heavy snow for 7 or 8 months of the year. At the lower levels of the road pine trees and scrub clung to the mountainsides. As we climbed higher the trees disappeared and the terrain began to take on the appearance of arctic tundra. It's so high, so windy and so cold for much of the year that nothing can grow up there. We reached the very highest point and stopped for a photo. We were both starting to get altitude headaches since we were over 2 miles up. It occurred to me that people skydive from lower altitudes than where we were. All about us we could see the snow and ice that never melts. We were there in October and it was getting colder, it would start snowing soon.

We traversed the road and descended to a lower altitude. We were also keen to see some of the wildlife that the park is famous for. The most celebrated animal residents of the park are the elk. They are magnificent huge deer-like creatures with absolutely giant antlers (on the males). The autumn is the start of the rut, which is the best time to see them. Dusk was approaching, which is the time when they often gather in the meadows. Sure enough, after a bit of driving we came across a large group of them. There was a park ranger and a few other people gathered around their cars keeping their distance from the twenty or so elk grazing in the adjacent meadow.

Elk are dangerous, especially during the rut, when the male elk will be particularly protective of his females. At this time, as they get ready to mate, the male elk will try and gather as many females as possible into his "harem". He then protects them for about four or five weeks as they prepare to come into heat and then he *ermmm* "gets friendly" with as many of them as possible, as often as possible, while they are willing to mate. The rut seemed like a busy and demanding time for the male elk. Just looking after the females seemed like a full time job to me. They are in constant danger of just wandering off or becoming detached from the group. We could see the male having to always keep an eye on them or bring them back to the herd when they strayed a little far. Being on constant duty seemed tiring and that's before he even summoned the energy to *seduce* as many of them as possible.

    The other threat to the male and his harem is other male elks who will try and steal some (or all) of the females. Clearly it's tough trying to keep 20 girlfriends at once. The only human I can think of who's even attempted it is Hugh Hefner. No wonder the gates at the Playboy Mansion are so big.

    During the rut the males will often fight, with a huge and violent clattering of their massive antlers. Eventually during all the tussling one of the males will break off the other's antlers (they'll grow back the following year). At that point the defeated one needs to make a run for it or risk getting gouged. The elk also pose a risk to humans. At one of the park visitor centres we watched an (unintentionally) amusing video of portly tourists being harassed by male elks. For the most part, elk simply try to chase people away, but sometimes if the male is particularly violent they can cause significant injury. This video though was more like a TV prank show. A male elk would appear out of nowhere behind some unsuspecting camera-happy, Hawaiian shirt-wearing tourist. Eventually the tourist would see the elk cantering towards them and (for the first time in presumably in many years) have to run away as fast as they could. It was strangely watchable.

In the park though as we watched the elk, the ranger pointed out a younger male elk across a small stream, a 100 metres further on from the male with the harem. The would-be interloper was watching carefully, clearly thinking, *I'm not greedy, I'd be happy with just 6 or 7 of them, just a small harem, nothing over the top!* But it was not to be, apparently he'd been chased off once and he didn't make another attempt while we were watching. We were also lucky enough to see some "bugling". During the rut the males (in an effort to show off their prowess) start making a calling noise, a long single note, which they do repeatedly (like a bugle). It's impressive to watch, the stag rears his head back, his huge antlers pointed to the sky and the sound echoes around the valley.

We stayed in Boulder which is a great little city (and is the 11th biggest city in Colorado – remember that for later). It's the home of Colorado University, and has a very liberal environment, with lots of parks, cafes and rooftop bars. The weather was perfect, sunny and cloudless every day. We went for a walk in the nearby Flatirons. These slate-grey mountains jut jaggedly out of pretty meadows of wildflowers and frame one side of the city. The blue skies and excellent views made for an excellent hike and we felt healthy and active (not always the case with so much driving to do).

Soon enough our thoughts turned to food, but while Colorado is famous for mountains and skiing, it's not the most obvious culinary paradise. If it does have a local speciality, it's probably "Rocky Mountain Oysters". Now these are euphemistically named and are not in fact oysters. The joke of course being that Colorado has no coastline and no oysters. What it does have are a lot of cattle and these "Oysters" come from bulls. To be clear – they are the testicles. Obviously, we weren't about to go on some grand "testicle tasting tour". So what else was there? Colorado is famous-ish for beer (home of Coors and various craft brewers), but we'd done beer. So the last option was tea. Boulder is home of Celestial Seasonings – the biggest herbal tea manufacturer in the US.

We went to the Celestial Seasonings factory just outside the city. It was a good tour, we could have as much free tea as we wanted beforehand, and they had about 50 different varieties so the selection was very widespread. There were exotic ones such as "Bengal Spice" (surprisingly fiery) to a tea that was meant to taste like coffee, "Roastaroma" (surprisingly pointless). Anyway they had a great many interesting and tasty varieties, and then the tour led us round the factory, the highlight of which was probably the mint room, where they kept all their mint in huge sacks; the smell was unbelievably strong. In fact the mint has to be kept in a separate room because the aroma alone would be enough to flavour the other teas.

So it was a good tour, but why is Celestial Seasonings in Boulder? Well because Boulder is at the foot of the Rocky Mountains, and it was founded by a bunch of people who (for unexplained reasons) were picking wild herbs in the Rockies in 1969. What type of people would be trying to make a living picking wild herbs in the mountains in the late 1960s? Your final clue is that the company they founded is called "Celestial Seasonings". That's right, they were hippies.

I can't think of many successful companies founded by hippies other than this one. To be honest I think hippy names are a hindrance from the off, I mean "Celestial Seasonings"? That would be fine for a company specialising in herbs and spices from outer space, but a tea company? Was everybody so high they didn't even notice that tea isn't actually a seasoning? It certainly wouldn't be my first choice for a name, but I guess that's why I'm not one of the many uber-successful hippy businessmen.

There's actually one other tea connection in Boulder, and that is the rather unusual "Boulder Dushanbe Teahouse", supposedly the largest Teahouse in the Western Hemisphere. It's a traditional central-Asian looking Teahouse, a huge beautiful building with hand painted tiles and ceilings and intricately carved pillars. We ate there and had some really nice exotic food and interesting teas. It was a pleasure to dine in what was a very tranquil and unusual setting.

But why does Boulder have such a huge central-Asian styled Teahouse? It's because Boulder is twinned with Dushanbe, the capital of Tajikistan, and they sent it over as a gift in the 1980s. A team of forty artisans in Tajikistan built it, doing everything by hand and it was shipped in crates to Boulder. One puzzling thing is; I can't really find any reason why the capital of Tajikistan is twinned with a much, much smaller city in Colorado, apart from the fact they're both near mountains. I can only imagine the following phone call took place:

"Hello, is this White House? We call from Dushanbe, glorious capital of Tajikistan."

"Err...ok how can I help you?"

"We want twin city, we think capital of United States, Washington DC perfect for us."

"Hmmm, no, we've actually already got a lot of twins for Washington. Don't worry though, I can find you somewhere else."

"Ok New York City also good."

"Ermmm, not sure *(covers mouthpiece and speaks to someone in the office) – who've we got available for twinning? I've got Kazakhstan on the phone – Who? What? Where's that? Some hippies in Colorado? Sure – he'll go for that (uncovers mouthpiece).* We've got a great city for you – Boulder, Colorado."

"Ahh ok, capital of Colorado."

"No, it's not the capital."

"Ahh ok is biggest city of Colorado."

"Not quite."

"2nd biggest?"

"No."

So anyway, like I said, I'm not sure how it happened, but it could have been like the above. Both Colorado and Boulder were a delight though and it seemed very liveable. The people appeared active and healthy, the sun shone and nature was right on the doorstep. Apart from the fact that Colorado gets very cold, I think it would be a very fine place to live indeed.

* * *

Jack and I were also driving west. We were in Oklahoma and were unable to take any more of the cassette and Jimmy Ray and all the other one hit horrors. We'd gone into an electronics store in order to find something that might allow us to connect my CD player or Jack's iPod to the tape deck. In the end we'd managed to find a little device which broadcast an FM signal from my CD player. We then tuned the car radio in to the correct frequency and finally we could listen to something other than the damn cassettes.

"Did you notice anything about that girl in the department store?" I said to Jack.

"What, do you think she liked me?" he asked.

"Don't be a fool, I meant she didn't notice we were British or anything, did she?"

"No I don't think she did," he said thoughtfully.

"We're in the middle of Oklahoma; do you think she's ever even met a British person before?"

I was slightly surprised really. One of the little pleasures about being British and travelling around the US is that in restaurants and shops the staff will often pick up on your British accent and ask excitedly if you are indeed British. It's like having a very low level of fame. Although it's a type of fame where you're not sure what it is you are famous for and even then something for which you have no real reason to take any credit.

The conversation normally goes one of two ways when a stranger asks if you are British. Once Britishness is confirmed then they often ask specifically where you're from. That one doesn't tend to be so good, because a lot of Americans only know two places in the UK: London and Scotland. So when you answer *I'm from the town of Northwhistle in the county of Crumpetshire*, they look disappointed as they haven't heard of it. So if you're from anywhere close to London or have ever even visited London I think it's probably best just to say London. This will then elicit a positive response because they'll have heard of London, or maybe even have been or perhaps plan to go someday.

The other way the *"You're British!"* conversation can go is a follow-up question or comment about a specifically British thing. It could be anything, but being British you will be expected to have some level of authority on or insight into the subject e.g. *Is Kate Middleton pregnant again?* It's hard to answer questions like that, although staring back seriously and saying *"yes but she's only 10 weeks in, so we're not really supposed to be telling people yet"* is a fun way to reply.

Sometimes the comment will be about something British that by dint of association you will be expected to be a fan of, or involved in. The following is a true example with a shopgirl in a mall.

"You're British!"

"Yes."

"That's so cool. I love British things!"

"Oh that's good, like what?"

"I just love Doctor Who. It's great, do you watch it?"

"Errmm not really, isn't it a bit geeky?"

Shopgirl looks hurt, "Oh I would have thought you would like it."

Me retreating, "Oh yeah, well I do kind of like it, I meant it's kind of cool and sci-fi geeky at the same time. So yeah I do like it I suppose *(pause)* anyway, I better get going."

I learnt pretty quickly that honesty is not always the best policy and it is better to just be open and positive, because it's always nice when people are a bit excited to meet you. Plus doing anything else would let down my country and also the Queen, who, since you've asked, yes I do know personally.

25. Wyoming: Cowboys

Wyoming is shaped like a big square, with no cities of note, and is the least populated state in the US (around 450,000 people). Despite that, I would recommend it heartily to anyone, which is surely the best way to recommend anything.

Wyoming is in the high plains, the terrain is wide and open. The distances are vast and signs of human life are few and far between. You have to drive about 500 miles in Wyoming to get from one corner to the other, and much of the time it is just plains: empty, desolate plains. There is a kind of beauty to it all, but also the feeling of being in a wild and barren land. However, Wyoming's star features are probably unsurpassed anywhere else in the nation. In the Northwest of the state there are two fabulous National Parks, one is America's first National Park, Yellowstone, and the other is the adjoining Grand Teton National Park. Both of them contain some of the most magnificent and stunning scenery we'd ever seen.

Yellowstone National Park is actually bigger than the two smallest states in the US (Delaware and Rhode Island) put together. In the height of summer though it seems like it contains more campervans and RVs than any three states combined. Despite being hundreds and hundreds of miles from anywhere and huge, it can feel a bit busy in certain areas, so if you ever go, plan for a quieter time of year – although not easy when it's closed nearly 8 months of the year for snow.

President Ulysses Grant designated Yellowstone as the first national park in the US in 1872. It was also the first national park in the world. Around this time large parts of the interior of the US were only just being fully explored by the US government. Yellowstone was noted immediately for its interesting geothermal features. Ferdinand Hayden was responsible for two thorough surveys of the region and became a great advocate for preserving it as a national park. He was spurred on by his concern at the commercialisation he'd seen at Niagara Falls (in the 1870s! Imagine what he'd think now.) He argued for setting aside the Yellowstone area "as a pleasure ground for the benefit and enjoyment of the people."

One of the things to make a big impact on the politicians back in Washington DC was the photographs that had been taken on the expedition (photographs were quite a novel thing at the time). There was actually a lot of resistance to the idea of protecting the area as a national park from some politicians who thought it would damage the economic prospects of the area. Fortunately these complaints were rejected and Yellowstone was created. This also paved the way for the creation of the National Parks Service and the fabulous national parks that the US now enjoys.

Yellowstone is absolutely massive, covering a similar area to *countries* such as Cyprus or Lebanon. It also has four distinct areas. We decided to stay in two different places during our stay. Yellowstone has plenty of accommodation within the park (and the park's sheer size means it makes sense to stay inside the park). You can choose from little cabins to big lodge hotels. We stayed in the Old Faithful Inn, which was the first hotel built in the park and is the largest building made from logs in the world. It was constructed back in 1902 and is quite a sight to behold, particularly so from the inside. The lobby and central area were vaulted and airy. The sheer scale of the wooden roof was very impressive, the logs in the roof and the cross beams were absolutely huge. The central fireplace measures 85 feet and weighs 500 tonnes. The place is massive, particularly considering it is almost entirely made of wood. It is four storeys high and the upper floors of the inn have a ringed balcony above the central area. Again all these balconies are also made out of logs. It's a unique place and certainly brought home the natural aspect of staying inside a national park.

    The inn is right across from one of Yellowstone's most famous features, the Old Faithful geyser. Yellowstone has about 300 active geysers and about 10,000 thermal features in total. Old Faithful is one of the most predictable geysers on earth, erupting every 90 minutes, hence its name. The geyser was the first to be named in the park (during the 1870 expedition) and the men found an unusual use for it - as a laundry. Garments were placed in the hole and then ejected "thoroughly washed" by the eruption. Sounds efficient but unfortunately some of the geysers in Yellowstone were blocked up in the early 20th century by tourists throwing things in so that they could see them ejected by the eruption. Over time these objects caused blockages and the geysers stopped erupting at all. Fortunately they are better protected now and Yellowstone is still blessed with lots of geysers, some predictable, most not. Old Faithful generally attracts crowds, since it erupts on schedule, and it is quite a sight, ejecting on average 23,000 litres of boiling hot water up to around 150 feet.

The park is justly famous for its geothermal features, including amazingly-coloured mineral pools, boiling mud pots and hot springs. It is also famous for wildlife as it contains the largest concentration of free roaming wildlife in all of the lower 48 states. It's particularly known for bears (both grizzly bears and black bears) and wolves. Bears do very occasionally attack humans, particularly when they are walking alone on trails. The typical scenario when this happens is when the bears are on a trail with their young and a hiker comes round the bend and surprises them. Fearing for their young they will attack (and often kill) the unfortunate walker. For this reason, the park advises you to make noise, sing, clap or otherwise indicate when you are approaching blind bends so that you don't surprise any bears. Robyn and I were walking along a trail and were conscious of this.

"Robyn there's a blind bend coming up, do you want to make some noise or something?"

"It's alright, you can do it," she replied.

"You're just embarrassed!" I said. It was true; while there was every reason to alert a bear that you were coming, there was a problem if there was no bear, but instead there were some walkers on the other side of the bend. In that case it would be pretty embarrassing to be heard singing (to the imaginary bears).

"Ok fine then," she said after a pause.

"Go on then."

Rather than clapping or singing instead she shouted out "Helloooo! Where's your bears? Wheerrree's yoouurrr beearrrs?" It seemed as good a thing as any to be crazily shouting out. After that, it became our standard blind bend bear-greeting.

One evening we went out wildlife-spotting in the valley over from where we staying. The bears and wolves generally come out at dusk or dawn, so as a wildlife watcher you need to be up early or stay out late. As we drove along we came across a herd of bison (also called buffalo), which were blocking the road. These huge creatures are fairly dim and slow and move around in big groups. They weigh between half a ton and a ton each, so when they're crossing the road *you* have to wait. They often create mini traffic jams, while they trudge across the road. Eventually they moved on and we got to the valley, where we were fortunate to spot a group of wolves, reasonably far away, but with a telescope we got a good view of them.

Dusk turned to darkness and we drove back over the hill out of the valley. Soon it was pitch black and the road was unlit. We drove along and suddenly I saw a glint a few feet ahead of the car at the edge of the road, a second later it was alongside the car, a couple of inches from the wing mirror. Robyn shouted "Bison!", at which point I realised it was a bison - a huge whacking great bison. We were literally a hands-width away from hitting it and totalling the car. I slowed right down and went to the middle of the road. At this point we saw a few more of them just lumbering up the edge of the road – clearly they were using it as a pathway to wherever they were going. We were lucky, it was pitch-black and they are very dark and hard to see. It was a fortunate escape, because the car would have been a write-off and he didn't look like he had insurance.

We also went to the adjoining Grand Teton National Park, the home of a stunning mountain range called the Tetons, originally named by French-speaking fur trappers as *les trois tetons* (literally meaning the three breasts, so now the name humorously translates into French as big breast national park). The park itself is spectacular. The Teton Mountains themselves frame most views, jutting dramatically up in the background with pretty lakes, streams and forests in front. We went swimming in a mountain lake and saw plenty more wildlife including moose and pronghorns. The pronghorn is an antelope-type creature, and is the fastest mammal in the Western Hemisphere, it can run 55mph which is the second fastest land animal in the world (behind the cheetah). The irony is that their predators and prey have changed so much that they now rarely bother to run anywhere near that quickly.

Wyoming (and this corner of it in particular) is also associated with cowboys – the Wyoming license plate even features a bucking bronco and a cowboy with his lasso. Because of this tourism is far from a new addition to the area. The original concept of the "Dude Ranch" originated in Jackson, Wyoming (near Grand Teton and Yellowstone). In the 1920s East Coast city-dwellers often wanted to come out West to try being a cowboy. Nostalgia for the bygone days of "the West" and the frontier led many to want to recapture that by spending their vacation on a grand trip west. The Dude Ranches gave them the chance to experience life as a rancher or a cowboy and so a number of ranches sprang up in Wyoming.

Perhaps because of this cowboy and frontier history Wyoming does not have any especially strong food traditions. It doesn't really have great immigrant influences or any natural advantages like seafood from having a long coast. In fact, our bible of foods (the 500 things to eat book), only recommends one thing in Wyoming: "ditch", which is what cowboys round these parts call whiskey and water. The book even makes clear that even at its recommended place to drink a ditch that, "There is absolutely no food of interest. Nor do we recommend ordering a frozen margarita or a Cosmo...you drink beer or whiskey."

Almost no fruits or vegetables grow in the high plains. The only common wild-growing fruit or vegetable on the plains are huckleberries. Even then they are only found in late summer. They are also beloved by bears (and I've mentioned what can happen when you surprise a bear, so just imagine how angry they'd be if you stole their berries). In the end we went to a chuckwagon, which is a very authentic cook-out, where a few locals play their fiddles and guitars and croon old cowboy songs – although thinking about it, there were hordes of tourbuses, an army of senior citizens, and two gift shops – so maybe it wasn't that authentic.

The idea of this very touristy, and somewhat cheesy event, is to feed you up in a way that resembles how cowboys on a cattle drive would have been fed, i.e. they brought a cook along who cooked up a big pot of beans and meat doled it all out together on one plate, along with bread and cake. The food cart back then was the "chuckwagon" and that's where these more modern touristy places get their name. The food was actually pretty good. They were cooking up steaks by the dozen on the open grill and the meal was a definitely a hearty helping of good old fashioned food.

Interestingly the owner who had bought the chuckwagon 50 years ago had originally run it as a cattle and horse ranch. They started doing horse rides in the summer and then they started having bonfires, playing some tunes and having cook-outs. Over time it became more profitable than the animals, so they turned it into a full-time tourist venue. Considering Yellowstone is mostly closed by snow except in the summer it tells you how profitable tourism can be compared to old-fashioned ranching. Regardless, Wyoming is still a great place to go to get a sense of the American West and has some of the most fantastic scenery and wildlife that the US has to offer.

* * *

For once I was driving. It was unusual, Jack liked to drive and I was happy to let him do it. I was the navigator, which, back in those days before satnavs and smartphones, was a tricky thing. We possessed a single large scale road atlas. It was fine for telling us which interstate led between which cities but when we got to a city it was about as useful as a concrete cushion. We would drive around, occasionally chancing on the correct street but more often than not we would have to admit defeat and stop and ask people for directions. At that point though as we continued west into Texas there was only one road for us to take and we were on it. There was no navigating for Jack to do and it was another long driving day, so I'd got a shift driving for a couple of hours.

Evening came and as we approached the town of Amarillo, Texas, we read the guidebook. It said that the town had a "lively street" and being bored of chain motels and fast food we were looking forward to having a night out. We left the plains behind and rolled into town. It was full of low-slung buildings and seemingly very little life. We boxed round the area we thought the particular street was in but couldn't really see it. Finally we drove down a street with one bar on it. At the end of the street we spotted that the street we were on was *in fact* the "lively" street. Resigned and with no other options we thought we may as well head to the only bar. We parked up and ventured across the traffic-less street. The smell of fried food hung oppressively in the air and the sounds of country music drifted out of the bar.

We put our heads round the door and looked in. It was empty.

"This doesn't look great. Shall we stay or not?"

"I can't take any more of this food," Jack whinged. I couldn't help but agree. I didn't know whether it was the deep-fried smell, the lack of customers or the mere fact the promise of life after days and days of nothingness had turned out to be a lie, but I wasn't interested either.

"Ok, let's go," I said. We turned quickly and scurried away before we were seen, feeling awkward - as though by simply opening the door we were somehow obliged to be customers.

We reached the car and got inside. At that point the bar door flung open and a big angry man in a vest looked out. His face seemed to say; *"What kind of varmints have just gone done opened my goddamn bar door?!"* He didn't look friendly and we didn't want to stick around. We headed back towards the interstate exit for signs of more life there.

26. South Dakota: Native Americans

We drove north out of Wyoming on our way to South Dakota. The route necessitated that we drove through nearly 500 miles of Montana but we didn't really do anything foody, not unless you count stopping at an Arby's to eat an "Arby-Q" burger, which, having eaten an Arby-Q burger, I wouldn't. Montana seems as lacking in food traditions as Wyoming, and again the only naturally occurring fruit and vegetable in that part of the plains is the wild huckleberry. That said the scenery was stunning as we emerged from the Yellowstone/Grand Teton area. We went through a winding, twisting descent and we were treated to views of mountains and valleys as far as the eye could see.

We drove on for a hundred miles or so and the terrain began to flatten out. After a few hours we stopped at the Little Bighorn battlefield (also known as Custer's Last Stand). It was absolutely fascinating. The site is located in the high plains, remote and at the edge of a Native American reservation. The earth had a brown scrub-like quality; it was exposed and covered with little ridges and rises. We could see a long way, although it was the same terrain that rolled out for mile after mile in every direction.

In 1876, the US was still expanding its effective control west and north across the continent. This was putting the federal government and the settlers in conflict with existing Indian populations. Native Americans had been pushed onto reservations where they were still allowed to hunt and govern themselves. Most of the land that they had historically lived on had been taken for settlers. However, even the reservations were being shrunk and relocated. When gold was discovered in the Black Hills in the Dakota Territory, the government wanted to relocate the Sioux tribe again. The US government insisted that by the beginning of 1876 all tribes not on the reservation would be considered hostile. Some consented while others decided to resist.

At this time Chief Sitting Bull, a leader of the Lakota people, who had spent periods on the reservations, decided that it was better to try and preserve their way of life off the reservation than be forced on to it. In 1876 he formed a coalition of Lakota Sioux, Cheyenne warriors and others who had refused the US government demands to live on the reservations. Various skirmishes and battles had already been taking place in the previous 10 years, aggravated by gold prospecting, railroad surveying and white settlement. By 1876 there was open conflict. On the other side was General George Custer, a Civil War veteran. He was leading the US army 7th Cavalry Regiment in the western territories. His group had been surveying for gold in the previous two years and were also charged with trying to force any non-compliant Native Americans back onto the reservations.

When we arrived at the Little Bighorn battlefield, a National Park Ranger was just beginning his talk. It was a sunny and clear day, the talk was outside with the crowd gathered on rows of benches, looking out at the battlefield. Before long everyone was enraptured by the ranger's dramatic and punchy narrative. We could see the site of the Indian encampment, where Sitting Bull had gathered a substantial village of followers; there were nearly 10,000, many of them women and children. The ranger continued to describe the events of that fateful day, building the tension towards the inevitably tragic conclusion.

On that June day in 1876 Custer was pleased to have come across such a huge group of Indians. He hoped to round them up and move them back to the reservation in one fell swoop. He split his group of 700 soldiers up to continue to survey the area and left himself with around 250 men. Not long after this he received information that some Indians had tracked his group's trail and were probably aware of his presence. Custer was concerned that the Indians might therefore scatter and was keen to act soon. Unfortunately he had massively underestimated the size of the Indian forces. Rather than wait for reinforcements Custer decided to seize the initiative and launch an all-out attack on them. As the guide explained, this was a catastrophic error. Sitting Bull and Crazy Horse, the two leaders of the Indians, had actually amassed a fighting force of over 2,500. This comprised their own fighters and warriors who had recently left the reservation to join them. They had been angered by a recent betrayal by the US Government. The Government had just disregarded an important treaty and begun to allow settlement and gold prospecting on sacred Indian land.

Sitting Bull had performed a Sun Dance in early June, a couple of weeks prior to the battle. This ritual required him to fast and sacrifice around 100 pieces of flesh from his arms. He'd had a vision of "soldiers falling into his camp like grasshoppers from the sky." The Indians were ready for a fight and vastly outnumbered Custer and his poor men. They slaughtered every single one of Custer's group. Many of them were scalped.

Custer's last stand has become a byword for military catastrophe and lost causes, but as the guide explained, the debate about why Little Bighorn happened as it did continues to rage. Custer's men fought bravely to the end, retreating to a hill where they tried to fend off attackers from all sides. It was in vain. The Indians were justly aggrieved, but it was a pyrrhic victory. An outraged US public ensured that many thousands more US soldiers were posted to the area and the Indians were forced back on to the reservations or fled to Canada. Our group was absolutely captivated, as the guide was a natural performer (he was a retired schoolteacher) and the story was fascinating. Seeing the battlefield before us as he spoke really brought the history alive and it left an indelible impression as to what forces have shaped modern America.

Onwards we drove to South Dakota. It has a thing that it's famous for, and boy does it like to go on about it. Not only does the licence plate have a picture of Mount Rushmore on it, the 'Welcome to South Dakota' signs also feature a picture of the four huge Presidents' faces carved into the stone of the mountain. Where else does it crop up? Oh yeah, in everything else to do with the state that you can possibly think of, such as the state quarter, the state nickname "The Mount Rushmore state", and even the flag, which has the words "Mount Rushmore" on there! Never before have I seen the name of what is essentially a tourist attraction on a flag. I don't recall Florida's flag featuring a tagline of: "Have you thought about coming to Disneyworld? If not, we also have Gatorland."

I say just go the whole hog and rename the state "Mount Rushmore, featuring other assorted land previously known as South Dakota." I wonder if anyone in South Dakota is sick of Mount Rushmore? I wonder if that's just completely taboo though, and peer pressure in South Dakota means no one could ever speak out about it, even if they did feel that way. It would be a tortured life though since you must see that same image about seventeen times a day when you're in South Dakota. I'd also like to know what South Dakota's thing was *before* Mount Rushmore (completed in 1940). Presumably the motto was: "South Dakota, nothing to see here."

Anyway, what did we do in South Dakota? Err... go to Mount Rushmore. Obviously we went there! We went during the day, and then stayed on into the evening. It was pretty impressive. The carved heads are each about 60 feet (18m) in height and loom suitably large. However, when we got close, they looked a little smaller than I imagined. If you go for the evening, then you get treated to a show, where they light the monument up. It was odd though, particularly if you are a foreigner. We were treated to (in no particular order): a park ranger singing "America the Beautiful" (a cappella), a mass "pledge of allegiance" from the whole crowd, group singing of the national anthem, a video entitled "America – you gave the world freedom" (or something similar), a five-to-ten minute continuous standing ovation for every veteran in the crowd who wanted to go down the steps to shake the park ranger's hand, and much more.

As always with lengthy overt displays of American patriotism, I felt trapped between awkwardness and a kind of respectful pride that America should still venerate its core values (which are undoubtedly noble) and so regularly honour people who have served. American culture is seemingly obsessed with honouring the military (or those who have served). I feel this is a good thing, in the sense that these people have put themselves on the line (and potentially sacrificed for the good of the nation). It's in direct contrast to Europe where there is a lot more ambivalence about the military, or they are simply ignored.

On the surface (to some foreigners) this type of overt patriotism can come across as an over-the-top display of nationalism. It's never clear if some are proud of the military because they think: *America is the best and American troops are an extension of our power*. I hope this is not the reason, since this would represent some kind of undesirable cultural superiority complex. If as a foreigner that is how you view it, then obviously it's going to grate, particularly since a lot of Europeans still associate the US military with the unnecessary adventurism of the Iraq war. However, I take Americans' pride in the troops to be something more virtuous. I wonder if it's a reaction and apology for how US troops were often treated on returning from the Vietnam war (protested against, harassed, abused) and a recognition that that was wrong. The troops do not decide where to fight, they simply offer themselves up (and potentially their lives) to defend the nation and the noble values it still stands for. In that sense all this patriotism can be a positive, and to be honest if you've chosen to go somewhere to stare at four gigantic heads of former US presidents then you can't really argue that it's an inappropriate place for it.

Anyway, Mount Rushmore was also the place where we had our South Dakotan food, which was bison (buffalo). Hundreds of years ago the bison had roamed by the million across the plains (estimates suggest there were as many as 50 million of them prior to the Europeans' arrival). They were brought to near extinction in the late 19th century as settlers shot and killed them with abandon. By the late 1880s there were only a few hundred left, with the only significant wild herd in Yellowstone. Stories exist of westward bound settlers shooting bison out of train carriage windows for fun, the corpses simply left to rot on the plains. Fortunately, thanks to that one surviving herd in the Yellowstone area and subsequent conservation efforts there are now half a million wild buffalo in the US. They are also now farmed for their meat, which means they are a unique and genuine plains food. It is a leaner version of beef with less fat and cholesterol, so it's actually a pretty healthy meat. There is even 'beefalo', a cross-bred version of cows and buffalo.

We had a rather tasty bison stew at Mount Rushmore. It didn't taste too different from beef stew, and we later had a bison burger (which again was not too unusual). Given the health benefits of bison, and the fact that 'exotic meats' like ostrich and so on are becoming more popular, I could see bison becoming more popular outside of the plains.

We also went to the town of Deadwood, a Wild West gold rush town, founded in 1876. At exactly the same time that Custer was chasing Indians there were illegal settlements springing up. People had heard that there was gold to be had and started flocking to the area. Deadwood, in the Black Hills (i.e. the territory that was disputed with the Sioux) exploded almost overnight to a town of 5,000 people. There were men, money and no real law, so prostitution and gambling mushroomed.

The town gained notoriety in August 1876 (six weeks after Little Bighorn) when Wild Bill Hickok was gunned down while playing poker. Intriguingly, when in a saloon, Wild Bill would always choose to sit with his back to the wall, facing the door. On this particular day, there was only one seat left, with its back to the door. Twice he asked another player to switch with him and twice he was refused. Before long, a buffalo hunter known as Crooked Nose Jack walked into the saloon and shot him (no one was ever just called "Steve" in the Wild West). Deadwood was interesting, although more for these kinds of tales than what it offers now (basically just tourism and small casinos).

There wasn't too much else to report apart from uncovering the bizarre stranglehold that once popular actor, Kevin Costner, now seems to hold over the town of Deadwood. We first noticed a flyer for an attraction called "Tatanka: Story of the Bison". The museum describes the westward expansion of the US through the tale of what happened to American's bison. The tagline strangely though was: "Kevin Costner invites you to experience Tatanka", that was odd I thought; what's he got to do with it? As I continued to read the guidebook more and more references to him kept appearing. Every time there was a name of an attraction it was followed by an ominous sentence: *owned by Hollywood actor Kevin Costner...* This included (but was not limited to) a casino called *The Midnight Star*, *Jakes*, a fine dining establishment, a theme bar, a trolley bus tour company, the list simply wouldn't end.

To get to the bottom of it, we went to the theme bar (the theme unsurprisingly was the movies of Kevin Costner). It was strange, it was almost empty, but it was like some kind of Kevin Costner hall of fame. There were cases of costumes from Kevin Costner films, and not just ones you've heard of like *Field of Dreams* and *The Bodyguard*, but little-loved and forgotten ones like *The Guardian* (swimming champion becomes a coast guard) and *Message in a Bottle* (hopeless romantic puts tragic love letter in a bottle). They were all there. Big glossy movie posters and memorabilia, with Kevin's face looking down at us from a dozen angles at once.

We tend to forget about him these days, but if you search on the internet movie database "IMDB Kevin", you'll find he's still the second most popular acting Kevin (one below *Spacey,* one above *Bacon).* But why has he taken over Deadwood? Apparently while he was filming *Dances With Wolves*, Costner took a shine to the town and started buying up businesses. So there you go, you thought *Waterworld* had finished him, and he was actually off buying whole cities in South Dakota.

He hasn't only been buying up Deadwood though, he's been up to all sorts. Did you know he's in a country and western band: *Kevin Costner & Modern West*? They've had one top 40 album. Did you also know that Costner was so concerned by the Exxon Valdez oil spill in 1989 that he began personally investing in machines which would separate oil from water? He spent $25 million on patents in 1995 and started developing the machines. When the BP oil spill occurred in the Gulf of Mexico in 2010 – BP actually started buying Costner's machines. At this point Costner's former business partners sued him on the basis he'd been *holding secret meetings with BP to sell them these machines and cut them out of the profits.* Kevin Costner. BP. I'm not making this up. No wonder his acting career went down the pan in the mid-90's, he had a lot of other stuff going on.

* * *

Jack and I were still in Texas miles from anywhere we wanted to be. Having been chased out of town by the angry bar owner we headed back to our boring chain identikit motel. These motels are the very model of efficiency, bargain rates, right off the interstate, with a big neon sign advertising their low nightly rate. That rate always turned out to be the single occupancy rate, but the rooms always had twin beds, so being low on both funds and scruples we used to always take the single rate. One of us would check-in as a single traveller and then sneak the other one in afterwards. This particular motel on the outskirts of Amarillo that we had chosen that night was particularly unsavoury. It looked like the type of place where you would arrange to meet your crystal meth dealer.

As we headed away from the city centre, back towards the interstate and our motel we still needed something to eat. Before long, the giant neon lights of the fast food logos reared up like some unpleasant hallucination. We'd been eating nothing but fast food for days and we wanted to sit down in a bar or restaurant and enjoy some wholesome food. Then, in between all the familiar signs, we saw it: a massive red neon lobster. It was the sign for *Red Lobster* – yes it was still a chain but it was a restaurant and it seemed infinitely better than the thought of another burger in a cardboard box. We circled around and continued boxing in closer and closer to the huge red neon lobster in the sky. Irritatingly we could never quite get to it, just as we thought we'd reached it we would suddenly be heading away from it again. I sometimes wondered if those huge neon signs could also include an address or a handy directional hint like *"Turn left at the Texaco!"* In the end we realised we were close to the motel, so decided to leave the car and walk to the restaurant.

At last we arrived. It was closing. We walked back out of the restaurant and frustrated I looked up to see the KFC Colonel leering at me, as if to say, *Here you come, crawling back, just like I knew you would. You'll be eating your dinner from a bucket tonight!* Just as despair started to hit and we were dragging ourselves reluctantly towards the Colonel we spied a Bennigans, which is a chain mock Irish pub/restaurant. Salvation! Something different! Something original at last! Relatively speaking of course, our standards were very low at this point.

We walked into the bar and they were still open, which was a good sign. In fact it was quite lively. Why weren't all these people at bars in the centre of town? Why were they all out here, near the interstate? We took some seats at the bar and ordered some food. The other customers all appeared to be playing some quiz with electronic screens that were mounted into the bar. We were unclear how it all worked and got chatting to two guys next to us. After they explained that it was a quiz (or trivia) that was being done centrally across loads of bars and that you participated on the screen in your own local bar, they made a sudden realisation.

"But you guys are British?"

"That's right," I answered.

"What the heck are you doing here?" one of them asked.

"We're driving Laura Glinski's car back to her," Jack added, almost deliberately unhelpfully. We then went on to explain about our journey and the driveaway to California.

"This calls for shots!" We weren't clear why it called for shots, but we obliged them and spent the rest of the evening drinking with our new friends.

Soon enough the bar was closing and we had to leave. They were surprised to find we would be walking back to our motel and insisted on driving us. We accepted even though it was only about two minutes in the car and the guy was a bit drunk. Again it struck me as odd that they had driven out to the interstate to get drunk, only to have to drive back into the city. Just before they dropped us off they began arguing about how much they'd spent on shots. We were in the back and it started to get awkward.

"Yeah but I was just trying to show the British guys a good time!" one of them practically shouted.

"Why did so we spend so freaking much?"

I tried to defuse the tension, "Guys we did have a great time, we really appreciated it."

"Well that's something," the angrier one said. We stopped at a red light on a quiet road and Jack spotted our opportunity to leave, "Actually our motel is just there," he gestured and opened the door. "We did have a great time guys, here's $10," and gave one of them the note. We both got out of the car.

"Well that was weird," he said.

"As always," I replied and we made our way to the motel.

Somewhat drunk and lively we returned to our crack den of a motel. We had some beers left in the room and decided to keep drinking. We played some poker and were talking and joking loudly. Before long we decided to put on some music through Jack's Macbook. We turned the volume up and began singing along loudly. All of a sudden there was a BANG BANG BANG on the door. A middle-aged man shouted through.

"What in the hell is going on in there? Quit the goddamn noise!"

Jack and I froze, and he jumped to turn the music down.

"Sorry" I shouted out in a meek voice.

The voice replied from the other side of the door. "I ain't coming back here, the next call I make is to the police!" We looked at each other horrified, this sounded a bit serious. Jack ran to the door and opened it. The guy looked angry.

He pointed at me, "This is a single occupancy room! What the hell is he doing in here?" he continued to gesture accusingly.

Jack tried to mollify him, "Ah yes, he's my acquaintance and is simply visiting, he'll be leaving shortly."

"Well it better be soon and he better be goddamn quiet about it!" The guy huffed.

"Most assuredly he will be," Jack said in an increasingly posh English accent.

"Well good," the guy said as he began to calm down. He gathered himself for one final rebuke, "but if I hear another peep, it's the goddamn police that'll come a-knocking." With that he slammed the door. We stayed frozen as we heard the steps retreating and then fell about laughing.

27. Washington: Popular culture

We continued west into the Pacific Northwest region. It lies west of the Rockies, bordered on the northern side by Canada and comprises all of the West Coast that's north of California. We visited Washington State first, not to be confused with Washington DC (which stands for District of Columbia). Apparently before it became a state, the territory of Washington State was called Columbia (being named after the local Columbia River). On being granted statehood in 1889 the name was changed to Washington, *so that people wouldn't confuse the state with Washington, District of Columbia*. Yet they chose to change its name from Columbia to *Washington*. Ongoing confusion between Washington DC and Washington State seems to be about the only thing they did achieve. How few brain cells did the people in that meeting have?

The biggest city of the region is Seattle, situated on an inlet of the Pacific coast only 100 miles south of the Canadian border. At first glance it seemed a little unkempt and grungy. There were lots of hippy cafes, a fair amount of graffiti, quite a few bums hanging about on the street corners, not typical homeless people, but drifters, the type of people openly smoking a spliff, but who might still ask you for spare change. Washington is one of two states (Colorado the other) to have legalised marijuana. Twenty-three states have legalised marijuana for medicinal use.

In Washington they have licensed shops to sell up to an ounce of marijuana to any citizen over the age of 21. Both states that have legalised marijuana have done so after a referendum, so it has been the will of the people (rather than the politicians) that has caused the change. However, one consequence for the state governments is that the taxes on the sale of marijuana are very lucrative. This is great for the individual states because they tend to be cash-strapped and reluctant to raise any other taxes. Estimates suggest the income is in the order of a hundred million dollars every year for each state. However, at the national level marijuana is still completely illegal, which puts these states in direct conflict with the federal government. They seem pretty chilled out about it though (although that might not be surprising, given what they're smoking there.)

Despite its grungy appearance I liked Seattle. It's right up against the water, it's got that West Coast free spirit and the museums were excellent. Being a modern city, founded in the late 19th century, its outlook is very different to the East Coast. Seattle has experienced three big booms during its 140 or so year history. The first was the Klondike gold rush back when Seattle was still really a frontier town, with an economy based on logging. In 1896 reports filtered through that gold had been found in Alaska. Since Seattle was the gateway to the Northwest, gold prospectors flocked to the town before making the treacherous journey north to Alaska. We learnt about the gold rush at the excellent little museum in the city centre. The story seemed very similar to that of Deadwood: although the only real way to get rich in the gold rush was to either be very lucky or set up a business selling supplies to the prospectors.

Seattle boomed again during World War 2 as Boeing, the aircraft company that's based in the city, began to expand significantly. After this, it wasn't until the late 80's and early 90's that it really experienced another boom, this time in both technology and culture. Bill Gates headquartered his tiny operation - Microsoft - in the Seattle area and its success was phenomenal. Other technology companies like Amazon and mobile phone companies followed suit.

From a cultural perspective though Seattle had never been the hippest place to be; yes it had a small and respected jazz scene and had given the world Jimi Hendrix but its cultural influence was still negligible. American music continued to be centred in California, New York and to a lesser extent, Chicago, Detroit, New Orleans, Memphis and Nashville. In the early 90's though, the rock band Nirvana were pioneering a new wave of music called grunge and the Seattle-based scene took the world by storm. Culturally they put the city on the map.

Seattle's technological boom and its music explosion are combined in the seriously impressive EMP – Experience Music Project Museum, founded and funded by Seattle native, Paul Allen (co-founder of Microsoft). It celebrates modern culture with massive exhibits on Seattle's musical legacy (with huge displays focusing on both Nirvana and Jimi Hendrix). After seeing so many excellent but traditional museums in the US (especially in Washington DC) it was really great to see a museum which dealt with modern culture rather than history and it didn't do it in a whizzy or tongue-in-cheek way. I really appreciated the way it took a really serious look at the cultural impact of Nirvana (and the grunge wave) and the immense guitar talents of Jimi Hendrix, along with a host of other interesting exhibits.

We left the museum and walked back through the city. Down a side street we could see a crowd gathering near a hotel. Being fond of having a nose-about when something interesting is going on I gestured to Robyn that we head down the street.

"But why?" she protested.

"Because something's going on!" I said, amazed I had to argue the point.

"Well, what specifically is going on?" she said, unmoving.

"I don't know what, but that's the point. They wouldn't all be gathered if it wasn't *something!*"

She relented and we walked down the street. We approached the crowd and I asked a guy what was happening.

"I don't really know but I think something's going to be happening *real* soon," he said enthusiastically. Robyn arched an eyebrow at me. I pressed on and found someone else to ask. The next person told us, "I think someone famous is about to arrive at that hotel."

"Who?" I asked her, pressing her for more information.

"I don't know, but it's got to be someone pretty famous, look how big the crowd is."

It was literally a self-fulfilling crowd. Some people had gathered – for whatever reason – and now more idiots like me had come along, not wanting to miss out. After some more asking around, we found out that some people were speculating it was the American football team, the Dallas Cowboys, who were in town to play the Seattle Seahawks. Others thought it might be some country music star who was playing in town that night. After about half an hour some of the crowd wavered and a few started to leave, although they were regularly replaced by newcomers who had been enticed by the prospect that there *must* be something interesting about to happen.

"Can we go now?" Robyn said, restless.

"But we've waited all this time now," I reasoned.

"Exactly, we've already wasted half an hour."

"We can't go now! What if they turn up as we leave?" I neglected to address the other half of that point, which is what would happen if no one turned up.

"Ugh fine – 20 more minutes."

"Come on, I know you want to see the Dallas Cowboys," I said pleased, misjudging her mood.

"We don't even know if it is the bloody Dallas Cowboys! It could be some country music person who we're not even going to recognise," she said, exasperated.

"Yeah, but at least we'll have seen them," I retorted weakly.

In the end it was someone very famous (Bill Clinton) so I felt partly vindicated. *On the other hand* he was whisked through in the back of a Range Rover in about 10 seconds and didn't stop for the crowd, so I wouldn't exactly say it was holiday time well spent, and I'm pretty sure Robyn wouldn't either.

As well as its modern outlook and culture, Seattle's food scene is very different from the pizzas, hot dogs and European immigrant influences of the East Coast and Midwest. Seattle is famous for two things food-wise – fish in the Pike Place Market – where the fishmongers inexplicably throw fish quite long distances between the counters to each other. I'm unsure why walking is a problem for them, but the throwing of the fish has become a rather strange tourist attraction. The other famous Seattle food and drink export is Starbucks coffee.

Fun fact alert! Originally the company was going to be called Pequod, after the whaling ship from the book *Moby Dick*, but this name was rejected by some of the co-founders. Instead the company was named after the chief mate on the Pequod - Starbuck. Names aside, Starbucks itself is a phenomenon; its rapid expansion means that it is undoubtedly one of the best known brands in the world. Starbucks opened in 1971 and only had one store all the way through until 1984! At that point they expanded slowly and then from the late 80's they started expanding at a much faster rate. In fact if you average out their expansion from 1987 till today – they've opened at a rate of about two stores *every single day for nearly twenty years* meaning they now have more than 20,000 stores worldwide. Aarrgh. That sounds like world domination to me.

What can I say about Starbucks? Well they're good business people; I think that much is unarguable. We went along to the first Starbucks store, next to Pike's Place Market and even that seemed like a good business for them. People were queuing out of the door! Regardless, when I got to the counter I continued my proud tradition of ignoring the Starbucks words for different sizes "primo", "venti" etc. I use a tried and tested technique, called English, and use the words "small", "medium" or "large". It seemed to work and Robyn and I enjoyed two Americanos as we walked around the market.

* * *

Jack and I continued pressing westwards; we left Texas and reached New Mexico, undoubtedly a western state in outlook. After a while the scenery began to improve dramatically, the brown flat scrub land that had been with us for hundreds and hundreds of miles began to transform into a desert. We began to see little hills and the earth turned a kind of pinkish yellow. Eventually we saw cactuses. Neither of us had ever seen them in the wild before. We were overjoyed by this change in scenery and decided to pull over and go for a walk. We'd been in the car for hours and fancied a leg stretch. We took the first side road we saw.

As we drove down the empty road, we could see there was absolutely nothing around us, no signs of life and the traffic from the main road was now a mile behind us in the distance. In England there are a lot of public footpaths where people have right of way to walk, even through private land. This is not the case in the US, where private land is private land. We stopped the car and got out. There was a thin barbed wire line, demarcating the edge of the road from the desert in front of us.

"Do you think we're allowed in there?" I asked Jack.

"Of course we are! We're just going for a little walk, aren't we?" he replied. I wasn't sure; there was the barbed wire for a start and I could see a little sign hanging from it, a good way in the distance.

"There's a sign over there Jack". I strained to read it, "I think it says Keep Out." I was unsure now.

"Just don't look at it Boss," Jack replied cheerfully, as he went underneath the barbed wire.

We walked up the hill. It was pleasant to be in the fresh air after all that time in the car. The terrain rolled out before us, with ridges as far as we could see. The main road stretched off, arrow-straight into the distance. We could see the strong sunlight glinting off the cars; they looked tiny in the distance. The landscape was dotted with cactuses. They were various shapes and sizes; they were pretty big (compared to what I'd seen in say a garden centre), but weren't comically large like I'd seen in old Westerns. I inspected one that was close by. It was curious-looking, almost fuzzy, but on closer inspection, you could see the needles. Unthinkingly, drawn like a moth to a flame, my hand reached towards the cactus. I suppose subconsciously my brain was simultaneously thinking *"Those needles look pretty sharp"* but also thinking *"I wonder just how sharp they are?"* On autopilot my brain elected to use the power of touch to get to the bottom of the issue. I felt a sharp pricking on my finger, my brain snapped to attention and I looked down - my finger was bleeding.

The bleeding wasn't bad, no worse than being pricked by a large pin, but my brain suddenly went into overdrive: *"Are cactuses poisonous?" "Why the heck did I just deliberately prick myself on a cactus?" "Where's the nearest town for medical advice?" "Did our Lonely Planet have a section on how dangerous the cactuses are?" "If not, why not?" "Would I be able to recognise this particular cactus, amongst all the different cactuses, in the Lonely Planet dangerous cactus section?" "Who would I leave all my possessions to, now that I was done for?"*

Back in the car, I demanded we go to the nearest town where I could ask someone at a pharmacy whether they were poisonous. Jack was being typically unhelpful.

"I wouldn't worry. Look, either it's not poisonous and you'll be fine, or it is poisonous and it's already in your bloodstream. Right? So not point worrying is there?" he was smiling again, pleased with how annoying he was. If I had a cactus right there I would have smacked him around the head with it. Instead I glared at him and muttered, "Not funny."

A few miles down the road we reached the outskirts of a town. As we drove through it started to resemble a Wild West town, the road opened into a big wide main street. Some of the shops had wooden fronts. We drove along and finally spotted a pharmacy. We walked in and I tried to seem unconcerned and unhurried. I approached the counter, where the pharmacist, a youngish woman, was looking at some prescriptions.

"Say, I was wondering if you could give me some advice."

She looked and up replied, "Certainly sir, how can I help?"

"Well," I said, unsure how to say it, "I'm afraid I just pricked myself on a cactus and I was rather wondering whether that would be a problem...you know, if it was poisonous or anything?"

"Why did you do that?" she asked, puzzled.

"Well I didn't do it on purpose!" I said haughtily, even though I clearly did do it on purpose - but I wasn't about to tell her that.

"Well, gee sir, I can't say that I know for sure, I'll get the senior pharmacist," She toddled away, in no particular hurry, and after a time the senior pharmacist emerged. He was a late middle-aged guy with greying hair. He was polite and spoke slowly.

"What seems to be the problem sir?" he asked in a vaguely concerned manner. I could tell that the lady had already told him my story but for reasons unknown he wanted me to repeat it. Perhaps he thought I was crazy. After I'd related my story to him he paused for a second and then said, "I'm really not sure if the cactuses are poisonous."

I was exasperated, "Don't any of you know whether cactuses are poisonous? You're the ones who live around here! They're everywhere!"

"Yes sir, but we don't normally tend to go around poking them."

28. Oregon: Pioneers

Robyn and I continued south down the coast to Oregon, also part of the Pacific Northwest region. Oregon is often overlooked by tourists but it has quite a lot to offer. Similarly to neighbouring Washington State it has a rather modernist liberal outlook in the cities but also vast rural swathes away from the coast in the interior. The rural towns seem to be mostly populated by lumberjacks and their associates. When I tried to search the internet for lumberjack food the only reference I found was that lumberjacks "won reputations for consuming large amounts of food", and you have to remember they won that reputation *in America*. So I can only imagine their consumption was pretty impressive. Apart from this info on the quantity of food there was no further information about what lumberjacks actually ate.

As we headed further into Oregon we veered away from the coast and went inland to Crater Lake National Park. Crater Lake is the deepest lake in the US and the 9th deepest in the world. What's interesting is that it's actually in the caldera of a volcano. Basically a volcano blew its top and the eruption hollowed it out, then water filled it in to create this really deep lake. Since the lake is in the "crater" of the volcano, the surface of the lake itself is actually higher than ground level below the volcano. As you drive up to it you're driving up the sides of the (extinct) volcano and you don't get a view of the lake until you go over the rim and look down into it. It's an amazing sight, the colour is such a pure blue and it is framed on all sides by the crater of the volcano.

We pulled up and were greeted by this phenomenal sight. Unfortunately we were not the only ones there. The sun was high in the sky and I don't think I'd ever seen a lake such a deep blue before. I'd certainly never seen a lake in the crater of a volcano before. It was impressive. However, all I could hear was a group of idiots yabbering away.

"Look at that dumb pigeon!"
"Dropped his piece of food. Huhuhuh."
"Stupid pigeon."
"Look at it now, near the tree."
"What a dumbass. Huhuhuh."

It was drivel. It was the most ridiculous nonsense, conducted at a volume level that I couldn't help but hear. The whole time I was trying to reset my mind on the amazing vision in front of me and all I could hear was the wittering of a group of Neanderthals. Their group almost certainly contained more people than brain cells. Clearly they had seen the view five minutes before, got bored and had then collectively turned their attention to a pigeon - something they could see anywhere in the world. It was beyond annoying. I felt like using them as guinea pigs to find out whether it was indeed the deepest lake in the US. Instead, being British, we simply glared at them and drove off.

We did enjoy some marvellous walks around the crater rim, with great views at every turn. It's certainly an arrestingly situated lake and was well worth the trip. We finished our walk and returned to the car. We drove on and later we passed a ghost town. Ghost towns are towns that have been abandoned (or mostly abandoned) because of economic factors (i.e. the jobs dried up) or because of manmade or natural disasters. The US has a lot of them, especially in the rural Great Plains and even in places like rural Oregon, where in many areas the population is still about a third less than it was in the 1920s. It was interesting because people had emigrated to these towns and then decided to uproot themselves again and move on (often pushing west).

A lot of settlers who went to the West Coast were already living in the US (as opposed to foreign immigrants). The West Coast (and Western half of the US) was not settled for the most part for over 100 years after the East Coast had been settled. In many cases these people who went West or "pioneers", as they were often called, were European immigrants or children and grandchildren of immigrants. It was striking that they or their recent relatives had already uprooted themselves from Europe to the US and then they chose to go West and uproot themselves again. The "Oregon Trail" was one of the most popular routes that pioneers from the eastern part of the US (east of the Mississippi River) would use to travel west. The trail, which was 2,200 miles over often difficult terrain, was first cut by fur trappers and then later used by the pioneers. Some stopped along the way to take advantage of US government incentives to encourage people to start farming the interior, in many cases prospective settlers were given hundreds of acres for free, if they were willing to farm it. Others wanted to go all the way to the West Coast.

The Oregon Trail was a pretty treacherous route. The pioneers rode in their wagons across sometimes hostile, and in some cases unexplored, territory. The trail was used by approximately half a million people between the 1830s and 1870s, at which point the railroad arrived and the final territories became states. While the trail was operating a lot of the land was still disputed, for the most part a lot of it was still inhabited by Native Americans (bear in mind that Little Bighorn happened in 1876). If you were travelling with your wagon on the trail in the 1850s then this really was the Wild West and you ran the risk of Native American attack, bandits and any number of accidents. However, increasing government control of the area and European diseases continued to decimate the Native Americans.

These pioneers found themselves in the "new world", but still had the inclination and motivation to upsticks and move again, despite the prospect of hardship and significant risks in making the journey. Various things drove the pioneers west: opportunity, land, the prospect of riches (e.g. the San Francisco gold rush) and even religious freedom (the Mormons).

The original Oregon Trail finished close to modern day Portland, twenty miles or so inland from the Pacific Coast. We visited Portland, which is now the largest city in Oregon. It struck us as hippy-ish, modernist and positively European: everyone seemed to be cycling, while organic and vegetarian food was everywhere. Portland even has a food tradition all of its own – food trucks. Portland has hundreds of them and there is a definite scene with various websites like *Food Carts Portland* and *Cart Attack* cataloguing all the different carts and giving recommendations. But these aren't your usual burger vans or chip vans that clutter up festivals, fairs and increasingly the car parks of DIY and home improvement stores. No, these food trucks are gourmet delights and there are an estimated 700 of them in Portland.

The food carts tend to cluster in outdoor food cart courts (often just a parking lot). The one we went to had at least twenty carts, so it was a little bit like a food court in a mall, except it was outside and possible to get something healthy. All the carts were brightly painted or decorated and looked very individual. They were like a collection of gypsy caravans. Each one seemed to be serving something tantalising and delicious. You could get a fresh smoothie mixed at one, Vietnamese street food at another and handmade chocolate at a third. The food cart culture really symbolises Portland's pro-independent, green-minded, liberal culture, standing in stark contrast to the dominance of chain restaurants in a lot of other cities.

In the end I had some kind of guava smoothie, which was mixed in front of me by a hippy (which is clearly the way a guava smoothie should be made). After that we approached a silver bullet looking caravan. In this one we actually went inside to order. It was a Norwegian themed food cart called "Viking Soul Food". That's right, it was Norwegian. That's not normal restaurant diversity. That's the kind of diversity you'd only get at the UN. Robyn had a meatball wrap while I went for a salmon wrap, with seasoning that the woman assured me was "Nordic". It was delectable and light and left enough space to take advantage of the homemade chocolates afterwards.

* * *

After my brush with death with the cactus, which by and large are not poisonous (they rely on their spines to keep people away, although clearly that doesn't keep *everyone* away), Jack and I kept on driving west. We stopped for a night in Santa Fe, the capital of New Mexico. It's a curious city. Early in the 20th century it was economically threatened when they diverted the railroad away. It was isolated and at risk of becoming a ghost town. Because of its significant historic past the city government decided that tourism would be the way to revive the city (this was pretty revolutionary, given it was only 1912 – there weren't many Japanese bus tours to attract back then). They imposed a uniform building style on the city – called the Spanish Pueblo Revival look – in order to maintain the historic heritage of the city and thus encourage tourism.

The city government decreed that all the buildings would be built out of adobe, a natural material made from sand, clay and water to match the original buildings. So everywhere we looked in Santa Fe all the buildings were in this yellow smooth adobe coating with wooden beams exposed on the outside. It was very distinctive and very traditional all at once. It suited the desert surroundings and brought home the strong Spanish and Native American traditions of the area.

Jack and I took a tour to check out the architecture and art scene that Santa Fe is now famous for. Unfortunately our tour guide suffered from a condition I call *robot voice*. Clearly he had given the tour so many times, that he had become the human equivalent of a tape on repeat. It was hard to make sense of. Every word, sentence and fact blurred into one impenetrable monotone. Luckily, the vistas of the city, combined with the desert and mountains in the distance, were more than enough to make the tour worthwhile.

Jack and I left New Mexico and entered Arizona. The desert continued rolling on by and always made for interesting viewing as opposed to the scrub and farmland of the earlier part of the trip. We were heading to Flagstaff, the closest town to the Grand Canyon. We'd been on the road for over a week and felt like a night out.

We arrived in Flagstaff, it wasn't much to look at. It was clearly a town that made its living through tourism for the Grand Canyon and the railroad. Unfortunately the railroad had been driven right through the middle of the town. This meant every thirty minutes or so huge freight trains would pile through the town, literally shaking its foundations. We arrived at the hostel, tried to check in and were told that it was full but they had another building elsewhere that we would be staying in. A minor annoyance, but one we could cope with.

After we'd settled and unpacked our stuff at the other hostel, we were ready to hit the town. It was a weekend night, but nevertheless we were surprised by just how busy it was. It turned out that it was "Cinco de Mayo" (literally 5th of May in Spanish). We hadn't realised but Cinco de Mayo is like St. Patrick's Day, but for Mexicans. What this means is that (exactly like St. Patrick's) everyone goes out drinking. The only real difference is everyone is drinking Corona beer instead of Guinness. A handful of people had also decided to go for the optional extra: the comically large sombrero.

Arizona (and the other Southwest states – New Mexico, California and Texas) are heavily influenced by their Spanish/Mexican past. This part of the US was originally Spanish territory, called "New Spain" in the first half of the 19th century. Spain then gave this territory to the newly independent Mexico. It was only following the Mexican-American war in 1848 that the territories were incorporated into the US.

Gradually these territories were turned into new states during the westward expansion and Arizona was the last to be granted statehood (not until 1912).

The Spanish-Mexican heritage can be seen everywhere in the region, from the architecture, the place names, to the people. A lot of the residents are descended from those who were living in the area while it was still part of Mexico in 1848. When the US incorporated the territory following the war they moved the border hundreds of miles south and lots of people found themselves suddenly living in the US. The Southwest has also been one of the areas that has attracted the highest levels of Hispanic immigration. This has reinforced the existing cultural legacy; as a result 24% of people in New Mexico speak Spanish as a first language (21% in Arizona). Therefore if anyone in the US is going to take the Mexican holiday of Cinco de Mayo seriously then it's going to be the people in Arizona and the Southwest.

Unaware of any of the history but nevertheless conscious that everyone around us was drinking Coronas, Jack and I were happy to get into the spirit of it. The bars were packed, people were friendly, everyone was in party mood. We hit a couple of bars and found ourselves attached to a group who suggested we move on to another bar. This one was even livelier than the previous one. A band started up on the stage, two of them had the comedy sombreros on, one even had a joke "Mexican" moustache. This won them instant favour with the crowd.

We drank more with our new friends, another bucket of Coronas was bought and before long we were dancing. We had a great time and the band finished at about 1am, although a DJ continued. I was tired and full of Corona; I was ready to go home, I asked Jack if he wanted to go but he seemed keen to continue talking to a girl he had been with for a while. We only had one key for our room. I am forever perplexed about why some hotels will only give you one key for a room when there are two of you – are keys that precious? They give you two glasses, two towels, two breakfasts, but only one key!? I told him to knock on the door when he got back.

After a couple of hours of drunken sleep I woke up. I looked at the clock - it blinked 3:50am. I looked over and Jack wasn't there. *This is unusual,* I thought. *Ah well, he can look after himself.* I closed my eyes and tried to get back to sleep. I kept trying, but my mind started to wander. *What if he couldn't get in to the hostel because he didn't have a key? What if he'd gone to the first hostel and couldn't remember that we'd switched to this one? What if he'd been pricked by a poisonous cactus?* None of them seemed likely, but I still felt a nagging guilt. It was 2005 and we were in a foreign country so we didn't have mobile phones. I couldn't get back to sleep so I felt I should probably get up and look for him. "Stupid idiot," I muttered as I put my shoes on.

First I went back to the bar, but it had closed long before so I wandered past the other bars. Most were shut and the last one seemed to be kicking out.

The final few revellers swayed by, beers in hand, comedy sombreros by now badly askew. I decided to go to the first hostel to see if Jack had gone there by mistake. I let myself in to the common room. There was no one there. I left and unsure what else to do, returned to our hostel. It was now after 4.30am, I decided to put a shoe in the door, so he could open it if he returned and went back to sleep.

The sun was streaming in the window, I woke up and looked over – there he was, in the bed. He was awake and grinning.
"Good morning Boss," he said, cheerily.
"Where the hell were you last night? I asked grumpily.
"I was talking to that girl, you know that," he said. I explained my night time adventures looking for him. Surprised, he explained how he had been with the girl for a few hours and then had returned to the hostel. The front door had been locked so he slipped through an open window in the common room and then found our room door propped open with the shoe.
"It's funny how you went to the other hostel, because I didn't go there at all," he said.
"Yeah hilarious," I said. "Where exactly did you go with the girl when the bar closed?"
"She invited me to the skate park," he said. It was a strange answer as we were talking about the early hours of the morning.
"What do you mean, skate park?"

"Yeah, well I was thinking it was odd. I was thinking, maybe, you know..." he smiled.

"I know what you were thinking."

"I was thinking that maybe she was thinking...you know."

"I know."

"But that's not what she was thinking."

"No? What was she thinking?" I was interested now.

"She was thinking...let's go to the skate park."

"And?"

"She was thinking about what you normally do at a skate park - she had her skateboard."

"Sounds kinky," I said.

"It really wasn't."

"What did you think?"

"I didn't know what to think! I mean, she got her skateboard out and we skated."

"While I was running around Flagstaff at 4am?" I said, still annoyed.

"Yeah," he said smiling.

"I wouldn't have minded going skating," I said.

29. Arizona: Geology

Robyn and I began the final part of our journey by driving down through Utah and into Arizona. There are a wealth of National Parks in the area, from the megafamous (Grand Canyon) pretty famous (Arches, Zion and Death Valley) to the almost completely unknown (Carlsbad Caverns and Capitol Reef). The scenery is absolutely fabulous. On a whim and just because it looked close (close in this part of the world is anything under a 100 mile detour) we went to Capitol Reef National Park. It was phenomenal and I've never even heard anyone even mention it. These parks contain some of the most fantastic geological wonders that you're ever likely to see and they're almost unheard of outside the region.

The general area is known as Red Rock country, and it really is. The scenery from the road was impressive but when we drove into Capitol Reef, a huge wall of red rock rose high above us. It was immediately obvious why they call it a reef; it's like a ribbon of rock that stretches off into the distance. It's actually a "geologic monocline" or in layman's speak, a wrinkle on the surface of the earth, but one that is nearly 100 miles long. It's the scale of these geological features that is so astounding.

As well as the incredible natural features, there's a lot of cave art, drawn by Native people around 3,000 years ago. These people irrigated crops like lentils, maize and squash and even stored grain in granaries, so they were pretty advanced. They weren't great artists though - pictures of stick-men? I mean come on.

I'm joking of course, it was really interesting to see the cave art and the depictions of people that were literally drawn thousands and thousands of years ago.

The Southwest is one of the few places where there are still sizeable numbers of Native Americans. In New Mexico, they comprise 10% of the population, with Navajo the third most spoken language in the state (after English and Spanish). In Arizona they comprise about 5% of the population. After Capitol Reef we proceeded on to the Navajo Nation and Monument Valley. The Valley is like a National Park except it is owned by the Navajo Native Americans. The valley is iconic, it's instantly recognisable and has been featured in dozens of films, from John Wayne westerns to *Easy Rider* to *Forrest Gump*. When you think of the American West you probably imagine Monument Valley. It's dotted with immense sandstone buttes (isolated hills, with vertical sides – they almost look like huge columns) that rise majestically from the pink-red desert floor.

The Navajo Nation is the largest Native-American governed territory in the US. It's huge; most of it is in Arizona, but it spreads into Utah and New Mexico. If it was a state, it would be bigger than the 10 smallest states. It has its own judicial system and police force and social services. It was created in 1868 (at a similar time to a lot of the other reservations), while Native Americans were still getting a very raw deal from the US government. Despite the creation of these reservations, native peoples continued to receive questionable treatment from the government. Even as late as the Second World War, some states (including Arizona) had "Indian schools" which were designed to assimilate Native Americans into American culture. Children were sometimes enrolled against their parents' wishes and attempts were made to suppress their Native American identities, giving them English names and cutting their long hair.

A lot of the shared history between Native Americans and the modern day US is extremely sad. The Trail of Tears – the forced relocation of Native Americans in the Eastern part of the US to Oklahoma in 1830 – is one particularly egregious example. Tens of thousands of Native Americans were forced out of their ancestral homelands to open up their lands for white settlement. Thousands died along the route. Elsewhere Native Americans in the West were forced on to reservations and later there was the forced assimilation through the Indian schools. It's still being resolved - in 2014 the Navajo won a legal landmark case and were awarded over $500 million as the US federal government had been mismanaging their lands and funds for decades.

We drove through the Navajo Nation and it wasn't an especially uplifting experience. The cars looked old, some were rusting in front of small and modest houses. It was a little unkempt and looked down-at-heel. It's a difficult dilemma for Native Americans who are trying to maintain a community and their traditions while living in places where the economic opportunities are limited. We saw a lot of Native Americans near Monument Valley trying to make a living selling trinkets and souvenirs. We ate in the only restaurant we could find (a McDonald's) and the place didn't feel unfriendly, but it doesn't say a lot that the only place to eat was a McDonald's.

On the plus side, tribes like the Navajo are finally putting the conflicts with the federal government behind them and being granted increasing autonomy. This is empowering them to take decisions for their communities. However, they struggle with internal politics like anywhere else. Certain jobs on the territory require complete fluency in Navajo. Unfortunately many of the younger generation aren't fluent, it's being lost as the older generation dies out. These restrictions in turn encourages some younger Navajo to move away. That said, the Navajo Nation has a population of 300,000 and it is young – the median age is in the early twenties. So there is definitely an opportunity for Native American populations to thrive in 21st century America, if they can seize it.

Robyn and I continued to the Grand Canyon. The Grand Canyon is a phenomenal sight and hard to describe. When you first come close to the rim and look over the edge into the canyon it genuinely takes a while to get your perspective right. In normal life your eyes just don't have to deal with that much space. The opposite rim seems really far away (and on average it's about 10 miles apart) but it's the cavernous space that you are looking down into that is so hard to comprehend.

The canyon itself was caused by the flow of the Colorado River. Over millions of years it cut a gorge, which got deeper and wider and longer (it's over 270 miles long). Scientists still dispute exactly how it formed, but fascinatingly, the canyon is so deep that it exposes rock layers that are nearly 2 billion years old. That's nearly half the age of the earth, so you can literally see the history of the world in the canyon walls if you hike to the bottom. However, it does take a full day's hike to reach the river on the canyon floor.

The walks along the rim were fantastic and while the visitor centres were busy, a 15 minute walk took us away from the crowds. We went to a talk on the endangered California Condor, a vulture that became extinct in the wild in 1897. Fortunately some were kept in captivity and had been reintroduced to a couple of places in the US (including the Grand Canyon). A knowledgeable Park Ranger was giving her talk on the reintroduction and how to spot them. She was describing how a lot of people spot what they think are Condors, but are actually just regular vultures, since the Condors are still very endangered and very rare. At that moment as if on cue, a Condor appeared, flying over the Canyon. It was a true pantomime moment as someone pointed out "it's behind you." Her scepticism turned to astonishment as the group evaporated and went to the rim to watch the majestic Condor soaring and wheeling above the canyon.

Robyn and I drove on to Flagstaff, the scene of my adventures with Jack 10 years before. We were keen to try some Mexican food, which is very common across the Southwest. We didn't have any special place in mind, so went to the first Mexican restaurant we could find. We ordered and were chatting away.

"So anyway, she got out the skateboard and he said that apparently she just wanted to go for a skate. Weird, huh?" She raised an eyebrow and looked unimpressed. I changed topic and we discussed our order. This particular restaurant, like a lot of Mexican restaurants in the US, veered more to Tex-Mex cuisine rather than traditional Mexican cuisine. Americans love Mexican food, but as in Britain where we have adapted Indian cuisine to our own tastes, Americans have done the same thing with Mexican food. Some dishes in Tex-Mex cuisine aren't really Mexican but instead were invented in Texas and the Southwest (e.g. fajitas and chili con carne). Other much more authentic Mexican dishes such as enchiladas, tacos and burritos are often served with an American twist. Typically this is characterised by a heavier use of grated cheese, meat and beans.

Robyn's eyes wandered down the menu and her face lit up. Everything seemed to come with cheese, which was ideal from her perspective.

"I think I might have the fajitas, what are you going to have?" I asked.

"Enchiladas, they sound great," she said happily.

"Oh yeah, why's that?" I asked.

"It says they are covered in cheese!" she said gleefully.

"Everything's covered in cheese," I replied.

"We should eat Mexican more often," she said simply, as if the logic of the plentiful cheese made it an unarguable point. To mitigate the incoming cheese we agreed on guacamole and tortilla chips to start, since it sounded like the healthiest thing on the menu.

A waiter came over and he made the guacamole in front of us at the table. I've seen this a couple of times in Mexican restaurants. I've always found it impressive, because, firstly, you know that it's as fresh as can be, and secondly, it's quite cool to watch it being made. Good guacamole is basically just mashed ripe avocados and seasoning (finely chopped tomato, onion, garlic and other ingredients are optional extras). Guacamole was first invented by the Aztecs at least 500 years ago, so it has a pretty good pedigree as a Mexican food. It's now also very popular in the US as a dip, with sales peaking on two days in particular: Super Bowl Sunday and Cinco de Mayo. This particular guacamole was zesty, fresh and with quite a kick.

The enchiladas and fajitas that followed were duly cheesy and meaty. It was a feast and by the end I was overly stuffed. I looked down at the empty plate. I realised, half with satisfaction and half with disappointment, that I'd stopped noticing the very large portion sizes in the US a long time ago. We made the huge effort of rising from the table and wandered out into the night.

* * *

Jack and I were making the same journey from Flagstaff to the Grand Canyon. Technically, according to the terms of the driveaway contract, we were not allowed to go to National Parks or drive the car on unsurfaced roads.

"Are you sure we should be going to the Grand Canyon?" I asked.

"Of course we should be!" Jack replied cheerfully.

"Yeah, but I mean the guy explicitly said we weren't allowed to go to National Parks."

Jack took his eyes off the road to stare at me at in the eyes. He said gravely, "It's what Laura Glinski would have wanted."

I sighed at the never-ending nonsense, "I'm serious! What if they find out?"

"Well they're not going to find out are they? I think it's fine, *What they don't know, won't hurt them.* Right? Ever heard of that?" he reasoned.

"You sound like someone pulling an insurance scam. Seriously, *What they don't know won't hurt them?* It's not much of a moral code to live by is it?"

"Well it's not so much a moral code, as just a code."

"This is my point. I just don't know about this."

"Ok, let's put it this way, do you want to go to the Grand Canyon?" he asked. He'd got me, I did want to go so I stopped protesting.

We arrived at the Grand Canyon and seeing it for the first time was awe-inspiring. We were now two and a half months into the trip and scheduled to leave in only a couple of weeks. It occurred to us that we had probably better get round to writing some postcards. Since postcards only have enough space for about 50 words, which is less than a word a day for the amount of time we'd been away, we went for some rather snappy summaries, "Weather good, driving lots, canyon big." With that job done, we departed the Grand Canyon and headed back out into the desert.

30. Nevada: A gamble

Nevada is pretty much synonymous with Las Vegas. In fact three quarters of Nevadans live in the Las Vegas area. Outside Vegas most of Nevada is a desert. Not many people choose to live there since most people think that living in a desert is a bad idea. Of course it's easy to forget amongst the dancing fountains and golf courses of Vegas that you are still in the middle of the desert, just a very unique part of it.

People first came to Nevada for the mining; even now the state is still the fourth-largest producer of gold in the world. However, mining is now a far less significant industry than tourism and gambling (the vast majority of which is centred in Vegas). Outside Vegas though, Nevada is characterised by vast swathes of emptiness, 85% of the land is federally-owned. There are all sorts of army bases, test facilities and of course the mysterious Area 51, where we all know that the government is inexplicably keeping hordes of captured extra terrestrials.

Nevada was a frontier state, even as late as the early 20th century. Hardly anyone lived there and those that did were miners. These miners were single men with time on their hands and money to spend. Perhaps inevitably the "vice industries" – gambling, prostitution and prize-fighting - flourished. In order to develop the local economy, the state government sought to capitalise on this reputation and legalised casino gambling. At this point, back in the 1930s,

Vegas was absolutely tiny, but with its relative proximity to Los Angeles (and the fact that no other states allowed gambling) it was able to attract a steady stream of visitors. From the 1940s Vegas began to grow steadily.

In the late 40's an unlikely combination of mobsters and Mormon bankers began to conspire to use Vegas casinos as a means through which to funnel large sums of money. The first to do this was the gangster Bugsy Siegel who opened The Flamingo casino (which still exists) in 1946. Bugsy died in a hail of gunfire in 1947 but the pattern was set. It was the perfect arrangement. Mobsters, millionaires and eccentrics piled into Las Vegas and a dozen more casinos were opened. By the 1950s Vegas started to use glitz and glamour to give itself a new image. Elvis Presley, Frank Sinatra and the Rat Pack were brought to Vegas to perform and visitors started turning up in their millions. Las Vegas was on the way to becoming the incredible spectacle and gambling Mecca that it is today.

Las Vegas truly is something else. Robyn and I walked down the Strip on our first evening (and the evening really is the time to see the Strip). We left our casino, Paris Las Vegas, and looked back at it. As well as the casino, with its frontage modelled on the Louvre, there was a half-scale replica of the Eiffel Tower, a two-thirds scale replica of the Arc De Triomphe and a huge old-fashioned French hot air balloon. All of this stuff was just jumbled up out the front. It looked as if the city of Paris had decided to hold a yard sale.

We turned to face the Strip and the lights of Vegas hit us immediately. Vegas is like an illusion. During the day it is difficult to tell that you are in the middle of the desert and at night it can be difficult to tell that it really is night time. There were bright lights, colourful neon and huge signs everywhere. Photography from the International Space Station shows that Las Vegas is the brightest city on earth. Las Vegas is even the main cause of light pollution in Death Valley National Park, even though it's about 100 miles away. The energy used to light, heat, cool and fuel Las Vegas doesn't even bear thinking about.

Robyn and I walked along the Strip, the main drag of Vegas. The casinos lined up next to each other in a parade of outlandishness. Each one seemed to be battling to be more over the top than the last. We walked along past The Bellagio, with its fantastic fountain show. The fountains "dance" to music from Pavarotti to Frank Sinatra. It was a fabulous show and like a lot of things in Vegas, it was free. We pressed on, stopping in The Venetian which incredibly features a reproduction of the canals of Venice. You can even ride on a gondola along the canal. It was even more impressive when I realised it was all inside and even more so when it dawned on me that it was not even on the ground floor. A canal? Inside a casino? On one of the upper floors? It boggles the mind.

We were on our way to a show. In the way that Las Vegas first started to enter the mainstream through its use of pop stars and entertainers, the shows in Las Vegas have now become a massive business. From TV magicians to residencies by singers like Celine Dion, Las Vegas hosts some seriously big names. In 2003 Celine Dion committed to three years of shows, five nights a week at Caesar's Palace. This was in a specially designed arena and earned around $400 million. Caesar's hosted over 600 Celine Dion shows, night after night, for over three years. That doesn't even bear thinking about.

Perhaps the biggest show of all in Las Vegas is Cirque Du Soleil and that's what we were on our way to see. Cirque Du Soleil is a phenomenon and tours all over the world but if anywhere is its home it's probably Vegas. There are 7 or 8 different Cirque Du Soleil shows on in Vegas at any one time. They are a fantastic and an incredible mix of circus, performance, music, stunts and much more. It's gaudy, over the top and expensive, but it's impossible not to be impressed. We went to see *"O"* which featured a 1.5 million gallon water tank on the stage. Nearly 100 performers did some of the most incredible stunts and acrobatics we'd ever seen. It was elegant and jaw-dropping at the same time.

The following evening we walked the Strip again, watching some more of the various attractions. We came to The Mirage which was the most expensive hotel-casino in the world when it was built.

Its construction in 1989 ushered in a new era of luxury showpiece casinos in Las Vegas. The Mirage featured the largest free-standing sign in the world and its unique gold windows were achieved by using actual gold dust in the tinting process. It also has an artificial volcano out the front which erupts every half an hour. They blast out the sounds of a real volcano erupting and in order to combat the smell of the burning gas apparently they pump in pina colada fragrance. Las Vegas is by turns ostentatious, incredible and ridiculous.

We proceeded on to the Treasure Island casino, just in time to see the nightly pirate show. This was a live action show with real actors on two ships outside the front of the casino. It was a bizarre spectacle; at first the rambunctious pirates were firing cannons at the sexy sirens on the other ship and the next moment, they were all dancing and singing together, as happy as could be. Firing cannons at strangers seemed like an unusual way to make friends, but hey what do I know about history?

By this time, slightly confused and definitely hungry, we decided to try the Treasure Island buffet. You really are spoilt for choice when it comes to dining in Las Vegas. Some of the finest restaurants in the country can be found in the city and every celebrity chef has a signature restaurant there. Where there's a lot of money, there's a lot of fine dining.

The real food tradition of Las Vegas is the buffet. It was originally conceived in the 1940s at the time modern Las Vegas was emerging. The El Rancho casino launched a $1 buffet, attractively priced and open at all times. It was designed to keep the gamblers in the casino and keep them gambling. In fact the "All-you-can-eat" concept, so beloved of buffets everywhere, can be traced back to Las Vegas buffets. Nowadays buffets are an absolutely essential feature of any casino. Many gamblers will choose their casino based on the quality of the buffet. Caesar's revamped their buffet in 2012 and spent $17 million on it! The buffet now features a scarcely believable 524 different choices.

    The quality, choice and cost of the buffet is generally directly connected to the quality of the casino. The more luxurious the casino (i.e. the more it costs to gamble there) the better and therefore more expensive the buffet will be. We chose Treasure Island which is a fairly midrange casino. The choice at the buffet was still phenomenal. The serving area was a huge concourse, with myriad counters and signs. Tasty-looking food was displayed everywhere, lobsters arrayed to our left, noodles sizzling to our right, shelves of pizzas in front of us.

    It's an odd thing though all that choice. You only have one stomach to fill up. Nevertheless it's tempting to try a little of everything. It's best though to have a plan of attack; go for the seafood, don't fill up on the bread, make the man on the omelette station cook something for you, save room for dessert. Regardless of how you do it, you're going to end up feeling stuffed and almost never having room for that dessert.

* * *

It was dark as Jack and I crossed the border into Nevada, but we'd heard that driving into Las Vegas at night was a striking sight. The inky black desert passed by until a golden spot on the horizon appeared. It grew bigger and brighter and soon we saw a beam of light. It was shooting straight up into the night sky. It was being projected out of the top of the pyramid-shaped Luxor casino and I learnt later that it is the strongest beam of light anywhere in the world. As we got closer we could see some of the other casinos, the tower of the Stratosphere, the huge block of the Wynn casino and the Eiffel tower of Paris. I looked at Jack and his eyes lit up.

We drove the Strip. The lights, colourful and bright, shone from every angle, the place was buzzing. Despite the fact that our battered car, the Glinski-mobile, was probably worth less than a ticket to the buffet at one of the luxury casinos, we felt cool. It was hard not to. We were on the Strip in Las Vegas. There was something instantly recognisable, but wondrous and new about it. I challenge anyone to walk or drive the Strip on their first night in Vegas and not feel a tingle of excitement. The place screamed glitz and glamour.

We checked into our lodging (unfortunately a hostel on the wrong side of the tracks rather than a five-star casino) and hit the town. We wandered from casino to casino and decided to play some blackjack, since that was the thing to do. It was a mistake and we both lost a crippling $100 each at The Mirage, which was a serious amount of money to us. Fortunately in Vegas, if you are gambling they will bring you drinks for free (if you tip the waitresses). Unfortunately if you're going to lose $100 in 15 minutes it's pretty hard to get your money's worth in terms of free drinks.

Only slightly dispirited, we decided to switch casino. We left The Mirage and headed to the much more downmarket Sahara, a vaguely Moroccan-themed casino (camel on the sign, flying carpet themed ride inside). They had a $40 poker tournament starting at 10pm. Poker was more our type of thing and we were significantly more confident, although it couldn't really go much worse than the blackjack had. We'd played a lot of poker at university, several nights a week in fact, so we were well-practised.

"This is our game Boss. I think we're going to do well," Jack said.

"Well at least I know how to play poker, so I think that puts me in a stronger position than the blackjack. How are you feeling about it?"

"Well I've been reading my Glinski book, so pretty good." He tapped his pocket, it was unclear if *David Sklansky's Theory of Poker* was in there now, but I wouldn't have bet against it.

"Do you want to go halves and share our winnings equally?" I asked. Jack looked at me sceptically and paused to consider the question for a moment.

Jack was much better at poker than me. His challenging and mischievous style of play made him tricky to play against. In our university house he used to win with such consistent and unrelenting regularity that eventually he began to feel guilty about it. Despite the small stakes we used to play for, the sheer frequency (almost inevitability) of Jack's wins meant that his earnings stacked up. Soon enough he used to start buying crates of beer for everyone out of what he called the "poker tax". My offer there and then to split our winnings in our first (relatively) big stakes game was a tough call. On the one hand, he was more likely to win than me. On the other, if we were splitting winnings it was more of a team effort. He spoke, "Ok, sure Boss, I'm happy to back you. Now let's win this thing."

The hundred or so players were split into about a dozen tables each with their own dealer. I'd never played with a dealer before. Some of the players looked like sharks, smooth gambling types, with shades, or caps, silent and tough-looking. There were a couple of more obvious tourist types, overweight, genial, wearing Hawaiian shirts or T-shirts with slogans like "Vegas Baby!" on them.

Jack's decision to back me got off to a shaky start almost immediately. I was dealt a pair of Queens on my first hand (a great starting hand) and I was forced to follow an aggressive bettor. He bet heavily before the deal of the community cards and then when they were dealt, he bet heavily again. To my dismay, he bet his total stack, which meant I needed to risk all of my chips on my very first hand. I was a cautious player and I had wanted to watch a few hands to get the lay of the land but I wasn't being given the opportunity. According to what was showing on the board, I had to call him, I couldn't fold the hand.

    I looked at him and he was staring me. I hadn't seen him play before (since this was the first hand) and so didn't have any kind of read on him. *Screw it,* I thought and called him, I put all my chips in. He turned over his cards and he had two Kings. He won the hand and all my chips. As soon as he turned them over it seemed obvious. Jack was not going to be pleased. I felt bad, but to my surprise I was immediately given the option to "rebuy", which means buying more chips to continue playing, sometimes an option in the first hour of a tournament. Being in Vegas for five hours by this point and seemingly already an inveterate gambler, I chose to "invest" another $20 and was back in.

    Fortunately the next couple of hours went a lot better for me, I accumulated chips steadily and players dropped out. When enough players had been eliminated they made the remaining ones join another table, in this way the number of tables reduced steadily. When we were down to 30 or so players, Jack came over, he was out. There was a break in the play and we chatted. It was getting serious now, there were only a few tables of players left. I asked Jack how I should play it and what Sklansky would say. Jack looked at me. "Well Sklansky would say you should only bet when you've calculated the pot odds, the implied pot odds, the stake, your table position, the size of the blind and your number of outs. But you've been drinking for about five hours now, so that might be difficult for you. My advice would just be to go for it."

In between some good cards, shrewd bets and my opponents' suicidal moves, I progressed to the final table. Now there were just eight of us. Strangely the guys in Hawaiian shirts and Vegas T-shirts had departed. These guys looked more serious, one of them spoke to the table.

"Is anyone here not from Vegas?" Only me and one other guy weren't. Clearly I was an underdog. The hands progressed and I stayed out of the big battles. One by one they fell to each other, until it was just me and another player, one-on-one.

It was about 3.30am and I was tired. I'd played hundreds of hands. I had a smaller stack of chips than he did and he tried to bully me out of our first hand, before the deal of the community cards. Lacking much will to go on, I went all in. It was a bluff really, I had a King and six, not terrible, but not good, especially not when he called me and he turned over his pair of eights, which was a much better starting hand. However, while poker is a game of skill, it also has an element of luck. The deal turned over a King and I fluked a win. I was elated, I was in pole position now and I won a tense final hand to win the tournament. I was overjoyed, Jack was delighted.

"I've won a thousand dollars Jack! I can't believe I've won."

"*We've* won a thousand! We really have!" We laughed, I didn't care.

The money was presented immediately and without ceremony. We left, it was past 4am, but if there's any city in the world where 4am is a pretty reasonable time to continue a night out, it's Las Vegas.

"What should we do now Jack?"

"Well it's Las Vegas and we've got pockets full of money. Let's go to another casino."

"Hmmmm," I was sceptical, "We lost $100 each earlier. If we keep gambling, we're going to lose all this money I've just won."

"I hear you Boss. What you're saying is we should go to a cheaper casino, so we don't haemorrhage money like last time."

"That's not quite what I'm saying, but whatever."

We were halfway along the Strip at the midrange, but still somewhat down-at-heel, Sahara casino. Up the Strip were the glitzy, glamorous casinos that had so thoroughly rinsed us earlier, down the Strip were the old casinos: smaller places that recalled Las Vegas's Wild West past, with names like

The Golden Nugget and The Gold Spike. We knew which way to go. We headed downtown and saw one casino that advertised $2 blackjack. It seemed like our kind of place. We got more drinks and toasted my success.

It was 5am but there were still people gambling. We came to one of the blackjack tables. There was a scuzzy-looking fat man in a dark, worn-out t-shirt. He had one of those caps with the foam front, it looked like he'd been wearing it non-stop since the 80's. The other man was scrawny, with a rat-tail hair style and missing teeth. They didn't look the type of men who had library cards. We started gambling and were doing a lot better than last time, not least because we knew how to play blackjack by that point.

It started to emerge that our two companions at the table were friends. The fatter one told us he was a trucker, whose truck had broken down a week ago. The scrawny one didn't say much except to guffaw at the trucker's jokes. The trucker asked us what we were doing and he was impressed by the tale of the poker win. The longer we talked to him, the less any of it made sense. Why had he been at a casino for over a week? Where was this mysterious broken-down truck? Parked in the casino multi-storey? Even more curious was the relationship between the two. It was unclear to say the least, until the conversation took an unexpected turn.

"What are you boys doing after this?" the trucker asked gruffly.

"Well, it's nearly 6am, so not much," Jack slurred.

"Do you boys want to come up to my room and have some fun?" he asked. It was incongruous. The scrawny one leered in, intrigued now. Even though I was tempted to ask him to elaborate, I don't think I really wanted to hear the answer. It didn't sound like he was talking about a friendly game of Monopoly. We declined and made our excuses to leave. It was clear that our night was over. We went outside in to the soft morning light. The sun was rising and it was time to go home.

31. California: The American Dream

Robyn and I drove into California and arrived at the giant redwoods, the tallest trees on earth. They can reach up to 380 feet (116 metres); that's longer than a football field, I mean a soccer pitch. Actually it doesn't matter because it's longer than both, whether it's soccer or American football. They were incredible. It was hard to get them in perspective when we looked at up at them, they were so tall and straight, not crooked or gnarled at all. They are also some of the oldest living things on earth, the oldest are over a thousand years old. They were 400 years-old when Joan of Arc was running around medieval France. Unfortunately 96% of the original old-growth forest was chopped down by voracious loggers in the late 19th and early 20th century. The "Save-The-Redwoods" campaign was founded in 1918. It was one of the earliest conservation efforts in the US and it's them we have to thank for what's left.

It was humbling walking amongst some of nature's grandest and oldest living things. The forest was a special place to go for a hike. It was quiet and awe-inspiring. This being America though, our car wasn't going to miss out on all the fun. Despite Robyn's protestations I made sure we went to The Drive-Thru tree, which as it says, is an opportunity to drive through a tree. Perhaps not worth $5, it was nevertheless an entertaining diversion. However, Robyn wasn't keen to stick around to watch others drive through the tree, regardless of my speculation that "someone might get stuck."

We pressed on to the Napa Valley. The US is famous not just for food (and for coffee and beer and everything else I've mentioned) but also for wine. Robyn had made the Napa Valley an absolute condition of the trip. Napa is around 40 miles long and we stayed in the north in Calistoga. Despite its proximity to San Francisco (only about an hour away) the valley is actually very rural. The area is of course fantastic for wine, which is grown throughout the valley; different microclimates within the valley even favour different wines. Sonoma, which is equally heralded for wine, is right next to Napa.

We decided to hire bikes to tour the vineyards. The bike hire place gave us a map with all the vineyards marked on and we began our leisurely pootle around, stopping wherever we pleased. The vineyards tended to charge a few dollars for a tasting, but they provided a decent flight of a few different wines, a fairly attentive server or barman and sometimes little extras like chocolate or other nibbles. At each different vineyard we asked where to go next and they were bursting with good advice. None of the vineyards were far to cycle and much to Robyn's liking the Valley was completely flat.

"Do you know? If it wasn't those pesky hills, I think would really rather enjoy cycling. It's just much easier this way," she said, happily.

"Well at least you're honest," I replied.

The weather was perfect and the scenery was idyllic. The hills jutted along each side and the fields were filled with endless neat rows of grapes. Sometimes the route called for us to ride right through the vineyards. It was the perfect way to tour the valley. Not only was it extremely pleasant but I'm not sure if the drink drive laws apply to bikes (I mean I didn't check and I know ignorance is no defence in the eyes of the law, but maybe it's different if you are both ignorant and drunk?) Not that I'm condoning drinking wine and riding a bicycle, but if you have drunk a bit and you fall off your bike into a load of grapes, I imagine they'd make a nice cushion.

Despite the lovely rural surroundings in Napa, California is actually the most populous state in the US: 1 in 8 Americans live in the state. Originally California was a territory of Mexico and following a short-lived revolution in 1846 it was even briefly independent as "The California Republic". That name is on California's state flag, even today. When it was incorporated into the US it was an almost unreachable frontier state, a few hardy people who braved The Oregon Trail and similar routes made it to the West Coast, but not many. Once the railroad arrived then California began to boom. It attracted migrants from all over the US and from outside the country.

California is also one of the most ethnically diverse states; amazingly 43% of Californians speak something other than English as a first language.

However, despite its tolerant and welcoming image now, there are some episodes it would probably rather forget, including the internment of Japanese-Americans during World War 2. When Pearl Harbor was attacked in 1941 and the US went to war with Japan the US government immediately suspected all Japanese-Americans of potentially being "the enemy within" and decided to confine them in camps for the duration of the war.

The vast majority of these Japanese-Americans were living on the West Coast, especially in California. Some had been there for several generations. In the end around 120,000 men, women and children were placed in internment camps for four years. 62% of these people were American citizens. The move was politically controversial and slightly bizarre, but was evidence of a general fear that was gripping America in wartime. The people - who were essentially imprisoned - were American citizens, but in some way, they were still perceived to be foreigners, solely on the basis of their race. Of course the US is changing now and it is no longer overwhelmingly white in the way it was during World War 2. The official classification in the census is "Non-Hispanic White" and they are still the majority in the US, but this is shrinking fast. In 2010, they still made up 64% of the population, but this has been dropping by about 5% every decade since the 70's. Hispanics are the quickest growing group, now making up 16% of the population.

This is having an interesting effect on a lot of America, from TV (plenty of Spanish language channels on US TV) to shopping (a lot of the signs in stores are in both English and Spanish) to the food (Mexican food is ubiquitous) and it is even having an effect on national politics. Hispanics are a lot more likely to vote Democrat, which is making it harder and harder for the Republicans to win the presidency, as their core vote (older white people) becomes a smaller share of the electorate. The other potential effect of this demographic change is that it might even be changing what it means to be American. Think for instance of someone born in the US, living in California, with Mexican parents and speaking Spanish at home and to some of their friends. That's no longer unusual and demonstrates how diverse America is now.

While there is significant demographic change going on, it is not spreading across the country evenly. The reality in Nebraska, New Hampshire, Iowa or a dozen other states is that they are seeing very little change; it's still overwhelmingly populated by Non-Hispanic White people. However, in areas such as the Southwest, West Coast, Texas, Florida and New York there is a disproportionate growth in the Hispanic population (and mixed race people – another fast growing segment). In these places the face of America is definitely changing.

For me California really represents the American Dream. When you think of America, odds are that consciously or subconsciously, your view is influenced by Hollywood, by TV and by music. You might think of wide freeways, big houses, beaches, surfing, deserts, road trips, rich people, you find all these things in abundance in California. It is a hopeful place though. If you walk around the towns of Southern California, the sun always seems to be shining and it looks like everyone around you is living the good life. It's no surprise that California's state motto is "Eureka!" which in Ancient Greek means "I have found it."

* * *

Jack and I approached the border to California, we'd made it. It'd been a long journey, both in the Glinski-mobile but everything before as well. To mark the occasion I suggested we played the song "California", Jack wasn't keen but I insisted. It was good, but it was a cheesy moment. The song finished and we put on Jimmy Ray for the millionth time. We agreed that this was probably the only time in the history of the universe when *Are You Jimmy Ray?* was less cheesy than the song before it.

We arrived in San Diego, about 100 miles over our limit and twenty minutes late, but Ms. Glinski didn't seem too bothered.

"Are you guys British then?" she asked.

"Yeah that's right," I replied.

"and how old are you?" she enquired, innocently enough.

"Twenty-two."

"Hmmm....the driveaway company promised me the drivers would be at least twenty-five."

"Don't worry!" Jack said, "We only crashed it twice!" he grinned, she didn't.

She took us to our hostel by the beach and we spent a relaxing few days doing nothing much in particular. It was the Southern California lifestyle, with the sun shining and lazy days spent on the beach. Before long we left for Los Angeles. By now we were only a week or so away from finishing our trip. The cabin fever had built up for a long time and it was fair to say that we were starting to get on each other's nerves. From my perspective, it didn't help that Jack seemed to take great pride in just how annoying he could be.

We returned to our hostel in LA from a day's sight-seeing and had arranged to join a walking tour that the hostel was arranging. It was starting at 6pm and it was already 5.58pm. We returned to our room to grab our stuff. We were walking up the stairs.

"Let's just be really quick, so we can make it back down to reception in time, yeah?" I said.

"No problem Boss," Jack replied.

"Oh and I need to use the bathroom." The dorm room only had one bathroom and I thought I'd better mention it, since we needed to be quick. We reached the room and I went over to my bed to put my day bag on it. In a flash, Jack ran into the bathroom, I looked up and I heard the door lock.

"Jack, what are you doing?" I asked.

He cackled madly and started singing a song about using the bathroom.

I was pissed off and shouted through to him, "What the hell is your problem?" I paused, "Why are you so deliberately annoying?"

"Don't worry I'll only be 5 minutes, then we can go straight out!" he shouted through the door.

I was beyond annoyed, "Come out now, otherwise I'm leaving."

"I'm just in the bathroom at the moment!" He began singing his bathroom song again. I'd had enough. I opened the room door, walked out and slammed it.

Perhaps we just needed some space and we decided to spend a couple of days apart. Refreshed, we made up and agreed to put 'the bathroom incident' behind us. We were into the last week of the trip and we wanted to make the most of it so we rented one final car to drive up to San Francisco. We couldn't face the Greyhound again. Back on the road we were happier. We made our way inland to Death Valley National Park, curious to see the hottest, lowest and driest place in the US.

We drove into the desert and it was astounding to think we were still in California, home of beaches and some of the most fertile farmland in the US. Out here, it was different. It was only mid-May but it was boiling hot. The average high in mid-Summer in Death Valley is 46C (114F), which we couldn't even imagine. We got out of the car and went for a walk, the desert sand looked almost white; we could see salt crystals on the surface. Our walk didn't last long, the heat was oppressive. We wondered if it was possible to both burn and melt at the same time. We didn't really want to find out, so we turned back towards the car with its precious air conditioning.

We'd had enough of being in the desert and decided to head back to the coast. As we left Death Valley we stopped at a gas station, there was a Subway restaurant there as well. I couldn't understand why anyone would live out there. It was so hot, you'd never be able to go outside and there was absolutely nothing there. Yet four hours away were some of the most idyllic conditions on earth: beaches, warm blue seas, palm trees, other people!

I wanted to shake the young guy in the gas station and tell him to get a Greyhound ticket immediately. It was hard to comprehend why he or anyone else stayed. Maybe he'd been on Greyhound before and reasoned that the prospect of a lifetime in the desert was preferable.

We reached the coast at Santa Cruz, where we relaxed at the beach and went to see the seals that live under the wharf. There was a colony of elephant seals; seemingly dozens of them lived on the wooden beams that crisscross underneath the pier. They were ungainly creatures. They were big and manoeuvred on the beams with great difficulty. When they tried to squeeze by each other, they would almost knock each other off into the rolling waves just beneath. Often they would get cross with each other and roar. It was an intriguing sight, although the unpleasant smell didn't inspire us to stick around for too long.

We reached San Francisco, our final destination. It was a great city to finish in. It's right on the water, and its multitude of hills give it a really unusual topography. It felt no matter which direction we walked, we'd be walking up a hill or down another one. It felt unique; the streets were so steep that I was amazed they could build houses on them. Sometimes it seemed like the houses were one storey taller on the low side than on the high side. We did all the touristy things: we went to Alcatraz, we took photos of the Golden Gate bridge and Fisherman's Wharf.

On the final night we went to one of the cafés where the beat generation used to meet. The most famous of them was Jack Kerouac, who periodically lived in San Francisco. He wrote *'On The Road'*, the classic tale of an American road trip, so it seemed like a fitting place for us to go. We decided to split up our meagre shared possessions, the Itrip FM receiver, our Lonely Planet, our road atlas. It was a bit like watching a pair of travelling hobos divorcing. We began to reminisce, especially about all the crazy people we'd met.

"I wonder if those types of people are just attracted to us," I said.

"Yeah there was an awful lot of them: the Crone, Don, Simon, those guys in Texas, that compulsive liar, Glinski, loads of them."

"I'm not sure Glinski would be happy to be lumped in that list, she was just a woman who wanted her car back," I reasoned, Jack gave a nod as if to say *"yeah I suppose."*

"It's been a good a good trip though Boss." Jack paused, "although I can't believe we've got to drive all the way back again." We laughed at the thought of it.

I had been looking forward to the end of the trip, but now it was really ending and we had to go home. We paused for a moment and relaxed into the silence, drinking our drinks and looking out on the rest of the people in the café. Thinking about it there and then, if we were given the keys to another car, at that moment, I know I would have found it difficult to turn down the open road.

* * *

My trip with Robyn was almost over and we had one classic journey left. We headed south down the California coast on Route 1. The road stretches most of the length of California, but the section we were driving between San Francisco and all the way down to LA hugs the coastline tightly. It was surprisingly wild, barren and beautiful. The road twisted and wound through Big Sur, a single lane with rocks on one side and the Pacific Ocean on the other. It was not quick but the beauty was in the journey. Finding a very sparsely populated, untamed, rocky coastline in the middle of California was one final surprise.

We had time for one last food stop and we were aiming for the beach town of Cayucos. We came over the hill from the long, snaking Route 1 and saw the ocean laid out before us. We were definitely in Southern California now, the clouds had cleared, the sun was in its final hour and it cast a warm glow on the Pacific Ocean. We saw the tiny town with its wide sweep of beach, hills in the background and a pier jutting out into the ocean.

We stopped the car next to the beach and walked along to Ruddell's Smokehouse. The place looked halfway between a surf shop and a beach hut, but it had a great reputation for fish tacos, a Californian twist on a Mexican classic. The guy said he wasn't far from closing. He was a surfer though and from Southern California, which is about the most laidback combination you can get, so he was happy to make us up some tacos. They were fresh looking with chunky fish, plenty of leaves and a liberal use of lime and herbs.

We took the tacos down to the beach and we sat on a little concrete wall and ate them. They were zingy and fresh, nothing like the average cheese-filled tacos that you normally get. We watched the surfers, cutting through the waves of the Pacific, there weren't many left now. On the end of the pier, two people hugged, silhouetted in the last light of the day. The sun was setting now, we watched it dip over the horizon and sink into the Pacific. We'd reached the end of the road. There was only ocean in front of us now.

Afterword

This book originally started life as a blog a few years ago, so it has been a long time in the making. I expanded those original entries significantly by adding all the other non-food based stories which weren't present before. I think the universal thing about food is it only really makes sense in terms of the people who make it and the place it comes from, so it all links together. There's no surprise that steak is big in Texas, that the hippies in California love vegetarian food or that New York is known for its pizza.

I want to thank all the people that have helped me with the book, especially my wife. I also want to thank the other people that read it before publishing and even those people who just encouraged me to write it! In terms of the actual travel and tracking down all these wonderful places and foods, I'd highly recommend the book *500 things to eat before it's too late.* More than any other resource, it was absolutely invaluable and it's well worth picking up a copy if you're going to the US.

Although the vast majority of the book is based on true events, some details have been changed. Any similarity to real persons, living or dead, is purely coincidental and not intended by the author.

Printed in Great Britain
by Amazon.co.uk, Ltd.,
Marston Gate.